T0097720

Ritual Sacrifice in Ancient Peru

Ritual Sacrifice in Ancient Peru

ELIZABETH P. BENSON
and
ANITA G. COOK
Editors

UNIVERSITY OF TEXAS PRESS
Austin

Publication of this book has been assisted by a challenge grant from the National Endowment for the Humanities.

Library of Congress Cataloging-in-Publication Data

Ritual sacrifice in ancient Peru / Elizabeth P. Benson and Anita G. Cook, editors.— 1st ed.
    p.   cm.
Includes bibliographical references and index.
ISBN 0-292-70893-9 (cloth : alk. paper) —
ISBN 0-292-70894-7 (pbk. : alk. paper)
    1. Indians of South America—Peru—Rites and ceremonies. 2. Indians of South America—Peru—Antiquities. 3. Human sacrifice—Peru. 4. Sacrifice—Peru. 5. Peru—Antiquities. I. Benson, Elizabeth P. II. Cook, Anita Gwynn.
F3429.3.R58 R58   2001
299'.84—dc21   00-051078

To Jeffrey Splitstoser,
WHO WORKED ON THIS BOOK
HARDER THAN ANYONE ELSE

Contents

Preface and Acknowledgments ix
Elizabeth P. Benson and Anita G. Cook

CHAPTER 1   Why Sacrifice? 1
Elizabeth P. Benson

CHAPTER 2   Decapitation in Cupisnique and
Early Moche Societies 21
Alana Cordy-Collins

CHAPTER 3   Blood and the Moon Priestesses:
Spondylus Shells in Moche Ceremony 35
Alana Cordy-Collins

CHAPTER 4   Blood, Fertility, and Transformation: Interwoven
Themes in the Paracas Necropolis Embroideries 55
Mary Frame

CHAPTER 5   Children and Ancestors: Ritual Practices at the Moche
Site of Huaca de la Luna, North Coast of Peru 93
Steve Bourget

CHAPTER 6   Ritual Uses of Trophy Heads in
Ancient Nasca Society 119
Donald A. Proulx

CHAPTER 7   Huari D-Shaped Structures, Sacrificial Offerings,
and Divine Rulership 137
Anita G. Cook

CHAPTER 8   The Physical Evidence of Human Sacrifice
in Ancient Peru 165
John W. Verano

Bibliography 185

Index 205

Preface

ELIZABETH P.   For many people in the modern Western world, mak-
BENSON &   ing a sacrifice means either giving without receiving
ANITA G. COOK   or giving up something valuable for a cause that may
                benefit others. For earlier societies almost everywhere,
offerings were made for the greater good. Animals were sacrificed, and
many kinds of treasured things were offered. The most valuable offering
was human sacrifice, and throughout the world, there has been ritual human sacrifice at some time in history. Blood was the symbol of life, of animation, of nourishment, the most important offering that could be given
to the natural and supernatural elements of the world that gave humankind nourishment and allowed survival. The sacrificial nourishing of sacred
beings made life possible. At certain stages in cultural development, it was
the way that a people thought that its cosmology could be made to work.
Understanding sacrifice is an important means of knowing a culture, its
worldview, and its religion.

The Andes had no known form of indigenous writing, so the evidence
for sacrifice and many other activities must come from other sources. The
early Spanish chroniclers recorded what had been described to them about
life in Inca times; their accounts include frequent references to "sacrifice"
and "offering." Some doubt has been expressed about these accounts, however, for they were influenced by a European, Catholic point of view, and
the chroniclers did not ask the right questions about many things that we
today would like explained. However, pictorial evidence for sacrifice has
long been known. The Incas made little in the way of figurative art, but
existing pre-Inca depictions give visual evidence for sacrifice on ceramics
and textiles, on wooden and metal objects. Examples of archaeological evidence are now accumulating in the data from recent excavations in a number of places. Most of the archaeological evidence for human sacrifice in
the Andes—most clearly among the Inca and the Moche—is very recent.

The contributions to this volume cover a range of time from Cupisnique,
early in the first millennium B.C., to the Huari Empire, which collapsed

at the end of the first millennium A.D., and there are also references to earlier cultures and to the Chimú and Inca empires. Each author addresses the theme of sacrifice in its various forms: images of ritual activities associated with these sacrificial practices, material offerings as sacrifice, and the physical evidence of human and animal sacrifice. This book should serve as a compilation of significant research on sacrifice and related practices. In each article, reference is made to depictions of sacrifice in mural art or on pottery and other media; now, in most cases, the authors can link the images with archaeological remains. With a growing body of knowledge about Andean forms of sacrifice, the authors of this volume begin to unravel the significance of sacrifice in the lives of the peoples studied. An analysis of the role of sacrifice in the Andes has yet to be written; with the research presented here, and with future work, this should be possible.

Cupisnique, Chavín, and Pucará sculptures, and later Nasca, Moche, and Huari images on textiles, ceramics, and other media, show supernatural beings holding human heads. The elaborately embroidered garments placed in rich Paracas burials in the south-coast desert depict beings with knives and human heads. Mary Frame explores this iconography on block-design, embroidered, mummy-bundle textiles. She describes the figures as engaged in bloodletting activities, including autosacrifice, and interprets the imagery as showing a process that transforms the recent dead to ancestor and animal counterparts. Paracas sacrifice iconography has until now eluded interpretation; this provocative reading opens new avenues for future research.

Painted Nasca ceramics portray deities whose bodies are decorated with detached heads. Donald Proulx indicates that, although "trophy" heads are found or depicted in many Andean cultures, the south-coast Paracas and Nasca peoples are the only known societies to have meticulously prepared severed heads. He reviews the evidence and suggests that warfare was endemic and that the Nasca practice of head-taking and the use of severed heads had ritual significance beyond that of war trophies, a situation in distinct contrast to the practices of the north-coast Cupisnique (Cordy-Collins, "Decapitation," this volume) and the Moche (Cordy-Collins, Bourget, and Verano, this volume).

The depiction of sacrificial rituals and related activities is a major theme in the repertory of images painted on fine Moche funerary ceramics from the north (see Bourget, this volume, and Cordy-Collins, both articles, this volume). Now, archaeological excavation and its forensic evidence are beginning to produce an accumulation of concrete examples of sacrifice. A rare and early cache of Moche trophy heads is discussed by Alana Cordy-

Collins (in her chapter on decapitation). Archaeological evidence for mass sacrifice at Moche is described here by Steve Bourget and by John Verano.

A recurrent theme in this book is the connection between sacrifice and funerary rites. Anita Cook addresses the subject of sacrificers in Huari imagery and their connection to death, funerary rituals, burial, and regeneration. In this instance, the iconography, above-ground temple architecture, and below-ground burial cists are linked in a cycle that suggests the involvement of the Huari elite class in human sacrifice.

The last stages of pre-Hispanic Peruvian culture are not covered in detail here, but there is strong evidence that quantities of bodies accompanied high-status Chimú burials at Chan Chan, in post-Moche times on the north coast (Benson, this volume), and a number of individual *capac hucha* offerings of young people have now been found throughout the Inca empire (Benson, this volume, and Verano, this volume). Child sacrifice is a recurrent theme not only in the Andes but in much of the world.

This book is based on a symposium organized by the Pre-Columbian Society of Washington in September 1997, covering more than a thousand years between Cupisnique and Huari. The "Spondylus" chapter, by Alana Cordy-Collins, was not presented at the Pre-Columbian Society symposium but at an earlier Denver Art Museum symposium, which was not published. The chapter is included here because its subject is related to sacrifice. Indeed, most of the chapters in this volume mention Spondylus (*Spondylus* spp.) in relation to sacrifice.

ACKNOWLEDGMENTS
Without the Pre-Columbian Society of Washington's symposium, this book would not have existed. We are grateful to the many people who worked to organize the symposium and make it a success. The Pre-Columbian Society of Washington is an extraordinary group of people, who have created a remarkable organization in a relatively short time. They are dedicated, imaginative, and well-organized people, and we are very appreciative of their good sense and hard work. Especial thanks go to Jeffrey Splitstoser, whose energy and determination are as impressive as his intelligence and affability. He contributed significantly to the organization of the symposium and especially to the editing of this book. In fact, the most serious editorial work on the volume, performed valiantly and expertly, was his, and he also prepared the introductory map and chronological chart. Paula Atwood, the society's president, and many other members of the society helped specifically in the symposium and contributed to the general high level of quality and performance of the organization in general. They include: Lloyd Ander-

son, Meg Athey, Sharon Bowen, Steve Daniel, Lea du Monde, Joan Gero, Marydee Gibbons, Steve Loring, John Lyon, Rosemary Lyon, Joanne Pillsbury, Bill Puppa, Merril S. Read, Dorothy Rogers, Abelardo Sandoval, Lucy Wilson, Scott Wilson, and Elaine Wolfire. At the time of the symposium, the Ambassador of Peru to the United States, Ricardo Luna, and the cultural attaché, Juan Pablo Vegas, were immensely helpful. All of us involved in the meeting and in this publication are grateful to them. We are very grateful to Walter Alva for the photograph on the jacket. We also thank Tim Miller for his efficient last-minute help in the preparation of the manuscript.

MAP 1. Map of Peru with sites mentioned in text. Prepared by Jeffrey Splitstoser.

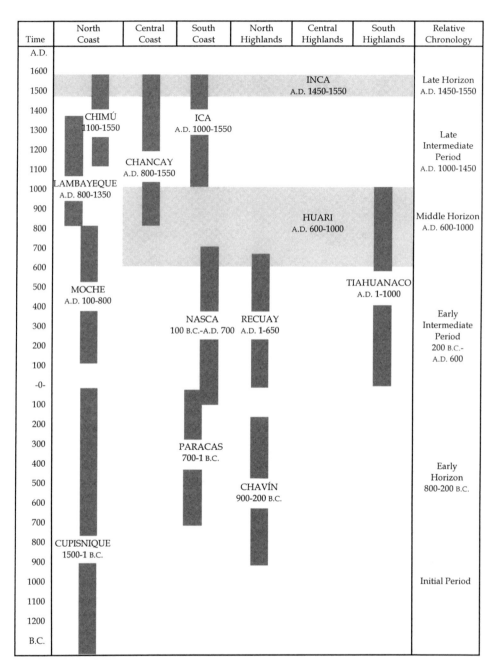

Time	North Coast	Central Coast	South Coast	North Highlands	Central Highlands	South Highlands	Relative Chronology
A.D.							
1600							
1500				INCA A.D. 1450-1550			Late Horizon A.D. 1450-1550
1400	CHIMÚ 1100-1550		ICA A.D. 1000-1550				
1300							Late Intermediate Period A.D. 1000-1450
1200							
1100		CHANCAY A.D. 800-1550					
1000	LAMBAYEQUE A.D. 800-1350						
900							
800				HUARI A.D. 600-1000			Middle Horizon A.D. 600-1000
700							
600							
500	MOCHE A.D. 100-800					TIAHUANACO A.D. 1-1000	
400							Early Intermediate Period 200 B.C.- A.D. 600
300			NASCA 100 B.C.-A.D. 700	RECUAY A.D. 1-650			
200							
100							
-0-							
100							
200							
300			PARACAS 700-1 B.C.				
400							Early Horizon 800-200 B.C.
500				CHAVÍN 900-200 B.C.			
600							
700							
800	CUPISNIQUE 1500-1 B.C.						
900							
1000							Initial Period
1100							
1200							
B.C.							

FIGURE O.I. Chronological chart. Prepared by Jeffrey Splitstoser.

Ritual Sacrifice in Ancient Peru

ELIZABETH P.
BENSON
Institute of Andean Studies

INTRODUCTION

In the depths of anyone's cultural heritage, all over the world, there is evidence of sacrifice—human and animal. Mythic supernatural beings were sacrificers and sacrificed. Ritual reenacts myth; human beings imitate what gods and sacred ancestors did. To sacrifice is to make sacred. Ritual may move far away from original myth, but the roots still appear in religious rites that people are familiar with today. The modern world, however, has generally lost the concept of sacredness and the deep meaning of ritual. Few of us believe that our rituals can change anything. In the past, people believed that the world could be coped with and changed through ritual. Today, we try to master it with technology alone.

In the ancient Americas, archaeological and skeletal evidence for sacrifice has been—and is being—found; there are also depictions of sacrifice on ceramics, mural paintings, sculpture, metal, and textiles; and there are written observations from chroniclers at the time of Spanish contact. The Andes belonged to this tradition. John Verano (1995:189) notes that various treatments of Andean bones "include human sacrifice, dedicatory burials, secondary offerings of human remains, and the collection and curation of human body parts." There were also offerings of animals and animal parts. Andean peoples generally believed that *things* had life, that there was animism in what we call inanimate objects. Objects, therefore, were also a kind of living sacrifice. Cloth, ceramics, metal, feathers, coca leaves, food, and other treasured things were valuable offerings.

María Rostworowski (1996: 9–11) cites seventeenth-century court documents that imply a clear difference between the indigenous Andean concept of the cosmos and the Christian one. An old native man accused of witchcraft testified that the sacred objects of the Spaniards (the figures of saints and the paraphernalia used in the Eucharist) were mute painted and gilded sticks, which did not speak or respond to requests, but the mummy bundles and the sacred objects of the Indians spoke and responded when sacrifices were made. These were *huacas*. A *huaca* (also *guaca* or *waka*) was a sacred place or object, or an ancestral mummy. An indigenous witness in a trial against idolatry noted that the Spaniards also had their *huacas*, but they did not feed them. The feeding of *huacas* was surely a major motivation for sacrifice in the Andes; although *huacas* were given other foods, blood was the most valuable nourishment. The Spanish chronicler Bernabé Cobo (1990 [1653]: 110-111), observing that the different sacrificial rites in Inca times were very varied but also carefully ordered, noted that "the most authoritative and important sacrifice was . . . human blood, but it . . . was only offered to the major gods and *guacas* for important purposes and on special occasions."

THE EARLY EVIDENCE

An early example of apparent Andean human sacrifice appears at Aspero, on the desert central coast of Peru, north of Lima, a site with artifacts dating back to 5000 B.C. and architecture dating to ca. 3000. Robert Feldman (1980: 114-117; 1985: 81) found in a temple there the body of an infant with some five hundred beads around its head, the remains of a special cap or hat. The body was wrapped and placed, with a bundle of textiles beside it, under a finely worked, inverted food-grinding stone, which had traces of red pigment. Probably the most elaborate burial known from the period, it may have been a dedicatory offering for sacred architecture (Burger 1992: 36). The site of La Paloma, near the coast south of Lima, was occupied at about the same time (5000-2800 B.C.). Jeffrey Quilter (1989: 66-67, 83) found there a number of child burials in houses or special structures. Again, these were the most elaborate burials at the site, and, again, they may have been dedicatory offerings. In the highlands, in the Alto Huallaga (Kotosh Chavín phase, 700-250 B.C.; Onuki 1993: 86), two child burials were found under the walls of structures. At Ancón, on the central coast, ca. 400 B.C., a child was interred beneath the corner of a semisubterranean stone house (Burger 1992: 74). The child's eyes had been replaced with mica sheets, its stomach supplanted by a gourd, and its heart by a clear rock-quartz crystal, a substance with magical qualities. Steve Bourget (this volume) writes of child sacrifice at the base of a sacred structure at Moche in later times. Vestiges of this practice remain. Today, in highland Bolivia, at the beginning of construction of a village house, offerings placed beneath the four corners comprise various things, especially animal fetuses, sometimes those of llamas (Arnold 1992: 50, 54). They are offered to the telluric aspects of "la Tierra Virgen." When the walls of the new house have been raised, a calf is sacrificed, and its blood is ritually sprinkled in the corners before the roof is put up. If the sprinkling is improperly done, a wall will fall.

In modern times, most of us are shocked by child sacrifice, but it has long been prevalent in many parts of the world. In ancient times, it was often a building-dedication rite. Patrick Tierney (1989: 106, 372) mentions, for example, two decapitated infant burials from ca. 3000 B.C. displayed in the Pontifical Museum of Jerusalem. The exhibit label reads, in part: "a few dozen infant burials have been found in the town area [near the Dead Sea]. They were invariably under house floors and were quite possibly foundation sacrifices, as encountered elsewhere in the ancient Near East." In the city of Carthage, in Tunisia, ca. 800 B.C., many apparent child sacrifices were placed in urns beneath limestone stelas (Tierney 1989: 396). Carthage seemingly had more child sacrifices than any other place in the ancient Old World; hundreds of apparent sacrifices have been found there.

SACRIFICE AND WARFARE
Cerro Sechín, a Casma Valley site on the north coast of Peru, with a C-14 date of 1519 B.C., provides possible evidence for another kind of sacrifice. Some four hundred sculptures, more than at any other early Andean site, are worked in granite, which was found nearby (Burger 1992: 77–80; Samaniego, Vergara, and Bischof 1985). The sculptures form a frieze of stones, a few of which depict a full-length profile figure with a band from the eye that seems to indicate supernaturalness; each holds a staff (Figure 1.1). Depicted near the profile figures are maimed bodies and decapitated heads and body parts in a "distressed and dismembered state" (Pozorski and Pozorski 1993: 56) (Figure 1.2). Even the upright, staff-bearing figures appear to have blood flowing from the waist. The frieze may represent ritual battle, with earth-nourishing blood, related to the ritual battle described in Inca and more recent times (see Bourget, this volume; Allen 1988; Hocquenghem 1978, 1987; Topic and Topic 1997; Urton 1993). It may represent actual military conquest (Pozorski and Pozorski 1993: 56), although the figures generally lack military attributes. Alana Cordy-Collins (1983) has argued that shamanic initiation is depicted in a death-and-rebirth metaphor.

Throughout Andean prehistory, there were certainly wars; there was surely at times purely ritual battle as well. War was a rite, even when it was fought to gain land to plant or to ensure water resources or trade routes. Some war was fought to defeat people in the next valley or upstream. Some war—and sacrifice—must have been regularly scheduled to be harvest- or rain- or solstice-related. Some would have been fought at the time of accession or death of a ruler, to mark the event or to gain captives for sacrifice.

FIGURE 1.1. Staff-holding figure with line through eye. Photographed by author in the Museo Nacional de Antropología y Arqueología, Lima.

FIGURE 1.2. Cerro Sechín. Section of wall with depictions of a man trying to hold his innards, a decapitated head, and an intestine(?). Photo by Elizabeth P. Benson.

A question that frequently arises is whether the sacrificial victim was a member of the sacrificing group or one of the defeated outsiders, probably a particularly capable, attractive, or high-ranking person, a worthy sacrifice. In different periods and places, there seems to be evidence for both situations. Cobo (1990: 111) noted that when the Incas conquered a people, they would select a large number of the most attractive individuals and bring them to Cuzco to be sacrificed to the Sun for the victory the Sun had achieved for them. There is also evidence of the sacrifice of conquered warriors at Moche (see Bourget, this volume).

RITUAL DECAPITATION

Decapitation was the common form of sacrifice in the Andes. Two repeated motifs in Andean (and other pre-Hispanic) cultures are an elaborate ritual object in a blade shape—there are many of these from very early cultures through Inca times (Lavalle and Lang 1977: 116; Rowe 1996: 313-315)—and a decapitated human head, a "trophy" head. Such a head was not what we think of as a trophy, but the most prominent, important, and valuable part of the body; human beings can get along without most body parts, but the head is essential. (The heart, another essential body part, was sometimes excised in sacrifice.) A small tomb found in the highlands in the Alto Huallaga, dating from before 800 B.C., was apparently constructed to hold only a head (Onuki 1993: 84). A gold crown decorated with trophy heads comes from an Early Horizon (ca. 400 B.C.) tomb at Kuntur Wasi, an architectural complex in the northern mountains near the Continental Divide and the city of Cajamarca (Millones and Onuki 1993: Lám. 1-1). Kuntur Wasi also produced a large sculpture portraying a split-faced, cross-legged supernatural being holding a tiny trophy head (Burger 1992: Fig. 102). Another sculpture, a wide-eyed figure—surely supernatural—from Pucará, a late Early Horizon and Early Intermediate site in the highlands (200 B.C.-A.D. 200), holds a small human head (Moseley 1992: Plate 40).

In the last two millennia B.C., a culture called Cupisnique, named for the Cupisnique *quebrada,* where it was first found, developed on the north coast. This culture, found at many sites, was ultimately influenced by the Chavín culture, which spread from the eastern slopes of the Andes. Sacrificial subjects appear in both styles (Cordy-Collins 1992 and "Decapitation," this volume). At least one sculpture at Chavín depicts a figure, with the fanged mouth of a god, holding a decapitated head (Burger 1992: Fig. 163). Trophy heads are a common motif on Cupisnique ceramics; a bottle from the Zaña Valley even takes the shape of an elaborately incised (tattooed)

FIGURE 1.3. Two views of a ceramic bottle depicting a man cutting off his own head. Cupisnique, Zaña Valley. Museo de la Nación, Lima. Photo by Elizabeth P. Benson.

man who is severing his own head (Figure 1.3; for autosacrifice, see Frame, this volume).

On the south coast of Peru, in the last centuries B.C., the Paracas style produced intricately embroidered textiles with compound figures holding a trophy head and wearing garments garnished with heads (Mary Frame, this volume; see also Lavalle and Lang 1977: 48–49, 52–53, 58–59). A Paracas ceramic piece represents a cut-off lower arm (Lapiner 1976: Fig. 160), a motif that appears in many later styles, as does a cut-off leg. On the post-Paracas south coast, the Nasca style, in the early centuries of our era, depicts compound supernatural figures, decorated with trophy heads, who appear to be engorging a head (Proulx, this volume, and 1983: Fig. 11). Donald Proulx (1996: 112) notes that, in Nasca art, there is "a close connection between the ritual taking and displaying of human heads and agricultural fertility." Both Nasca and Paracas heads were severed with obsidian knives. Obsidian appears in most early Peruvian sites (Burger 1992) and was probably used for sacrifice also in earlier times.

In contemporaneous Moche art of the Early Intermediate north coast, complex sacrifice scenes often show cut-off, rope-tied lower arms and legs floating, along with decapitated heads (Hocquenghem 1987: Figs. 25 and 187). Clay vessels depict legs, forearms, and hands (Purin 1990: Figs. 68–74). Extra body parts have been found in some burials, and in others there are bodies without appendages (Bourget, this volume; Alva and Donnan 1993). Copper knives were the sacrificial implements. Did the human bodies found with some important Moche burials—at Sipán, for example (Alva and Donnan 1993: 55, 122 [Tomb 1], 143, 159–161 [Tomb 2])—have sacrificial meaning? Humans accompanying an important burial might not have been sacrifices in the strictest sense—that is, offerings—but those who served the dead, although they may have been considered offerings taken along by the primary burial figure. A child's body found near the head of the coffin in Tomb 1 at Sipán and a child in Tomb 2 were more likely offerings than servitors (Alva and Donnan 1993: 120, 159; Bourget, this volume).

At Tiahuanaco, in the highlands of Bolivia, tenoned into the wall of a temple are apparent stone trophy-head replicas (Kolata 1993: Figs. 5.30 and 5.31). In the Akapana, the main ceremonial structure at Tiahuanaco, a sculpture representing a large feline, seated like a man, holds a human head with long hair (Kolata 1993: Figs. 5.23 and 5.24). The Middle Horizon site of Huari, near Ayacucho—which has some symbiosis with Tiahuanaco—influenced virtually all contemporaneous art. The Huari style was essentially new, but the subject matter was not; trophy heads are a frequent motif (Cook, this volume, and 1983).

In the Late Intermediate Period art of Lambayeque (Sicán) and Chimú, on the north coast, there is some evidence of sacrificial activity. Large painted textile panels from the north and central coasts show captives with ropes around the neck (Figure 1.4; Porter 1991; Lapiner 1976: Figs. 627–646); an occasional object portrays a large figure holding small trophy heads (Figure 1.5); effigy objects of gold and/or silver or ceramic take the form of an arm or leg (Figures 1.6 and 1.7; Cordy-Collins 1996: 195–198; Lapiner 1976: Fig. 620; Purin 1990: Figs. 196–199); elaborate knife-shaped objects of gold and silver are frequent (Lapiner 1976: Figs. 647 and 649). These offerings with sacrificial implications are important grave goods in Lambayeque and Chimú times, as objects with sacrificial depictions were in the Moche era. In general, however, the act of sacrifice is a rare motif in later Andean art, and trophy heads are not common. At the same time, Chimú multiple burials of a sacrificial nature have been found (Conrad 1982; Verano 1986 and this volume), and the numbers of dead accompany-

FIGURE I.4. Textile with nude figures tied with ropes, and vultures attacking a splayed figure. Chimú? 68½″ × 72½″ (174 × 184.2 cm.). Courtesy of The Textile Museum (1962.30.4).

FIGURE I.5. Wooden mirror handle with gold, turquoise, and paint. Chimú, north coast, ca. A.D. 1200. 11⅝″ × 5⁹⁄₁₆″. Courtesy of Brooklyn Museum of Art, Gift of the Ernest Erickson Foundation (86.224.4).

FIGURE 1.6. Hammered gold hand and forearm, with inlays of turquoise and silver (fingernails). This is not a glove; the end is closed. 20.2 × 3.35 cm. Lambayeque (Sicán), north coast. Courtesy of Dumbarton Oaks Research Library and Collection, Washington, D.C. (B-463).

FIGURE 1.7. Ceramic vessel in form of a lower leg and foot with sandal. Chimú. Courtesy of Staatliche Museen zu Berlin, Preussischer Kulturbesitz, Museum für Völkerkunde, VA 3775. Photo by Dietrich Graf.

ing high-status burials appear to increase greatly. At Las Avispas, a burial platform at Chan Chan, Thomas Pozorski excavated thirteen bodies, all of young women, stacked in layers (Rowe 1995: 30). He did not open up the entire mound, but he estimated that there were probably some three hundred young women interred there, perhaps with a ruler. The Laberinto at Chan Chan yielded remains of at least ninety-three individuals, with the smallest cell holding thirteen complete skeletons "stacked like cordwood" (Conrad 1982: 99). There may have been several hundred more burials in the platform. Other Chan Chan burial platforms yielded, among other offerings, bones of human juveniles, mostly female (Moseley 1992: 259).

ANIMAL OFFERINGS

In the Callejón de Huaylas, between the main cordilleras of the Andes, excavations at Huaricoto (2000–200 B.C.) produced a burned animal sacrifice with four pieces of clear quartz stuck in the remains (Burger and Salazar-Burger 1980: 28). In later times, the deer hunt, a common theme in Moche art, was clearly an important ritual sacrifice, related to vegetation and fertility (Benson 1988, 1997; Donnan 1997). Sea-lion hunts were also rites, and there is evidence on the offshore islands for ritual activity implying sacrifice, both human and animal (Bourget, this volume; Benson 1995; Hocquenghem 1987: 131; Kubler 1948; Rostworowski 1997).

Cobo (1990: 113–116) points out that the Incas, at a later time, sacrificed only domesticated animals, not wild ones. The Moche offered both. One or more llamas were commonly placed in Moche and other tombs (Donnan 1995). Llamas were offered for sacrifice in many times and places. At Tiahuanaco, in the main ceremonial structure, fourteen disarticulated llamas were found carefully arranged and accompanied by special objects (Kolata 1993: 119). In the forecourt of the Laberinto at Chan Chan, the Chimú had buried a large number of llamas (Conrad 1982: 100). At Túcume, in the far northern coastal desert, thirty-one llama burials were encountered in the Inca-period Temple of the Sacred Stone (Heyerdahl, Sandweiss, and Narváez 1995: 112–113, 177). Llamas were the prime Inca sacrificial animals; different quantities of llamas of different colors had their throats cut, usually at Inca calendrical rituals. At the end of October, a black llama was tied to a pole, without food or water, to implore for rain; in February, one hundred black llamas were killed in order to stop the rains (Zuidema 1992: 22–23). Llama organs were used for auguries about crops (Cieza de León 1959 [1553?]: 268–269). Llama sacrifices are still offered, and fertility rites for llamas and other herd animals are important festivals in many highland places. Alan Kolata (1996: 180–181) describes blood from llamas beheaded with obsidian knives and the blood then being caught in cups, carried in four directions, and poured on the earth. In Inca times, stone llama and alpaca vessels contained llama blood and fat offerings. Placed in pastures, these vessels were thought to ensure the fertility of a herd.

Dogs were sometimes sacrificed and often appear in burials, where their role was probably most often one of helping the deceased to the other world (Benson 1991a). The sacred and valuable Spondylus shell was a common offering in elite graves and caches over a long period of time (Alva and Donnan 1993; Heyerdahl, Sandweiss, and Narváez 1995: 216; see Cordy-Collins, "Blood and the Moon Priestesses," this volume). Red Spondylus shell has strong associations with sacrifice. Guinea pigs were—and still are—common sacrificial offerings.

THE NATURAL AND THE SUPERNATURAL

What did people in ancient Peru want to achieve through sacrifice? One assumes that they were making a contact and contract with gods or supernaturals, perhaps sacred ancestors; a supernatural being was an ancestor of the tribe, and the ancestors belonged to the supernatural world. The rulers who ordered sacrifice had priestly powers or instruction. They were divine rulers, as European rulers were thought to be not so long ago. Why did the ruler and/or the priest who regulated the ritual that benefited the people perform sacrifice? What was to be gained positively? What was to be prevented?

The primary need of human beings is sustenance. You need plant foods, and the sun and water to grow them. You need protein, usually meat, for which ancient man hunted and fished. From the Peruvian coast, you want to go to sea safely in your reed-bundle raft, and you want the fish to be plentiful. You want to take from the offshore islands fish, sea-lion pelts, and guano for fertilizer. Perhaps you want to conquer enemies or protect your people from raids and conquest. You want to ward off illness. Tuberculosis has been identified in mummified remains from Peru, and various viral, bacterial, and parasitic diseases are indicated (Verano 1992). There must have been epidemics. Simple curing practices were not enough.

Who and what were the gods or supernatural beings of the Andes? As Rostworowski (1996: 9) and others have observed, no word exists for "god" in the Quechua language of the Incas, although there seems to have been a major cosmic-deity concept with various names and somewhat different attributes or aspects in different places and times. There may have been one such being or possibly more at any given time. Somewhat conflicting reports from early Spanish writers indicate that there was a major god —perhaps a succession of powerful creators (Rostworowski 1996: 21–60; Zuidema 1992)—and a few lesser deities, as well as beings with supernatural power. Images from earlier cultures show a similar pattern. "Gods" had forces of nature as attributes, and there were personified aspects of nature; all nature was alive. These were the deities and spirits of the people and their cosmos. They may also have had aspects of culture heroes who taught people how to deal with nature. One way of understanding the supernaturals is to observe the nature that they created and in which, by which, they were created. The attributes of supernatural beings and the significance of rites would depend to a great extent on the environment and its exigencies.

In the natural world of the western Andes, there is a dichotomy and balance of high mountains and deep sea. The cold Humboldt Current, flowing up from the Antarctic, normally provides one of the world's richest fishing grounds. The cold air of the current condenses warm ocean breezes offshore, preventing rain over the coastal land. The mountains block moisture from the Amazon basin to the east. The coast, therefore, is one of the driest deserts in the world. The coastal people live pinched between the sea—the immense Pacific, into which, in the past, men ventured in rafts—and the Andes, some of the highest mountains in the world. Water and sun come to the coast from the mountains. Beyond the mountains lie the vast expanses of the Amazon forest, with resources to be sought and perils in the seeking. It is a rich system of environments, but its benefits do not come easily.

Only 2 percent of the land in Peru is suitable for cultivation (Burger 1992: 12). Much of the mountain landscape is desert with few cultivable valleys. Humans construct terraces on hillsides too steep to walk up. Water has to be captured and controlled in these terraces. For millennia, people have lived in the Andes at altitudes of 10,000–14,000 feet, above the timberline, with all the vicissitudes of that elevation. Most crops there are tubers and rhizomes. In slightly lower altitudes, maize is grown, but hail can destroy a crop in no time. Drought can also be a critical problem in the mountains (Kolata 1996; Moseley 1992).

The narrow, arid strip of coastal desert is watered by often-seasonal rivers carrying water from the mountains, water that must be controlled, canalized, and conserved for irrigation. The coast requires abundant mountain rainfall, but heavy rain can cause urgent problems in the highlands. There, I have driven past a moist field, only to return a few hours later to see a river rushing downhill where the field had been.

The Andean region is also earthquake country, where the earth is alive and moves. Earthquakes can wipe out populations on the coast and in the mountains; in addition to damaging structures and landscape, severe earthquakes can bring tidal waves (see Tierney 1989: 105–106). Less likely, though possible, is volcano eruption.

A major cause of anxiety is the occasional severe El Niño event. El Niño is a warm countercurrent that flows occasionally, usually for a brief time, southward into the cold Humboldt Current. It can come and stay, however, raising the offshore water temperature enough to cause heavy rain on the coast, with disastrous flooding that destroys irrigation ditches, crops, houses, and roads (Burger 1992: 14–16). Archaeology indicates that many coastal desert sites were destroyed or damaged by water in ancient times. Steve Bourget (this volume) has evidence of direct association between sacrifice and torrential rain on the north coast of Peru. El Niño also drastically changes the life of the sea. The common local fish cannot find their usual nutrients; they either die or go elsewhere, and are replaced by warm-water species. When fish disappear, sea lions and seabirds have no food, or they have food to which they are not accustomed; they die or go away. Human life is greatly affected by sea changes.

The Andes is an environment of strong spirits of nature. Gods and supernatural beings may have had identity as mountains, sky, thunder, earth, earthquake, caves, lakes, sea, etc., or some combination of these. Mountains are still sacred in the Andes, still personified, sacralized, deified, still the homes of ancestors (Allen 1988: 41-44; Sherbondy 1992: 58; Zuidema 1992: 30). Mountains were major water sources, and mountain lakes were thought of as ancestral places of origin—Lake Titicaca, for example (Sherbondy 1992: 56-62). The sea, believed to underlie the entire earth and provide water for the lakes, was the ultimate source of life for all Andean peoples. Cobo (1990: 111; see also Salomon and Urioste 1991: 4-9) speaks of sacrifices to springs, so that the sown crops could be harvested, and of sacrifices to the Sun to make the plants grow and to Thunder to make it rain and not hail or freeze. Thunder is a voice from the sky, a god voice. There was thunder on the desert coast in the severe 1982-1983 El Niño. One should remember that the Greek Zeus was a creator god associated with mountains, thunder, and lightning.

Thunder "acts mostly as a mountain god . . . considered to be a brother of Venus, the morning and evening star, and may even be equated with this planet" (Zuidema 1992: 18, see also 26). Andean gods surely had some astronomical identity: Sun, Moon, Venus, Pleiades, Orion, etc. As Tom Zuidema (1992: 17-18) and others have noted: "The Sun seems to have been central in Andean thought." Astronomical/astrological ritual calendars were important in the Inca period and must have been so in earlier times. Calendars are based on important sky events—solstices and equinoxes, new and full moons, for example (see Hocquenghem 1987; Zuidema 1992: 19-21)—and on such regular events as the beginning of the rainy season, the cleaning of irrigation canals, the running of fish, the harvesting of crops. There must also have been rites on the accession or death of a ruler, a temple dedication, etc., as well as rites to prevent ill-boding astronomical events—eclipses, conjunctions, etc. Certainly, many of these ritual occasions would have required sacrifice.

In modern times, in the highlands near Cuzco, Catherine Allen (1988:

182–184, 203) has observed that "The height of the rainy season [February] is a time for offerings and ritual battles," which produce bloodletting, a custom also in Inca times. The earth and the mountains are still thought to need the nourishment of the bloody sacrifices of ritual warfare. When the mountains are hungry or irritated, they have ways of showing their displeasure. Gary Urton (1993: 117–118, 128–129) also notes that ritual battles "often occur around the time of Carnival . . . from early February to mid-March," just before the plowing for the communal potato planting. Trees and unripened fruit figure in these rites. It is clear that part of the motivation for battle is the shedding of blood and the offering of it to nourish the earth to produce a good harvest. Human blood furnishes the earth with food and drink, as the earth provides humankind with food and drink.

In Inca myth, dismembered godly body parts relate to origins of agriculture. Pachacamac, an important Andean god, was a son of the Sun; he killed another son (by another woman) of the Sun and planted the body parts (Uhle 1991 [1903]: 49). The teeth produced maize, the bones yucca, and the flesh vegetables and fruit. This theme recurs in recent myths from lowland South America (Tomoeda 1982). Mircea Eliade (1968: 189–190) cites Oriental creation myths in which food-bearing plants are created through the sacrifice of a deity. Eliade also notes a sacrifice made by the Khonds of India, in which a voluntary sacrificee lived well until he was drugged, strangled, and cut into pieces. Each village received a fragment of the body for burial in the fields; the remains were burned and scattered over the land.

Supernatural beings are receivers of sacrifices. Also, gods or other supernaturals are often sacrificers themselves. Human beings are almost never shown performing sacrifice. In Moche art, a huge anthropomorphic owl, surely supernatural, holds a knife to the throat of a small man (Hocquenghem 1978: Photos 5–7; 1987: 124). An anthropomorphic owl or bat has a knife in one hand, a head in the other. Some scholars describe the sacrificers as masked humans. Actual sacrificers probably wore masks (like hangmen or beheaders in our culture, not too long ago), but I believe that the art generally depicts a mythic, supernatural realm.

This sums up some of the knowledge of pre-Inca sacrifices and prevailing motivations for sacrifice. Information regarding the Incas is a little different, because of the documents written by early Spaniards, some of whom denied that there was Inca sacrifice. Some sources describe Inca sacrifice, however, and a considerable amount of recent archaeological excavation has confirmed these sources.

CAPAC HUCHA

A hundred years ago, Max Uhle, one of the earliest archaeologists in the Americas, worked at Pachacamac, a site on the coast in the Lurín Valley, south of Lima. Pachacamac was important from the Middle Horizon through Inca times, probably as a trading and fishing center and as a religious place. It was the seat of an important oracle, it had rich cemeteries, and it surely saw its share of sacrifices. Uhle (1991: 86–87) found there an Inca Temple of the Sun with a cemetery containing only the burials of sacrificed women, dressed in Inca clothing and strangled with a cloth. They came from the house of weavers, women who had been chosen to serve the Inca, who was both the Sun and the state. Weaving women were sacrificed in this period also at Túcume, where archaeologists found them buried in a building that was then filled in; after this, heavy rains came (Heyerdahl, Sandweiss, and Narváez 1995: 97). The events of sacrifice and rain were clearly related.

Children, however, were the most common sacrifice found at Pachacamac (Uhle 1991: 86). From Inca times, remains of an essentially standardized pattern of child or youth sacrifice, known as *capac hucha,* or *capacocha* (translated as something like "solemn sacrifice"), have been found throughout the long Inca empire, from the coast of Ecuador south to the mountains of Chile and Argentina, in what must have been sacred places, often on snowy peaks and, in high-altitude Lake Titicaca, under water (Benson 1991b; Dransart 1995; Duviols 1976; McEwan and Silva 1989; Mostny 1957; Purin 1990: Figs. 372–378; Reinhard 1992, 1996, 1997; Rowe 1996: 302–303; Schobinger 1991; Silverblatt 1987: 94–100; Tierney 1989: 24–59). In this rite, children and young people were sacrificed with offerings that usually included one or more gold, silver, or Spondylus-shell figurines, human male or female—what an early Spaniard, Cristóbal de Molina (1959 [1575?]: 92), called "persons of gold and silver" (Figures 1.8 and 1.9). Some of the figurines were dressed in miniature clothing. Occasionally, dressed figurines seem to have been offered without a child (Heyerdahl, Sandweiss, and Narváez 1995: 103, 107–111). Sacrifice is not a theme per se in the generally nonfigurative art of the Incas, but there is a fairly large sample of *capac hucha* figures.

One such sacrifice, frozen and so the best preserved of those known, was a young woman discovered by Johan Reinhard (1996; 1997) and others atop the Nevada Ampato volcano in southern Peru. Two other sacrifices found nearby had been struck by lightning after their death. Lightning (*Illapa*) was an Inca "ambiguous divinity responsible for the fertilizing rains, as well

FIGURE 1.8. Silver female *capac hucha* figure, dressed in textiles and feathers. Inca. H. 7.1 cm. (2¾"). Private collection.

FIGURE 1.9. Silver female *capac hucha* figure. Inca. H. 15.75 cm. (6⅛"). Department of Library Services, American Museum of Natural History, B/9608.

as the thunderbolts of death" (Dransart 1995: 20). This being can be referred to as Thunder-Lightning (Silverblatt 1987). The face of a *capac hucha* boy who froze to death on top of Cerro El Plomo, in Chile, was painted with red ochre and four jagged yellow lines, which may represent lightning; the motif is found also on some of the miniature garments worn by the small figures that accompanied *capac hucha* burials (Dransart 1995: 6, 13, 20; Mostny 1957).

Juan de Betanzos (1996 [1557]: 46–47), an early chronicler who referred to this custom, described the dedication of the Temple of the Sun in Cuzco, the most sacred structure in the Inca capital. The Inca—the ruler, who was the son of the Sun—ordered the lords of Cuzco to have ready within ten days maize, llamas, fine garments, and boys and girls to make a sacrifice to the Sun. He then ordered a big fire, into which the heads of the animals, the garments, and the maize were thrown. The boys and girls, well dressed and adorned, were buried alive in the temple built around the statue of the Sun. (The Sun had come to the Inca in his sleep in the form of a shining child, and the statue was made to resemble this.)

Betanzos (1996: 132) tells us that on another sacred occasion, as part of the elaborate mourning rite after the burial of the Inca, it was decreed that "they should send out throughout the entire land and have a thousand girls and boys brought. All . . . should be from five to six years of age. Some of them should be the children of caciques [chieftains]. They should be very well dressed." The children would be carried in litters (a sign of high rank). The Inca also ordered that, as the children were sacrificed, it would be said that they were going with the Inca to serve him. "They would be buried all over the land in the places where the Inca had established residence" (Betanzos 1996: 132). The early sources often mention the pairing of boys and girls in the ritual, although this patterning is not clear in the archaeological remains.

Pierre Duviols (1976: 13), in his study of the rite, describes the solemn and majestic procession in which the children, with many offerings, were taken to Cuzco on Inca roads, accompanied by *curacas,* priests, and captains, all of whom could meet the Inca himself to present the offerings. The return journey—made in as straight a line as possible in that rugged landscape—led to the place where the sacrifice was made, accompanied by gifts from the Inca.

Various scholars have examined the *capac hucha* as a rite defining the sacred and political geography of the Inca empire and linking newer communities with Cuzco and the old Inca realm (McEwan and Silva 1989: 181–182; Dransart 1995: 20–24). Duviols (1976: 29) views it as a system of social control and integration of the empire, and sees Cuzco as the sacred heart of the Inca empire, with a circulatory system of veins and arteries, through which blood flowed, metaphorically and literally. One link of the cultural whole was this sacrifice, which was thought to irrigate the land and nourish the realm. Earlier peoples had used child sacrifice to dedicate and ensure the sanctity and security of a building; the Incas used child sacrifice to ensure the stability of an empire.

Rodrigo Hernández Príncipe (1923 [1621]; Dransart 1995: 20–21; Silverblatt 1987: 81, 94–100; see also Molina 1959: 91–92) wrote of *capac hucha* that, every four years, four children, ten to twelve years old, one each from the four parts of the empire, were taken to Cuzco and feted. (The Inca empire was the World of the Four Quarters.) The children were then taken back to their places of origin for a rite described as a "sacrifice to the sun." One girl from the central coast was dedicated to the Sun and died with objects given to her by the Inca. The parent of such a child often had special status to begin with, and this girl's father, after her death, was made a lord or governor of his community. Inca child sacrifices may have been, among other things, a means of gaining higher status for the family. The children acquired special supernatural status through the ritual; the dead girl in Hernández Príncipe's account became a venerated "goddess," embodying forces of fertility (Silverblatt 1987: 100).

According to Cobo (1990: 111–112):

> In the human sacrifices that were most frequently made, they offered the children that the Inka collected by way of tribute throughout the kingdom. In addition, because of some grave necessity that came up, some children would be voluntarily offered by their parents . . . there were some males and some females . . . they were sacrificed by being strangled with a cord or by having their throats slit.

The archaeological record indicates various sacrificial methods. Cobo (1990: 8) also wrote that the Inca people

> sacrificed even their own children . . . though this was an only child, it was a major offense to show any . . . sadness; . . . they were obliged to do it with gestures of happiness and satisfaction, as if they were taking their children to bestow upon them a very important reward.

All cultures that practiced child sacrifice seem to have believed in some sort of afterlife, and the persons sacrificed were usually specially chosen for this glorification, which united them with the sacred ancestors.

In many other parts of the world, there are examples not only of child sacrifice, but of parents offering their own children. In Greek myth, Minos, king of Crete, caused a severe plague in the city of Athens (Grant and Hazel 1993: 223). As a result, the Delphic Oracle declared that the Athenian king,

Aegeus, should send to Crete each year (or every nine years, depending on the version of the story) a tribute of seven boys and seven girls to be sacrificed to the Minotaur. (The trouble was caused initially because the bull that was the father of the Minotaur had not been sacrificed, as it should have been.) Eventually, Theseus, one of those taken to Crete for sacrifice, killed the Minotaur and caused the death of King Minos.

The Greek goddess Artemis delayed the sailing of Agamemnon's fleet for the attack against Troy, demanding the sacrifice of his daughter Iphigenia (Grant and Hazel 1993: 189–190). In one version, Iphigenia was killed. In another, she was rescued by the goddess and taken to her temple, where the girl's duty was to prepare for sacrifice all strangers who came there. Greek myth also describes gods who ate their children to keep a child from wresting power from the father (Grant and Hazel 1993: 93). An Andean myth describes an early deity or *huaca* who demanded that people have only two children, one of whom he would eat (Salomon and Urioste 1991: 43).

In the Book of Genesis (Chapter 22), God told Abraham to sacrifice his son Isaac as a burnt offering on a mountain. Abraham took Isaac to the mountain and prepared the fire, bound his son, put him on the altar, and took out his knife—then an angel appeared to point out a ram to sacrifice instead. Many people feel that the angel was a later addition to the text (see Tierney 1989: 372–373).

In *The Golden Bough* (Frazer 1981 [1890]: 235–236), there are several examples of a practice among "the Semites of Western Asia" in which the king, in a time of danger for his nation, gave his son to die as a sacrifice for the people. In times of pestilence, drought, or defeat in war, the Phoenicians sacrificed children to Baal. James Frazer also cites the sacrifice of firstborn children by groups in New South Wales and in Africa.

SACRIFICE AND COSMOS

The relationship of sacrifice and environment is basic; other aspects of sacrifice involve the sacred ancestors and reunion with them (see Bourget, this volume; Frame, this volume). Being sacrificed, you become worthy of the sacred ancestors. Verano (1995: 189) observes that the ritual offering of human lives, or of human remains, appears to have been an important means of mediation between the living and the dead. There is a further contract with the gods that may be implied. If a god created mankind, then mankind owes the god a debt. Gods can—and have, in myth—become dissatisfied with a current creation of man, destroy it, and try to make better people in a new creation. The god must be given his due and must be satisfied. It is not only man's needs that are to be met.

Zuidema (1992: 32) has written: "Man's connection with the cosmos was effected through sacrifice." The study of sacrifice helps us to understand ancient man's cosmos, the world in which he lived, and the rules for surviving in it.

Acknowledgments

I am grateful for suggestions from Alana Cordy-Collins, Edward Dwyer, Cynthia Pinkston, Nancy Porter, and Jeffrey Quilter.

CHAPTER 2

Decapitation in Cupisnique and Early Moche Societies

ALANA CORDY-
COLLINS
Anthropology Department,
University of San Diego

INTRODUCTION

The Cupisnique cultists (ca. 1500–1 B.C.) of the prehistoric Peruvian north coast were remarkable artists in clay, and their goldwork was the finest of very early metal production in the Andes. Their ceremonial architecture, decorated with sculpture, was impressive. They were one of the earliest cultures to record decapitation graphically. A study of their art reveals five distinct supernatural head-takers: a spider, a bird of prey, a monster, a fish, and a human (Cordy-Collins 1992). The artists represented these decapitators according to the esoteric but formal canons dictated by their religious tradition.

This tradition is most frequently referred to as a cult. There are two intertwined reasons for this. First, there is little direct evidence of Cupisnique patterns of social organization, demography, or subsistence strategies. What is known concerning these areas has been inferred, in large part, from the architecture and art. The architecture can be termed "corporate," indicating that it was planned and ordered (see Moseley 1985). The systematic arrangement of structures in Cupisnique sites (such as the Los Reyes complex in the Moche Valley) indicates the presence of an organized, stratified society of—at least—architects and designers, skilled artisans, and manual laborers. Base personnel of farmers, fisherfolk, hunters, or traders also must have existed to support the upper echelons of the society, but almost nothing can be said about such groups at the present stage of research. The second reason for referring to a Cupisnique cult is that, beyond the formal and structural regularities of Cupisnique architecture, many buildings were embellished with painted and incised stucco relief work depicting surreal creatures. The archaeological sites of Los Reyes, Cerro Blanco, Punkurí, Moxeke, Cerro Sechín, and Garagay all display buildings with such decoration.

In addition to the architectural ornamentation, supernatural creatures and their disembodied parts permeate virtually all other forms of Cupisnique art. All media lack commonplace representations. Naturalistic objects do appear in Cupisnique art, but analysis has shown them to exist within a supernaturalized religious context (Cordy-Collins 1977, 1979a, 1979b, 1980, 1982; Lathrap 1977). For these reasons, Cupisnique society is seen as one strongly rooted in and absorbed by religion. Following Anthony Wallace (1966), who classifies all religious institutions as one of four types of cults, it seems fair to refer to the Cupisnique people as a "cult," probably a shamanistic one. However, although a decided commonality exists in the artistry at the various Cupisnique sites, there is no reliable evidence that they were united other than through a similar religious practice. Therefore, to call the Cupisnique more than a cult stretches the available data.

The Cupisnique (also known as coastal Chavín) sphere of influence radiated outward from the Quebrada de Cupisnique, a region these people seem to have dominated for a millennium or more. The impact of their ideology extended from their coastal homeland to the eastern side of the Andean cordillera, but—eventually—the Cupisnique tradition waned; other emerging north-coast cultures that had experienced Cupisnique influence went on to develop their own character. Thus, the epi-Cupisnique period witnessed the rise of the Moche, Salinar, Vicús, and Virú (Gallinazo) cultures. Of these, by far the most vigorous and enduring was the Moche, spanning almost six centuries (ca. 300–800 A.D.).

A great deal more is known about Moche society than about Cupisnique. Several Moche archaeological sites are well excavated and they tell a consistent story. The society was highly stratified; it incorporated a base population of farming and fishing folk, a middle class, and an elite population of extraordinary wealth (Donnan 1978; 1990). And, while there was a definite distinction in the material culture between the Moche of the north coast and of the far north coast, there was a religious commonality which transcended time and space (Donnan 1990).

Not only were the Moche the most dynamic of the societies that followed the Cupisnique, but they seem to have been the ones most interested in the Cupisnique iconographic message. Intriguingly, the old Cupisnique supernatural head-takers—the spider, bird of prey, monster, fish, and human—are the same ones that the Moche chose to render in their religious art, with the addition of a supernatural crab and a scorpion. This narrow cast of characters is particularly striking because both cultures—the Moche in particular—represented a range of their local animals in other contexts. By contrast, decapitation imagery is extremely circumscribed.[1] This similarity between the Cupisnique and Moche head-takers argues strongly for a continuing tradition of belief (Cordy-Collins 1992).

THE PROBLEM

Although the variety of decapitators is small, it does seem curious that both the Cupisnique and Moche represented more than one kind. All perform the identical task, the severing of heads. Why the multiplicity, small as it may be? The current study aims squarely at this question, and then presents archaeological evidence for ritual activity paralleling the artistic depictions.

Certain rationales may be proposed for the presence of the several characters who functioned as head-takers. One is temporal. Perhaps each decapitator presided over a certain segment of the Cupisnique and Moche ritual calendars. Another is spatial. Different locales may have had their patron head-taker. A further possibility is that the decapitators were group-specific, referring to lineages or occupations. Alternatively, some combination of the above explanations might be valid. We can explore each of these suggested rationales to a limited degree.

Although intriguing, the first possibility—chronology—is the least productive avenue of investigation because we know next to nothing of the way the Cupisnique and the Moche divided time. They certainly were agriculturists, so they must have had a planting/harvest cycle. But they were also fisherfolk, so time may have been counted by phases of the moon as well. And there may have been even more complicated rounds. To explore a chronometric link for each of the decapitators is not particularly productive.

The two other proposed rationales potentially are more fruitful. Although there are no unequivocal proveniences for the Cupisnique material, there are a few for the Moche (Figure 2.1). These attributions are suggestive.

1. In 1967 the Huanchaco Project excavated a Supernatural Scorpion Decapitator in the Moche Valley (Iriarte 1967; see Cordy-Collins 1992: Fig. 13).
2. In 1968 the looting of Loma Negra in the Piura Valley produced a cache of Moche metal objects, some with Spider Decapitators (Lapiner 1976: Figs. 350, 363, 382).
3. In 1987 the Sipán Project recovered multiple examples of the Supernatural Spider Decapitator in the Lambayeque Valley (Alva and Donnan 1993: Figs. 121–123, 125, 126, 228–230).
4. In 1992 the El Brujo Project in the Chicama Valley found a wall painting of two partial Supernatural Spider Decapitators (Figure 2.2; Franco, Gálvez, and Vásquez 1994).
5. In 1994 the Dos Cabezas Project excavated a bowl with Supernatural Fish Decapitator representations in the Jequetepeque Valley (Figure 2.3; Donnan 1994). It is especially intriguing that this bowl was found in a barrio of fisherfolk.

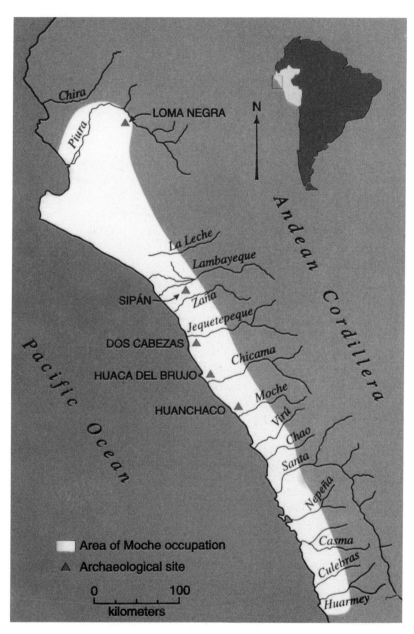

FIGURE 2.1. The north coast of Peru, showing Cupisnique and Moche sites mentioned in the text. Map by Donald McClelland.

FIGURE 2.2. Moche Supernatural Spider Decapitator excavated at Complejo El Brujo, Magdalena de Cao, Chicama Valley. Photo by Alana Cordy-Collins.

FIGURE 2.3. Moche ceramic bowl with four Supernatural Fish Decapitator images, excavated in the fisherfolk barrio, Dos Cabezas, Jequetepeque Valley. Photo by Alana Cordy-Collins.

What this spacing suggests is that—perhaps—the seven Moche decapitators were patrons of specific valleys, settlements, or groups. The limited number of archaeologically recovered objects with decapitator imagery is a hindrance in developing the proposal further, but it can serve as a basis

FIGURE 2.4. Moche ceramic bottle reported to have been found at
Dos Cabezas, Jequetepeque Valley. Enrico Poli Collection, Lima.
Photo courtesy of Christopher Donnan.

for testing the suggestion as more decapitator representations are found in
the future. At this point, three items of support are worth mentioning:

1. Only one type of decapitator has been found at any single site.[2] Local informants in the Jequetepeque Valley state that, prior to 1994, another find
   was made of a Supernatural Fish Decapitator at Dos Cabezas (Figure 2.4).
2. The presence of Supernatural Spider Decapitator images in three different
   sites does not necessarily undermine the lineage- or occupation-specific
   rationale. After all, there are only seven known decapitators, while there
   are many Moche sites. Furthermore, there is some evidence that the Supernatural Spider Decapitator was more important than the others. In the

Cupisnique sample fully half the decapitator representations are the Supernatural Spider (Figure 2.5a, b, c; Bonavia 1994: Figs. 21, 23, 25 [second from right]; Cordy-Collins 1992: Figs. 2, 3; Salazar-Burger and Burger 1982: Figs. 8, 10–14). In the Moche sample, Supernatural Spider Decapitators appear across media: in ceramics, wall murals (Figure 2.2), and metal (Lapiner 1976: Figs. 350, 363, 382).

FIGURE 2.5A–C. Cupisnique ceramic bottle with details incised and resin-painted. Each side shows a trio of severed heads, blood pouring from the wounds. A supernatural spider caps the end opposite the spout. Photo courtesy of David Bernstein Pre-Columbian Art.

3. In the Moche sample there are multiple scenes of the Supernatural Human and Monster in combat (Cordy-Collins 1992: Figs. 9 and 10; Lapiner 1976: Fig. 365). This could refer to competition between two Moche settlements, or groups within a settlement, each with a different decapitator patron.

ARCHAEOLOGICAL LINKS

The 1994 excavations at Dos Cabezas not only found the Supernatural Fish Decapitator bowl mentioned above, but made a startling discovery in one room of a small temple. At the south end of a long, narrow chamber lay eighteen severed human heads (Figure 2.6). Although the heads were completely fleshless when found, the articulation of mandible with cranium—

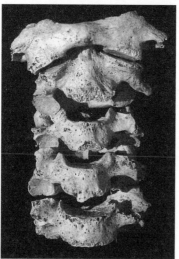

FIGURE 2.6. Moche severed heads in the "Cuarto de los Cráneos," Dos Cabezas, Jequetepeque Valley. Photo by Alana Cordy-Collins.

FIGURE 2.7. Cut marks on cervical vertebrae from the "Cuarto de los Cráneos," Dos Cabezas, Jequetepeque Valley. Photo by Rose Tyson.

FIGURE 2.8. Moche ceramic bottle of the Supernatural Human Decapitator gripping his victim by the hair with one hand, while preparing to remove the victim's head with the *tumi* in his other hand. Museo Rafael Larco Herrera, Lima. Photo by Alana Cordy-Collins.

and some cervical vertebrae in several instances—indicates that they may have been freshly severed when placed in the room. A detailed taphonomic study revealed that the heads had not been moved since their deposition in the room (Tyson 1995). Most importantly, close inspection of the cervical vertebrae shows clear cut marks across the throat of at least four individuals (Figure 2.7). If the cuts resulted from attempts to remove the heads, in these cases the procedure was not successful on the initial attempt. Conversely, those heads without cut marks on the vertebrae may have been cleanly severed through the disc cartilage on the first try. The cut marks appear on the anterior portion of the fourth to sixth cervical vertebrae, or at about the location of one's Adam's apple. Moche art clearly shows us decapitation in just this manner—front to back. Artists illustrate the knife aimed directly at the victim's throat (Figure 2.8). This find at Dos Cabezas marks the first recorded episode of Moche decapitation.

However, although we had found the victims, we were left with the classic mystery question: "Who dunnit?" The answer had to wait a year until our 1995 excavation season was well under way.

That season, as we cleared a ramp which led to an upper story of an architectural complex just south of the 1994 temple, we made an unex-

FIGURE 2.9. Moche ceramic face-neck jar fragment found in the Decapitator's grave, Dos Cabezas, Jequetepeque Valley. Photo by Christopher Donnan.

pected discovery: a burial lay entombed in a narrow space below a floor and between two walls. We expected that excavation would reveal either a post-Moche interment (not uncommon in this architectural zone) or a simple dedicatory burial for the building. Neither proved to be the case. Clearing away the overburden, we found that the body was neither in the flexed upright position of late burials nor in the characteristic north-south extended Moche posture. The individual had been laid out with the head to the east and feet to the west. This uncommon arrangement suggested that we had chanced upon a special interment. The gilded copper triangular pec-torals and elaborate headdress ornaments we encountered next confirmed it. Moreover, the iconography and technology of the ornaments identified this individual as a member of Moche society of the third century A.D.

A single piece of pottery lay near the body on the north side: the snapped-off neck of a small jar with a little modeled human head (Figure 2.9). The ceramic fragment was a puzzle. It seemed so inconsequential an item to be the only ceramic object entombed with an individual of such rank. It was clear that the tomb's inhabitant, an elderly man, had been of considerable importance in life because of the quantity of gilded copper ornaments that covered his head and chest. The jar neck lay almost casually just outside the man's right hand. Had it been accidentally dropped in the tomb and overlooked as the interment took place; or could it even have been placed there as some sort of prehistoric joke to which we were not privy? Other than the apparently standard copper pieces that lay over his feet and under his hands, there were no other grave goods. It was a puzzle that we had no expectation of solving.

Yet solve it we did. Upon removal of the left femur, which had partially obscured his left hand, we learned that the little ceramic head was only half of an unmistakable message. For the thick copper object that the deceased gripped in his slender left hand, its fingers marked with arthritic ridges, was a *tumi*—the crescent-bladed knife used by decapitators (Figure 2.10). No other *tumi* had ever been excavated held in a Moche person's hand.

The only reasonable interpretation is that this diminutive old man, so unassuming in death—with his arthritic bones and few remaining teeth— had in life been a formidable and deadly individual. It appeared that we had unearthed an actual Moche decapitator. That inference, derived from the *tumi*, was heightened by the placement of the little ceramic head near the man's right hand. We now understood that what had seemed such a trivial funerary item was in fact an integral part of his burial paraphernalia; together with the *tumi* it formed a dyad communicating to the future the role the deceased had performed in life: the severing of human heads (Figure 2.11). But had *he* actually decapitated the individuals in the 1994 temple, we wondered?

The answer to that question we probably will never know; however, additional evidence leaves little doubt that he could have. First, the building in which he was buried and the one in which the heads were placed are contemporaneous. Second, the knife he held is heavy and strong. Unlike the soft gold and silver *tumis* worn on the neck of Sipán's Warrior Priest (Alva and Donnan 1993: Figs. 94 and 98), this man's copper *tumi* was functional. Third, although the man was only 135 cm. in height (4′ 5″) and his bones were delicate, the interosseous crests of his forearms exhibit extremely heavy muscle attachments. This fact tells us that the deceased performed some kind of strenuous repeated activity with his lower arms. Moche art illustrates that decapitation was accomplished by seizing the victim by a topknot of hair and dragging him backward to sever the head with a *tumi* (Figure 2.8). To remove a human head with a handheld knife would require considerable strength; the muscles of the neck are dense and fibrous. Although we can't know how frequently a decapitator would have been called upon to ply his trade, it is worth noting that the osteological evidence is not at odds with the other data.

FIGURE 2.10. Moche copper *tumi* gripped in Decapitator's left hand. Dos Cabezas, Jequetepeque Valley. Photo by Alana Cordy-Collins.

FIGURE 2.11. Burial of the Moche Decapitator excavated at Dos Cabezas, Jequetepeque Valley. Photo by Christopher Donnan.

Thus, there is little doubt that our excavations had indeed unearthed an actual Moche decapitator. Unfortunately, other than his bones, no organic material remained in the grave. Even the decorative gilded copper plaques that adorned his body were so deteriorated that only a general idea of their original appearance could be determined. Therefore, we cannot say if this man functioned as a "Fish Decapitator" or not, and—for the time being, at least—the hypothesis of settlement- or group-specific decapitators remains untested. However, it seems extremely unlikely that we could have been fortunate enough to discover the only real decapitator in all of Moche society throughout its six-hundred-year history. Future excavations may well reveal other such individuals, and we should remain attentive to any clue of decapitator-type affiliation. Furthermore, because of the correlation between the Cupisnique and Moche decapitator types, it is a real possibility that the practice, as well as the variety of individuals, was part of Cupisnique society as well. Future excavation of Cupisnique sites may well support this view.

Acknowledgments

I extend my sincere appreciation to Christopher Donnan and Rose Tyson for allowing me to use their unpublished data, and for their help in the preparation of this paper.

Notes

1. Here, as in my earlier study (1992), I identify decapitators narrowly as only those individuals shown with a severed head in hand.
2. Looting in the Loma Negra area of the Piura Valley in the late 1960s produced several decapitator artifacts, including a bird of prey, spiders, a human, and a monster. However, the lack of recording where these pieces actually came from requires that we not assume they were from precisely the same site (see Lapiner 1976: Figs. 350, 363, 365, 382, 385).

CHAPTER 3 *Blood and the Moon Priestesses: Spondylus Shells in Moche Ceremony*

ALANA CORDY-
COLLINS
Anthropology Department,
University of San Diego

INTRODUCTION

Archaeological and artistic evidence informs us that a primary ceremonial focus in Moche society was the ritual bleeding of bound males, captured in combat, and the drinking of their blood (Donnan 1978; Alva and Donnan 1993; Donnan and Castillo 1994). The only female in the roster of elite participants in this ritual is a priestess, one who, we can now suggest, was a major functionary in a cult of the Moon. The inquiry leading to her identification as a Moon priestess is multilineal, but is closely tied to the rather abrupt appearance of symmetrical *Spondylus princeps* shells late in Moche cultural evolution.

THE SACRED SHELL

One of the most intriguing symbolic objects from the ancient Peruvian world is the Spondylus shell (Figure 3.1). Known colloquially as the spiny oyster or the thorny oyster, and scientifically as *Spondylus* spp., this spectacular bivalve has been an item of ritual importance in the region for well over four thousand years. The earliest archaeological remains are a few tiny fragments recovered from Formative Period sites (ca. 3000–2500 B.C.) along the Peruvian coast. Through time, the amount of Spondylus in use in Peru increased until, by the time of the Chimú Empire's apogee (ca. A.D. 1400), vast quantities of the shell were in evidence. Aside from its physical beauty, two characteristics of the shell are noteworthy: (1) it is *not native* to the cold waters of coastal Peru, and (2) it is found *always* in ritual contexts there.

The mollusk is indigenous to both coasts of the Americas, where six species or subspecies, all living in warm-water habitats, are recognized by malacologists. Those closest to Peru are found in Ecuador's Gulf of Guayaquil. There, two species are local: the larger *S. calcifer*, with its interior border of reddish-purple, and the smaller *S. princeps*, with its crimson inner rim. *S. princeps* is the deeper dweller, found as much as 50–60 meters below

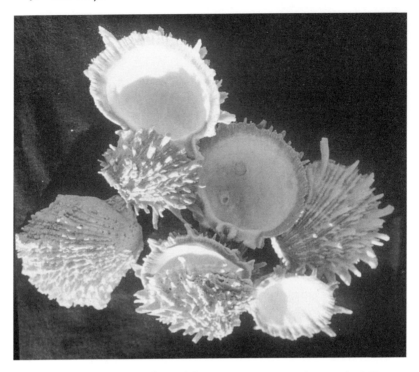

FIGURE 3.1. Open valves of *Spondylus princeps*. Photo by Alana Cordy-Collins.

the ocean surface. Despite the obvious difficulty in collecting the shellfish at such depths—or perhaps precisely because of it—*S. princeps* was the species most utilized by the ancient Peruvians.

My long-term study of Spondylus shells in pre-Hispanic Peru has revealed a clear pattern: from the beginning of the Initial Period (ca. 1800 B.C.) through the end of the Late Horizon (ca. A.D. 1530), Peru's ancient cultures consistently allocated the thorny oyster to four specific ends. They presented it whole or in part in petitions to the gods, interred it as elite mortuary offerings, worked it into jewelry and ornaments for their nobility, and infused its image into all high-status media, including ceramic, textile, and metal. It is widely associated with sacrifice, in part, surely, because of its reddish color, and also because of its significance as a sacred substance.

THE PUZZLE

The one apparent rupture in this social continuum occurs with the Moche (A.D. 100–800). It would seem that the Moche studiously avoided any rep-

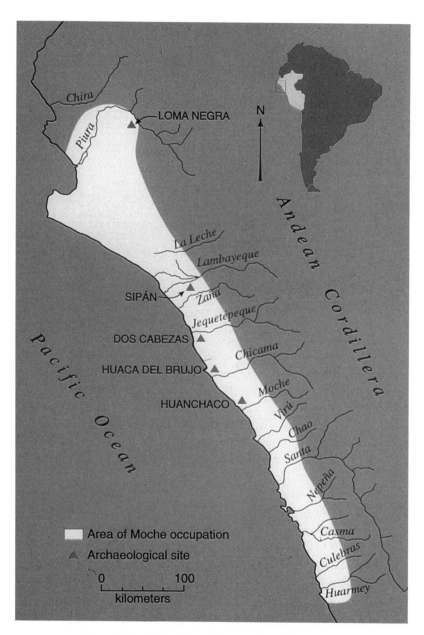

FIGURE 3.2. Map of South America with area of Moche occupation highlighted. Map by Donald McClelland.

resentation of the Spondylus in any medium. Indeed, until the archaeological discoveries at Sipán were made in the 1980s, we were inclined to believe that Peruvian access to the shell somehow had been curtailed during Moche times. We now know that this was not so.

Notable numbers of the bivalves were found among the sumptuous burial goods of Sipán's Warrior Priest, an aristocrat who lived and died in the Lambayeque Valley around the third century A.D. (Alva and Donnan 1993: Fig. 57). His cohorts, the Bird Priest and the Old Lord, were also buried with respectable quantities of the exotic shells (Alva and Donnan 1993: 145–147, 170–171). Subsequently, and to the south in the Jequetepeque Valley, excavations have revealed that the early Moche nobility of La Mina and Dos Cabezas also were sent to the afterlife with an array of Spondylus (Fig. 3.2). Moreover, four hundred years later in Jequetepeque, the elaborate tombs at San José de Moro have demonstrated that the Moche elites of the eighth century still were laid to rest accompanied by thorny-oyster shells. This presence of actual Spondylus shells in clear-cut Moche ritual contexts presented a real conundrum: there can be no question that the Moche revered the porcelaneous mollusks; the puzzle was why they did not represent them—unless they did so in a highly symbolic manner which we have not been able to recognize. To investigate that possibility, we need to examine the associations of Spondylus among other cultures. Here, we arrive at an intriguing discovery. We know that the Inca imported Spondylus shells[1] for water rituals, wherein they were referred to as "daughters of the sea" (Cobo 1956 [1653]: 85). Two millennia before the Inca the Cupisnique and Chavín people of northern Peru revered the thorny oyster, along with the conch, *Strombus galeatus,* as a dyad. In one clear instance, they associated Spondylus with left-sidedness, a characteristic that usually pertains to women, while, in a second instance, it is associated with femaleness directly (Cordy-Collins 1979b). To the north in Mesoamerica, the ancient Maya employed the Spondylus in ritual bloodletting, where it was associated with high-status women (Taylor 1992: 522). We begin to see a picture emerging wherein the shell is linked with femininity. This picture assumes a sharper focus if we look to the present-day Kogi Indians of Colombia. They inter two genera of shell with their deceased (Reichel-Dolmatoff 1974). Each has specific meanings and regimented associations within Kogi belief. One is a univalve whose association is with maleness and the right. The other is a bivalve and pertains to femaleness (as among the Chavín, Inca, and Maya) and the left (as among the Chavín). This complementarity of opposites, dividing the world into polar pairs, was an ingrained perception among many New World cultures. Might the relationship between females and thorny oysters have existed among the Moche?

If it did, a careful examination of paraphernalia and symbolic elements associated with women in Moche art should reveal it.

MOCHE WOMEN AND THE PRIESTESS

Overall in Moche art, women are not prominently featured. Certainly, they are represented, but almost always in a secondary role.

The only women of obvious importance in Moche art are priestesses. Although she is best known from the Sacrifice Ceremony (Donnan 1978; 1988), a priestess is also one of the two paramount individuals in the Tule Boat Ceremony (Cordy-Collins 1972, 1977; McClelland 1990). Priestesses also appear prominently in the Burial Ceremony (Donnan and McClelland 1979) and in the Animated Objects Ceremony.[2] Multiple representations in the Burial Ceremony suggest the existence of several priestesses, perhaps a sisterhood. Indeed, the excavation at San José de Moro of two females buried with the exact accouterments shown with the priestess images in the art supports the inference that a number of real Moche women enacted this role (Donnan and Castillo 1992; 1994).[3] If the Cupisnique/Chavín, Inca, Maya, and Kogi analogies are valid for the Moche, this priestess figure— as the female par excellence—should be represented with Spondylus shells.

THE PRESUMPTIVE OYSTER

For us, the most salient feature of the Spondylus shell is its spiny exterior surface. This was also an important characteristic for many ancient societies, from the Chavín through the Inca, a fact that allows us to identify it in their art. Thus, we have presumed that the Moche also would have emphasized the prickly surface if they represented the shell. But what if they chose to focus on another of its characteristics, such as its color or its form? Unfortunately, because Moche pottery is essentially a red-on-cream ware, the shell's red color would not be a clue—either for us or for the Moche. Another more promising characteristic is its form: cuplike. Then we must ask: are the priestesses ever shown with a cup? The answer is yes, in two clear instances:

1. The classic Sacrifice Ceremony scene illustrates prisoners' blood being collected in stemless "cups" by two individuals, one of whom is a priestess (Figure 3.3, bottom right).[4]
2. A Tule Boat Ceremony scene (Figure 3.4) shows a priestess being handed an identical "cup" by a secondary figure. Although they are omitted from this painting, all similar tule-boat scenes illustrate, below the main deck, bound human prisoners and/or bound jars, which are cognates of the prisoners (Figures 3.5–3.8).

FIGURE 3.3. Sacrifice Ceremony Scene on a ceramic bottle. Priestesses appear twice, once in the upper register, once in the lower. Drawing by Donna McClelland.

FIGURE 3.4. Type 1 Tule Boat Ceremony on a ceramic bottle. Priestess appears on the right, where she is handed a cup. Drawing by Donna McClelland.

If these "cups" are encrypted Spondylus shells, there should be some further association. And, indeed, there is. An article of priestess attire can be identified confidently as a stone weight of the type used in diving for Spondylus shells. It is oval to rectangular in shape, and appears on her dress—usually near the waist or hem (Figures 3.5, 3.7, and 3.9). Actual examples of such stone diving weights were found in excavations of a Spondylus processing workshop on La Plata Island in Ecuador (Marcos and Norton 1981: 149). The form and relative size of the excavated examples are comparable to objects worn on the waist of Spondylus divers in the Moche-derived art of Lambayeque (Cordy-Collins 1990: Figs. 2 and 15). Both the Ecuadorean and Lambayeque weights are comparable in size and form to the object the priestesses wear in the Tule Boat Ceremony and in an abbreviated example of the Sacrifice Ceremony (Figure 3.10, top left; McClelland 1990: 89).

Thus, evidence does seem to argue for the Moche having represented the Spondylus shell in their art after all, but in a very limited context and in a very limited time period. All examples of the priestesses in the art are late, whether they appear in the Sacrifice, Tule Boat, Burial, or Animated Objects Ceremony. Furthermore, the only known burials of Moche priestesses are also late, ca. A.D. 720. This period—the eighth century—was a time of tremendous change and upheaval within Moche society. Climatic shifts may have been a factor (McClelland 1990), and rather suddenly the

FIGURE 3.5. Type I Tule Boat Ceremony on a ceramic bottle. Priestess appears on the right, wearing a diving weight on the hem of her skirt. Bound prisoners and jars appear in the hold of both boats. Drawing by Donna McClelland.

FIGURE 3.6. Type I Tule Boat Ceremony on a ceramic bottle. Priestess appears on the right wearing insect wings on her headdress train. Lower portion of her boat is missing because of spalled paint, but in the hold of the other boat appear bound prisoners and bound jars. Drawing by Donna McClelland.

FIGURE 3.7. Type I Tule Boat Ceremony on a ceramic bottle. Priestess appears on the right wearing a diving weight on her waist. Bound prisoners and bound jars appear in the hold of each boat. Drawing by Donna McClelland.

FIGURE 3.8. Type I Tule Boat Ceremony on a ceramic bottle. Priestess appears on the right. Bound prisoners and bound jars appear in the hold of the boat at the left. Drawing by Donna McClelland.

old frontiers dissolved, perhaps within a few generations or less. Foreign pottery from the central coast and highlands of Peru made its way into the Moche sphere (Donnan and Castillo 1992; 1994). A new burial pattern mixed with the indigenous Moche one (Cordy-Collins 1993; 1994a). Exotic deities appeared (McClelland 1990). Long-distance commerce developed and the Mexican hairless dog was brought into the Moche realm (Cordy-Collins 1994b). A new, apparently non-Peruvian, loincloth type appeared in the cultural inventory. Instead of the traditional baggy breechcloth, worn consistently heretofore on the north coast, the looped Mesoamerican garment type came into vogue (Figure 3.11). And the Spondylus? Even it changed. All Spondylus shells recovered archaeologically from the early Moche period, be they from Sipán, La Mina, or Dos Cabezas, are characteristically misshapen (Figure 3.12; Alva and Donnan 1993: Figs. 164 and 167). Yet, from 700 A.D. on, all Spondylus from datable contexts are curved, symmetrically shaped shells (see Figure 3.1). It would seem that even the source of Moche Spondylus shifted.[5] All the Spondylus beds lie to the north of Moche territory; the new locus must be in that direction. Elsewhere, I have argued that Ecuadoreans of this time period were instrumental in introducing increased quantities of the marine mollusk into Peru

FIGURE 3.9. Type 2 Tule Boat Ceremony on a ceramic bottle. Priestess appears on the left wearing a diving weight on her torso. Bound jars appear in the hold of each boat. Drawing by Donna McClelland.

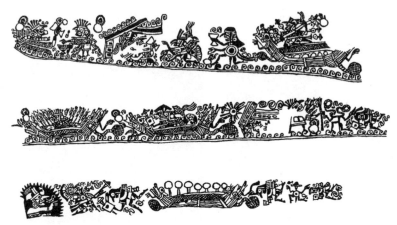

FIGURE 3.10. Composite of three ceremonies on a ceramic bottle: sacrifice at top left and center; tule boat at top right and center left and center; animated objects at center right and bottom. Priestess appears in all three as indicated. Drawing by Donna McClelland.

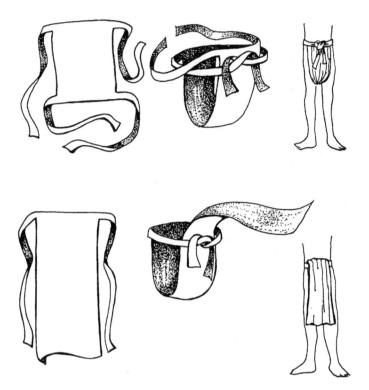

FIGURE 3.11. Top—traditional loincloth worn on the Peruvian north coast through the end of Moche times (note sash at both ends, allowing the garment to be tied front and back); bottom—"new" loincloth type worn on the Peruvian north coast following Moche times (note single sash tied in front, allowing plain end to drape over it). Drawing by Donna Kindig.

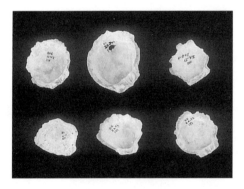

FIGURE 3.12. Sipán Spondylus shells inside (a) and outside (b). Photo by Alana Cordy-Collins.

(Cordy-Collins 1990). Moreover, there is unequivocal evidence to support an Ecuadorean commercial exchange with West Mexico at this time (Hosler, Lechtman, and Holm 1990). Therefore, we may question what Mesoamerican attitudes or beliefs regarding Spondylus might be relevant to the Moche priestesses and their involvement with the shell.

THE MAYA

Among the Maya it is intriguing to learn that sacrificial blood was sometimes collected by females using Spondylus valves as collection cups, as a scene at Bonampak suggests (Taylor 1992: 522, Room 2 mural). Such a practice plainly parallels that of the Moche priestesses in their Sacrifice Ceremony duties (and perhaps those in the Tule Boat as well). Might the Moche idea of females collecting human sacrificial blood in Spondylus shells have had its origins among the Maya? Exploring the Maya practice still further, we learn that those females were associated with the Moon Goddess. We have strong circumstantial evidence of a Moche lunar deity.

A PERUVIAN LUNAR CULT

We can establish at least five salient points of support for Moon worship on the coast of Peru in ancient times:

1. Soon after the Spanish conquered Peru, the Spaniards recorded a north-coast belief in a moon deity known as *Si.* This deity was female, and was worshipped in a special temple called *Si-an,* "House of the Moon." *Si-an* (also known as *Signan* or *Siñan*) still stands today, located just outside the town of Guadalupe, in the Jequetepeque Valley, less than two kilometers from the place where the priestesses of San José de Moro were buried. The chronicles tell us that her disciples worshipped her through human sacrifice (Rowe 1948: 49–50).[6]

2. The Spanish also documented that the Inca, while primarily worshiping the (male) sun, which was symbolized by gold, venerated the moon. The moon was associated with silver and with females, a belief the Inca may have co-opted, as they did other cultural elements when they conquered the north coast in the fifteenth century. A creation myth recorded from the north coast states that noble women emerged from a silver egg (Davidson 1980: 27).

3. Among the eighth-century Moche, silver clearly was associated with females, specifically with the priestesses. The two recovered at San José de Moro were interred with silver body sheathing (Donnan and Castillo 1994).

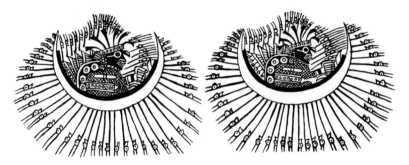

FIGURE 3.13. Type 3 Tule Boat Ceremony on a ceramic bottle. Priestess appears in both boats, now reduced to crescents with rays. She wears a diving weight on her torso. The rayed crescents may represent Spondylus shells. Drawing by Donna McClelland.

4. As far back as the third century, the Moche recognized a silver/gold duality wherein silver was associated with the left (Alva and Donnan 1993: 221, 223), the female side among the Kogi and the Spondylus side among the Chavín.

5. The priestesses' tule boat is often reduced to a crescent shape (Figure 3.13) which some researchers have suggested represents a crescent moon (Benson 1985, 1989; Lavallée 1970: 103, 106–107). Heretofore, I have argued against this interpretation, citing the lack of associated lunar attributes (Cordy-Collins 1977). However, in light of the data currently at hand, that argument seems less tenable; I think it is very likely that the boat represents a moon after all. Furthermore, most examples of this crescent are embellished with spiny projections. Such an image could have been intended to represent the spiny oyster itself.[7]

By compiling the salient features of these five points, we produce a Moche iconographic complex in which are associated Spondylus shells, noble females, blood, silver, and the moon. This complex almost exactly parallels that of the ancient Maya.

THE PRIESTESS-PRIEST

An interesting ambiguity exists in the terminal representations of the priestesses, as Moche society made a transition into the Lambayeque tradition. They became increasingly modified by male characteristics—including a Mesoamerican loincloth. Hybridized images of the priestesses (always identifiable by a characteristic plumed headdress) were created, whereby they were conflated with the male counterpart in the Tule Boat Ceremony (who is identifiable by his characteristic aura of clubs and shields). These hybridized individuals wear a loincloth and the priestesses' plumed head-dress, and are haloed by clubs and shields (Figure 3.14; Donnan 1976: Fig. 6). Another example of this hybridization is evident from archaeo-logical excavations. The two priestesses recovered at San José de Moro had been interred with over-life-size masks made of silvered copper. These masks were prototypic of the over-life-size gilded copper masks associated with males in Lambayeque burials (Cordy-Collins 1993, 1994a; see exam-ples of the latter in Shimada and Griffin 1994). Silver masks are unknown from the later period, however, and it could be that the role and duties of the old Moche priestesses were co-opted by the new Lambayeque priests. It is interesting in this regard to note that, among the Maya, males sometimes donned female attire for bloodletting ceremonies, thus merging gender in a comparable fashion.[8]

The question then arises: Did the Maya, with their long-standing sac-rifice of royal prisoners, introduce the Sacrifice Ceremony to the Moche? The answer is somewhat equivocal; excavations at Sipán have established that the Moche Sacrifice Ceremony is old, dating back at least to the third century. Decapitator images interred with the Warrior Priest, the Old Lord, and the individual in the looted tomb suggest that the practice of human blood sacrifice on the north coast extends even further back into Cupis-nique times (Cordy-Collins 1992 and this volume). Yet, it is notable that Sipán has yielded no priestesses. Those at San José de Moro lived some five hundred years after the Sipán priests. It is tempting to speculate that the priestesses may have been latecomers, part of the cultural practices that ebbed and flowed between Mesoamerica and the Andean area during the seventh and eighth centuries A.D. If their Moche origin lies in the Maya cult of the Moon Goddess, it is easy to understand why their association

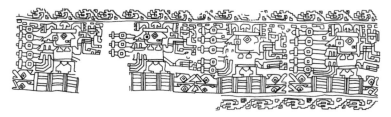

FIGURE 3.14. Tule Boat Ceremony on a textile in the Museo Amano, Lima, Peru. The Priestess and her male counterpart have been conflated. Note her loincloth and the clubs and shields behind her. She holds a goblet and wears her floppy headdress. Drawing by Alana Cordy-Collins.

there with human blood sacrifice would have provided a strong motive for their adoption into the Moche Sacrifice Ceremony of ancient Peru.

ADDENDUM

The Priestess

There are two major points that can be made about the Moche priestess. First, it can be demonstrated that she is the same character who officiates in three apparently interrelated ceremonies shown in the art: Sacrifice, Tule Boat, and Burial. Second, it is demonstrable that "she" is, in fact, "several"; there is good evidence that more than a single Moche woman filled the priestess role, both synchronically and diachronically. Examination of her clothing details and associations in Sacrifice Ceremony scenes allows for her positive identification in the Tule Boat, Burial, and Animated Objects scenes.

Sacrifice Ceremony

The most characteristic trait of a Moche priestess is her headdress, which is a band with large plumes. These number two (Donnan 1978: Figs. 241 bottom, 243, and 250), three (Donnan 1978: Fig. 254 left), or four (Cordy-Collins 1972: Fig. 28a). Another feature of her headdress, shown in two Sacrifice Ceremony scenes (Figures 3.15 and 3.16; Donnan 1978: Figs. 243 and 254 left), is pertinent to our analysis. This is a headcloth that forms a train down her back. In Figure 3.15 it has small attachments at the bottom, while in Figure 3.16, its vertical axis is ornamented with elongated oval elements, which seem to be insect wings.

Tule Boat Ceremony

There are three essential variants of the Tule Boat Ceremony (Cordy-Collins 1972; 1977). However, there is an internal consistency of the priestess depictions within each. For convenience, these variants are categorized here as Types 1–3. In the most detailed, Type 1, the priestess stands in a tule boat (Figures 3.4–3.8). Her headdress in three of these examples is nearly identical to what she wears in the Sacrifice Ceremony. In Figure 3.4 it is a band with three plumes, the left and right ones drooping down, and the central one upright. An undecorated headcloth trails down her back. Figures 3.6 and 3.7 show a headdress with a similar central upright plume, but with three and two (respectively) smaller drooping plumes to the left and right. In Figure 3.5 the bottom of the headcloth train is decorated similarly to the one she wears in the Sacrifice Ceremony scene shown in Figure 3.15, while

FIGURE 3.15. Fragmentary Sacrifice Ceremony on a mural at Pañamarca, Casma Valley, Peru. Priestess appears at the extreme left. Drawing by Donna McClelland.

FIGURE 3.16. Sacrifice Ceremony. Priestess appears second from bottom right. Design incised on a metal rattle at the American Museum of Natural History, New York. Drawing by Patrick Finnerty.

FIGURE 3.17. Type 2 Tule Boat Ceremony on a ceramic bottle. Priestess appears on the right drinking from a goblet and wearing a train with insect wings. Bound jars appear in the hold of both boats. Drawing by Donna McClelland.

in Figure 3.6 the train is ornamented with the elongated oval elements much like those in the Figure 3.16 Sacrifice Ceremony scene.

Three associations further equate the priestess in the Tule Boat Ceremony with the priestess in the Sacrifice Ceremony. The essential character of the Sacrifice Ceremony is the bloodletting of bound prisoners and the collection and consumption of the blood by elite individuals using special vessels (Donnan 1978: 158–173; Donnan 1988; Donnan and Castillo 1992, 1994). Figures 3.5–3.8 illustrate tule boats with prisoners bound together below the deck, along with a group of similarly bound jars—apparent prisoner cognates. In Figure 3.4 the priestess is handed a cup of the same form used to collect the prisoners' blood in the Sacrifice Ceremony (Figure 3.3).

The Type 2 Tule Boat Ceremony scenes offer less detail (as in Figure 3.9), but one scene is especially noteworthy (Figure 3.17; also see Hocquenghem 1987: Fig. 114). The priestess is shown without prisoners, but with bound jars. Furthermore, she imbibes from the same sort of goblet used by the elite blood-drinkers in the Sacrifice Ceremony (compare Figure 3.3 and Donnan 1978: Figs. 240–243, 249–250, 254–255). Moreover, in this same example, she wears a headband with plumes (in this case, the large ones appear to the back and front, whereas the smaller ones are in the center), and a train with the elongated oval elements drapes down her back. In shape and marking, these are most similar to the wings of dragonflies as shown in Moche art. Given the role of the priestess in the Sacrifice Ceremony, this voraciously carnivorous insect is an apt insignia for her. Here, as in most Types 1 and 2 Tule Boat Ceremony scenes, the priestess is paired with a second individual

(Figure 3.9 right; Cordy-Collins 1972: 14–17), a male (the short garment argues for such an identification), who usually is surrounded by an aura of clubs and shields. Occasionally, this aura is shown also around a prominent male figure with whom the priestess is closely associated in the Sacrifice Ceremony (Cordy-Collins 1972: Fig. 28a; Donnan 1978: Fig. 241). Thus, both her garb and her associations indicate that the Tule Boat Ceremony priestess is the same character as the Sacrifice Ceremony priestess. Most Type 2 Tule Boat Ceremony scenes depict the priestess dressed differently, but consistently, in what appears to be a net garment (Figure 3.9 is representative). She is often shown wearing a cape that is ornamented with circular elements (see also the Type 1 example in Figure 3.7). Her headdress is a simple band with several small plumes (the exact number varies) and a segmented train. Many examples illustrate her with an elongated oval object, horizontally located at waist level (e.g., Figures 3.5 and 3.7–3.9) and shown with one or more vertical elements that apparently attach the object to her costume (Cordy-Collins 1977: Figs. 1, 3, 5, 12, 13, 16, and 18). It is this object that I have identified as a diving weight (see discussion in body of text).

Type 3 Tule Boat Ceremony scenes are abbreviations of Type 2 scenes, where the boat is reduced to its simple crescent shape (Cordy-Collins 1977). Sometimes the Moche painted a crescent (Figure 3.13), while at other times they let the lower part of the vessel chamber represent the crescent three-dimensionally. One of these illustrations (Cordy-Collins 1977: Fig. 17) is especially noteworthy because the priestess is depicted with a mouth emanation which can be identified as a dragonfly "antenna," based on its characteristic inward curl (Donnan 1978: 41). Again, this would seem to refer to her Sacrifice Ceremony role.

Burial Ceremony

There is great consistency in the Burial Ceremony representations (Donnan and McClelland 1979), but there are important variations that relate to the priestess. She most frequently wears the net costume with segmented train in which she usually appears in the Tule Boat Ceremony. However, there are also illustrations of her clothed in a dotted or circle-decorated garment like the one in the Tule Boat scene of Figure 3.17, wherein she has dragonfly wings (compare with Donnan and McClelland 1979: Figs. 10–11). Often she also wears a cape with dots, as in the Tule Boat Ceremony scenes cited above. Almost invariably the priestess's headdress is the simple band with small plumes usually found in Tule Boat Ceremony representations. Two exceptions show her wearing a headdress with a pair of floppy plumes similar to what she wears in the Sacrifice Ceremony (see Donnan 1978: Figs. 241 bottom and 243). Another example shows her with a dragonfly "antenna" emerging from her mouth (Donnan and McClelland 1979: Fig. 6).

Animated Object Ceremony

In these scenes, the priestess is involved in the apprehension of anthropomorphized objects such as clothing and other personal gear (Figure 3.10, center right; Donnan 1978: Fig. 278). In this ceremony she is clothed in a dress and the floppy-plumed headdress. She also wears a diving weight on her skirt. Thus, the overlap of features among the four ceremonies argues strongly for the equivalency of the priestesses depicted therein.

Multiplicity

There are two categories of evidence for the priestess having been more than a single individual. Archaeology has produced diachronic evidence. Excavations at San José de Moro unearthed burials of two priestesses who appear to have held the office sequentially (Donnan and Castillo 1992; 1994). The synchronic evidence for several priestesses derives from the art,[9] where multiple priestess images appear in all the Burial Ceremony scenes. Especially convincing is one such scene in which a standing priestess exchanges a conch shell with a seated priestess (Donnan and McClelland 1979: Fig. 10). Particularly supportive of the argument is that the two priestesses wear different versions of the standard clothing. It may be that this costume dichotomy was intended to convey a differential status between the women. The seated one may be a "Mother Superior," and the other an acolyte.

Yet another example of multiplicity is found in a vignette of the Sacrifice Ceremony wherein a seated priestess quaffs (we suppose blood) from a goblet apparently just handed her by a standing priestess—the cover of the goblet is in the hand of the standing woman (Figure 3.10, top left). The pose and activity of the seated female are akin to those of the priestess in the Tule Boat Ceremony shown in Figure 3.17. In the current example, the clothing of the two priestesses is similar, but the seated individual wears a zoomorphized cape or mantle. That, along with her having been attended by the standing woman, indicates a differential status between the two.

In closing, it should be pointed out that the Figure 3.10 depiction of the priestess engaged in three of her roles on a single bottle is unlikely to have been coincidental (she is shown in a tule boat at the top of the center register). A more likely explanation is that it indicates an overlap of events in the mental template of the Moche artist.

Notes

Author's note: A preliminary version of this chapter was presented as a paper in the symposium "Parallels, Patterns, and Politics: Art of the Moche and the Maya" at the Denver Art Museum on October 15, 1994.

1. Probably by way of the Chincha-controlled coastal trade network (see Rostworowski 1975).

2. The Addendum to this chapter contains a detailed discussion documenting the case for the woman in these four contexts being the same character.

3. Documents attest to there having been, in the northern Moche territory (Jequetepeque Valley–north) during the sixteenth century, a high-ranked order of women who commanded the services of lesser-ranked females (Netherly 1977: 232–233).

4. Daniel Arsenault (1994) has made a very convincing argument for this figure's being an anthropomorphized carding device symbolic of the priestesses.

5. Jorge Marcos informs me that the smooth and misshapen shells can be found together in the same beds; the former develop in sandy spots, while the latter grow around rocks. Each locale literally makes its imprint on the shells (personal communication, 1999). Because the two shapes can occur together, it would seem that a selection process dictated which forms were sent to which markets.

6. Folklore has it that children were sacrificed there to the deity.

7. I would like to thank an anonymous woman in the audience at Denver who suggested this to me.

8. Similarly, among the historic Mapuche shamans of Chile, males could assume female guise to practice their craft (Tom D. Dillehay, personal communication, 1995).

9. The two priestesses from San José de Moro may have been partially contemporaneous.

CHAPTER 4   *Blood, Fertility, and Transformation:*
Interwoven Themes in the Paracas
Necropolis Embroideries

MARY FRAME   The Necropolis of Wari Kayan on the Paracas Penin-
Vancouver, Canada   sula is the source of an extraordinarily rich textile leg-
                     acy. Four hundred twenty-nine bundles were exca-
vated at this south-coast site during the late 1920s by Julio C. Tello and
his team. The funerary bundles were concentrated in two areas, or nuclei,
on the flank of Cerro Colorado, where they had been placed within abandoned dwellings. The largest bundles, when unwrapped, revealed exqui-
sitely embroidered fabrics (J. Tello 1959; Tello and Mejía 1979; Carrión
Cachot 1931, 1949). Despite nearly two thousand years of being buried in
the sandy desert, many of the fabrics are still bright in color and in excellent
condition.

Questions persist as to who is buried at the Necropolis site and where
the textiles were made. Water is scarce on the peninsula, the habitation site
near the beach is small, and no signs of the spinning, weaving, and embroi-
dering activities so evident in the Necropolis bundles have been unearthed
there. In the adjacent valleys of the south coast, three cultural traditions
were interacting between about 100 B.C. and A.D. 200 (Paul 1991a: 22),
the time span represented at the Necropolis. Ceramics of the Paracas, Topará, and Nasca traditions overlap in time and spatial distribution in the
area from the Cañete Valley to the Nasca drainage (Silverman 1991). Several embroidery styles occur at the Necropolis, and they are mixed together
in some of the bundles. While some embroidered figures resemble figures
on Nasca ceramics, it is Topará ceramics that are found at the site. These
and other puzzling facts have generated divergent hypotheses to explain the
Necropolis burials: a local peninsula population who used the burial site
continuously (Paul 1990); a population living in the adjacent valleys who
buried their dead on the peninsula (Peters 1991; Silverman 1991); secondary
depositions of bundles removed to the peninsula from Pisco Valley burial
sites (Rowe 1995); a regional cult drawing textile tribute from south-coast
populations in a number of valleys for rituals and burials on the peninsula
(Frame 1995). While final answers to the most basic questions await further

archaeology, the embroidered fabrics and the bundles in which they were placed provide a window into the myth and ritual surrounding the burial of the dead at the Necropolis site.

Of the 429 bundles excavated at the Necropolis, about 65 were large or medium in size and contained the majority of the richly embroidered fabrics. The large bundles have some consistency in their layered construction and the range of offerings they contain, although each bundle is quite distinct. The embroidered textiles interleaved in the bundle layers have the form of garments, but it seems likely that they were new when placed in the bundles (Carrión Cachot 1931). Some bundles have matching garments, but they may also have high numbers of a single garment type and an absence of other types. The sizes of garments are variable, ranging from miniature to gigantic, and there is little discernible pattern in the distribution of sizes, beyond the occurrence of the largest mantles and shirts in the outermost layer of the largest bundles. Large bundles, such as Bundle 89 (Paul 1991b), can include the smallest garments, aside from the packets of truly miniature garments that accompany bundles. The apparent newness of the garments, the mixtures of embroidery styles in some bundles, and the odd distribution of garment types and sizes draw into question the assumption that the textile offerings pertain solely to the person in the bundle. The character of bundles may relate more strongly to what the people who constructed the bundles ritually were expressing through the medium of clothing. The construction of the bundles has a degree of correspondence with the themes represented in the embroideries, and both will be discussed in more detail.

Numerous studies have been devoted to the description of the intriguing imagery on the more than one thousand fabrics with figurative embroidery. Many have contributed to the identification of animal, plant, costume, and supernatural attributes of figures, or to the description of some figure types. Labels such as mythological beings, demons, impersonators, trophy-head warriors, supernaturals, and cult objects have been used by researchers to describe the human- and animal-like figures and to suggest meaning. However, relatively little work has been done on the interrelationships between figures[1] and the underlying themes, which will be the focus of this chapter.

This chapter will look at three layers of references that recur in textiles embroidered in the "block-color" style:[2] blood, fertility, and transformation. Bloodletting is implied in many figures through the severed heads and knives they carry. Images of predation, autosacrifice, and evident wounds also indicate bleeding. Fertility is expressed primarily through references to plants. Plants sprout from figures; seeds, particularly beans, repeat within figures or replace entire bodies. Although the references to blood and fertility are not fully developed in single figures, they emerge as pervasive themes or metaphors when examples from different bundles are grouped together.

The third theme—transformation—also can be illustrated by grouping figures on textiles from different bundles. Varied figures with overlapping, but not identical, traits can be ordered to show transitions and transformations. The overlapping of traits between figures suggests sequences in a pictorial narrative. The central strand of this narrative follows the transformation of scantily clad, backward-bent figures to richly dressed and adorned figures that then take on the attributes of animals, particularly major predators. The general drift of the sequences of images appears to be the mythic transformation of the dead to ancestor and animal counterpart. The interconnected references to fertility and blood interweave with the narrative and will be discussed throughout the presentation of figure sequences.

CONVENTIONS OF THE EMBROIDERED IMAGERY

The block-color style of embroidery uses curved lines to define shapes (Dwyer 1979: 112) and separately colored areas to depict a wealth of figural detail in costume, ornament, pelage, and plumage. This style is most closely related to the Nasca style, as a comparison of ceramic and embroidered figures illustrates (Lapiner 1976: Fig. 469; Stone-Miller 1992: Plate 12).

Although the block-color style is detailed and depictive, the reflection it provides of the ancient world should be recognized as a distorted one, mythic in content, couched in artistic conventions, and overlaid with visual metaphors. Embroidered figures, which may be distinguished from each other by traits of earthly animals, are separated from living species by nonnatural traits. These include the attachment of streamers to figures (Lyon 1979: 97), improbable or impossible combinations of species and postures, and the animation of inanimate objects. Visual metaphors or substitutions abound, and the pervasive themes of blood and fertility, here called metaphoric lines,[3] parallel and interchange, endowing figures with multiple allusions. Artistic conventions imbuing figures with movement sometimes provide consecutive motions or startling, instantaneous transformations. The artistic conventions that animate figures and the metaphoric lines reiterate major themes, and this discussion of them will be interspersed with the presentation of figures making up the sequences of mythic transformation.

GARMENTS FOR THE ANCESTORS

The embroidered Necropolis textiles are generally in the form of garments: shirts, ponchitos, loincloths, wraparound skirts, headcloths, and mantles (Carrión Cachot 1931: 75–85; Tello and Mejía 1979: 474–477; Paul 1990: 47–58). They have neckslits, armholes, and ties appropriately positioned for the human body, although the dimensions are not always appropriate. Apertures may be too small for arms or heads, or simply not opened (for example, Paracas Necropolis[4] 114–31, American Museum of Natural History, New York, 41.2/8768; PN 89–26, Museo Nacional de Arqueología, Antropología, y Historia del Perú, Lima, 2489; PN 190–27, MNAAHP 3198), and a number of loincloths with two to four corner ties are too small to be wrapped around the hips and tied (Paul 1991b: 205–210). Some are suitable for giants, like the fringed shirts that dressed some of the largest effigy bundles (Bennett 1938: 121). Miniature versions of skirts, tunics, ponchos, and mantles, often between five and fifteen centimeters in the longest direction, occur as interior or exterior offerings. Packets of the diminutive garments accompanying no less than twenty of the opened Necropolis bundles have been referred to in published reports, and several have been described in detail (O'Neale 1935; J. Tello 1959: Lám. LXVII A,B, and Figs. 37–39; Tello and Mejía 1979: 360, 437–440; Yacovleff and Muelle 1934: 108–112).

A careful reading of the dimensions of garments from different bundles reveals that a wide range of sizes is present even among those that might be thought of as human-size, either child or adult.[5] Four- to sevenfold differences in the area of ponchos and turbans, respectively, suggest that, on one conceptual level, the clothes refer to growth stages. As most garments appeared to be new or even unfinished according to those who unwrapped the bundles,[6] the allusions to growth more likely refer to a growth cycle envisioned as taking place after physical death rather than during life. Excessive concentrations of a single garment type in some bundles[7] also suggest these are primarily offerings, and not the personal wardrobe of the interred, perhaps "offered to the corpse as marks of its new status as deceased" (Dwyer and Dwyer 1975: 160). Collectively, the garments that span miniature to gigantic sizes could refer to a mythic growth cycle that begins as tiny as a seed and progresses to well beyond human size.

The largest of the mummy bundles echo, in their very construction, the growth cycle hinted at by the differently sized garments. The seated dead, naked or nearly so, is wrapped in multiple layers of folded or draped garments, alternated with layers of plain wrapping cloths, until the bundle attains a height of five feet in some cases.[8] The bundles are purposefully layered, as if emphasizing stages in the growing size. Sometimes headbands are wrapped around a knoblike false head of bunched cloth in all of the plain-cloth layers (Bennett 1938: 123), giving the impression of nested human effigies of successively larger sizes. In the outer layers, the huge conical bundle might be "dressed" in a shirt, mantle, turban, and sometimes a cape of bird feathers or a fox skin, and provided with a staff and feather fan, as if it were a seated giant (*Peru durch die Jahrtausende* 1984: 48–49; Paul 1990: 37–41; J. Tello 1929: 131–141; J. Tello 1959: Lám. XI–XXI; Tello and Mejía 1979: Lám. III–X).

The corpse at the center of the bundle is transformed into an effigy of a much larger and more richly dressed personage in the completed bundle. The intermediate stages in the transformation are represented in the layered, interior structure of the bundle. I am calling the corpse within the bundle the "recent dead" and the transformed mummy bundle an "ancestor" effigy, to distinguish initial and later stages in the transformation cycle after physical death.[9] A parallel expression of growth and transformation of the recent dead to ancestor is contained in figures embroidered on the fabric offerings in the bundles. Although I consider the embroidered figures both supernaturals and mythical beings (Lyon 1979; Proulx 1968), the terms "recent dead" and "ancestor" suggest both a kinship with the living and a staged transformation cycle. The living begin the mythic cycle of transformation, in both the funerary bundles and the embroidered depictions, at the point where their earthly life cycle ends.

THE BACKBENT FIGURE AND ITS WOUNDS

On the garments, the seminal figure of the mythic transformation sequences is acutely backbent and nearly naked. A cluster of traits often occurs in the figures that initiate the transformation cycle: the extraordinary posture, the skeletal ribs, the loose hair, the little skirt the figure wears, and the baton and fan in the hands (Figure 4.1a–d). Many researchers have commented on this figure, variously describing it as falling, flying, diving, drowning, dancing, or trancing in shamanic ecstasy.[10] Everyone seems to agree, however, that the skeletal ribs indicate a connection with death, at least symbolic death.

The acutely bent posture is also one that exposes the most vulnerable parts of the body, the neck and the viscera, and the figures exhibit signs of wounds. Some figures of this type have a neatly defined square at the throat and a projection from the uptilted chin (Figure 4.1c, d). The flanged shape of the projection and its position suggest that it depicts a neck vertebra[11] and the square at the throat the hole into which the vertebral column would have fit before decapitation.

FIGURE 4.1. Variants of the backward-bent figures from embroidered garments illustrate the minimal traits usually associated with this figure (drawings by Mary Frame): (a) Paracas Necropolis 91–92, Museo Nacional de Arqueología, Antropología, y Historia del Perú, Lima, 2493, loincloth; (b) PN 243–17, MNAAHP 0892, poncho; (c) The Textile Museum, Washington, D.C., 91.159, mantle; (d) Boston Museum of Fine Arts, 31.501, mantle.

Other depictions of the backbent figure flick back and forth between two representations, one with its hand on top of its greatly expanded chest and the other with a skinny torso and arms outflung (Figure 4.2). The alternation suggests that they represent sequential action, most likely related to the difference in chest size. Both figures have a square or circle, possibly a hole, represented in the area of the sternum. This pair of figures occurs on a number of border fragments (Paul and Turpin 1986: 24), often with the death aspect heightened by the depiction of a defleshed nose (Anton 1987: Fig. 59; Frame 1995: Fig. 9) or a head that is not quite connected to the body (Figure 4.2).

A figure pair with abnormal chests from Bundle 382 is more explicit: a gaping hole in the chest of the larger figure is depicted by leaving the area unembroidered on the figures in the mantle field (Figure 4.3a). The figure seems to be withdrawing a heart-shaped fan from the hole. It alternates with a smaller-chested figure that brandishes the fan/heart aloft (Figure 4.3b). The two figures, like successive frames in an animated cartoon, ap-

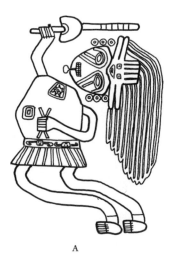 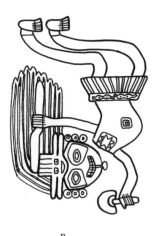

A   B

FIGURE 4.2. Two backbent figures, one with an expanded chest (a) and one
with a slender torso (b), are embroidered on the field and borders of a mantle.
Paracas Necropolis 38–14, Museo Nacional de Arqueología, Antropología,
y Historia del Perú, Lima, 1269.

A   B

FIGURE 4.3. Figures during and after the autosacrificial act. The
unembroidered area depicting the hole in the chest (a) is shaded. Paracas
Necropolis 382–9, Museo Nacional de Arqueología, Antropología, y Historia
del Perú, Lima, 1671, mantle.

FIGURE 4.4. A feather fan was placed in the area of the effigy's heart in many large and midsize bundles. Paracas Necropolis Bundle 114, American Museum of Natural History, New York, before it was unwrapped. Courtesy of Department of Library Services, AMNH, neg. no. 2A 7351.

pear to capture a particularly grisly act of autosacrifice by tearing one's own heart out and displaying it. A similar pair of figures repeats on several garment borders in Bundle 49, and one pair has been published in color (Lavalle and Lang 1983: 79).

The association of fan and heart in these depictions is made not only on the basis of a similar shape and location and a seeming action. The feather fan is an offering found in many bundles (Frame 1995: Fig. 2; J. Tello 1929: 133; Tello and Mejía 1979: Lám. IVc, 476–478; Yacovleff 1933b: 149–156). It is most often placed in the area of the heart in the outer layer of the bundle, where the bundle is dressed in garments and made into a humanlike effigy (Figure 4.4). As if it were the animating force of the nearly completed effigy bundle, the fan is consistently positioned to substitute for the heart, operating like a visual pun or metaphor for heart in the effigy bundles as well as the embroidered images.

In some representations of the backbent figure, the fan is much smaller and could be seen as a knife (Figure 4.1d). Multiple substitutions that visually pun on some common feature, such as shape, or on a thematic connection, such as the knife used to cut out the heart, are normal in this densely allusive art.

A three-dimensional representation, found in a cast of a vessel reportedly from Cahuachi,[12] gives another view of the backbent figure as arched across a vessel (Figure 4.5). The figure does not seem to be dancing, drowning, or flying but rather, exposed and vulnerable, prepared for sacrifice. The spouts protruding from the chest echo the grievous chest wounds of some of the embroidered figures. The carved handrest of a bone spearthrower in the Cleveland Museum of Art depicts the head and torso of a backbent figure and is incised with details of loose hair, skeletal ribs, and a cut across its exposed throat.[13] This type of wound parallels that on the figures with a protruding neck vertebra (Figures 4.1c, d).

Wounds that would have bled profusely are depicted in the embroideries, in addition to the neck and chest wounds of the backbent figures. A self-inflicted wound is clearly shown in a figure who drives a hafted knife into its distended stomach (Figure 4.6a). Wounds are also inflicted by seemingly innocuous adornment elements. The arm of one figure is being severed by an animated forehead ornament, a golden diadem more usually worn on the head of embroidered figures (Figure 4.6b). Another has a Spondylus (*Spondylus* spp.) shell pendant emerging from a gaping hole in its stomach

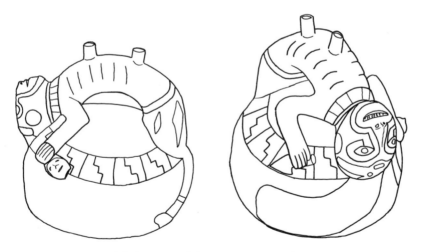

FIGURE 4.5. A modeled version of the backward-bent figure suggests the attitude of sacrifice. Two views of a cast of a double-spouted bottle said to be from Cahuachi. American Museum of Natural History, New York, 41.0/5404.

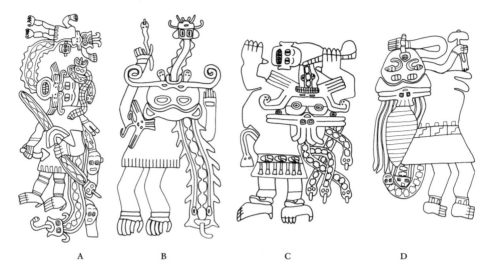

A   B   C   D

FIGURE 4.6. Depictions of wounds being inflicted by a knife (a) and by animated ornaments (b, c). The shell pendant (d) has an implied role in the wound. (a) Paracas Necropolis 38–13, Museo Nacional de Arqueología, Antropología, y Historia del Perú, Lima, 2710, mantle border; (b) PN 253-62, MNAAHP 3140, mantle border; (c) The Textile Museum, Washington, D.C., 91.76, tunic(?) border; (d) Peabody Museum of Archaeology and Ethnology, Harvard, number unavailable, mantle border.

(Figure 4.6c). Although many embroidered figures wear pendants around their necks and diadems on their foreheads, it is clear these bodily adornments also have bloodletting associations in the art, just as the fan and knife do.[14] Shown in a cutting context, shell pendants and gold forehead ornaments may substitute for knives by virtue of their hard, sharp qualities. Some figures hold the ornaments in their hands like knives, rather than wearing them. A backbent figure, shown with two deep cuts in its chest, holds a shell pendant that hovers just above the lacerations (Figure 4.6d). The proximity of pendant and wound implies a connection that is made clearer by an almost identical figure who holds a pointed knife above its lacerated chest (*Alt Peru* 1959: Fig. 92).

Other figures suggest bloodletting by unknown agents. A masked figure has a dart lodged in its hip but there are no indications as to how it got there (Figure 4.7a). A variant of this figure occurs on another border in this bundle, but it lacks the dart. It is shown with its loincloth askew, as if drawing attention to the area of the wound (Paul 1990: Figs. 6.2, 7.23, and I.23). An unusual figure displays a branching pattern of veins on its thighs, suggesting that they are flayed (Figure 4.7b). Flaying appears to be depicted in some small versions of the backbent figure that are appended to the headdress of elaborately accoutered figures (Paul 1979: Cover and Plate 21). The legs and feet are rendered as shapeless tubes without joints.

The most arresting example of wounding in the mythic realm occurs in a headless figure with a neck stump who carries either its own head or a mask, in addition to a suspicious knife (Figure 4.7c). The decapitated and obviously dead figure is depicted as very much alive, standing upright, wearing human clothes, and, seemingly, carrying its own head and the instrument for removing it. A similar figure with a neck stump, who holds a fan rather than a knife, is repeated on another embroidery (Carrión Cachot 1949: Plate Xg).

The variety of wounds, weapons, and possible agents in the embroideries suggests that bloodletting was of mythic and probably ritual importance. However, the references are not specifically to acts of human sacrifice or to war but seem to belong to a more encompassing category of fertile fluids, of which blood is a major one. Saliva, semen, and excretions appear to be grouped together with blood through the streamers that emanate from bodily orifices, as well as the sites of wounds in other figures: head, neck,

A   B   C

FIGURE 4.7. Wounded figures with a dart in the hip (a), flayed thighs (b), and a neck stump (c). (a) Paracas Necropolis 378–7, Museo Nacional de Arqueología, Antropología, y Historia del Perú, Lima, 2673, mantle border; (b) PN 290–39, MNAAHP 1710, mantle; (c) PN 364–2, MNAAHP 7723, mantle border.

and torso (Figures 4.6a, b, d; 4.7b). Blood and bodily fluids operate as a metaphoric line and are alluded to in a wide spectrum of figures through references to weapons, wounds, handheld ornaments, severed heads, and emanating streamers. In this densely allusive art, blood and bodily fluids are one, but not the only, set of references carried in the streamers and disembodied heads.

The backbent figure performing the autosacrificial act of removing its own heart may be a visual euphemism for death, both natural and unnatural, as well as a pivotal image for indicating the transition to a new cycle as young ancestor. The vulnerable posture used in the art may be borrowed from observations of animal behavior, where the "I give up" signal is rolling over and exposing the neck and viscera. The posture may also be that of human sacrifice, but perhaps carrying a more generalized reference to death in the embroideries.[15] The embroidered backbent figures likely refer to the recent dead who are wrapped in the bundles, as both the figures and the corpses are beginning new life cycles after death. The recent dead have also given up their bodies to be ritually prepared for a staged transition to ancestorhood as the funerary bundle is constructed into an effigy. This staged transition is given another expression in the following sequences of embroidered figures.

THE NARRATIVE STRAND OF MYTHIC TRANSFORMATION

The sequence of figures composing the narrative strand appears to begin with the simplest backbent figures, who wear only a skirt, carry a fan and baton, and are acutely backward bent (Figure 4.1a–d). Figures that continue the sequence illustrate a gradual transformation along a number of trajectories. The trajectories of progressive change include the addition of garments, ornaments, and weapons; a shortening of the hair; a straightening of the posture; and the acquisition of animal traits and sproutlike streamers. The changes on different trajectories are not necessarily synchronized, but the direction of change seems to be confirmed in a number of figures. There is a general clustering of attributes from different trajectories that are at a similar stage in the transformation.

Figures that have evolved slightly wear anklets, forehead ornaments, and shell pendants (Figures 4.2, 4.3, and 4.8). Some also wear discs in front of the ears and a short tunic, in addition to the skirt, and exhibit face-painting and a circle or square at the sternum (Figures 4.2, 4.8c). The hair is still long and loose, but the posture can be less acutely bent, especially on figures with abnormally shaped chests (Figures 4.2; 4.3; 4.8b, c).

The sequence continues with figures who have midlength hair (Figure

A   B   C

FIGURE 4.8. The gradual evolution of the backbent figure includes acquiring head ornaments, pendants, and a tunic: (a) Dumbarton Oaks, Washington, D.C., B-508, mantle border; (b) Paracas Necropolis 49-42, Museo Nacional de Arqueología, Antropología, y Historia del Perú, Lima, 1292, tunic; (c) PN 94-41, MNAAHP 2850, mantle.

4.9a, b) and short hair (Figure 4.9c, d). They still wear the skirt and carry the fan and baton, but they may also carry pendants, forehead ornaments, and severed heads. The figures' backs are less arched, but the head is inverted (Figure 4.9a) or angled (Figure 4.9b–d). Serpentine streamers emanating from their mouths and bodies usually terminate in animal heads, although half- and fully formed figures occur on some streamers (Figure 4.9b). The same figure acquires the feet and ears of an animal, beginning a transformation toward an animal counterpart. Two of the figures are almost identical (Figure 4.9c, d), except that the first has a naked torso and the second wears a colored tunic, indicated here by lines at the shoulders. This pointed difference suggests that there is a significance attached to the progressive acquisition of garments.

Another figure (Figure 4.10a) is closely comparable to the previous examples (Figure 4.9c, d), except that its hair is completely hidden beneath a corona headdress. This figure is one of a pair from the same mantle.

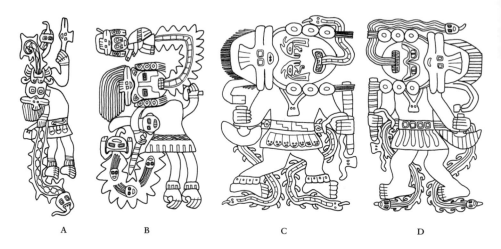

A   B   C   D

FIGURE 4.9. Backbent figures with midlength hair (a, b) and short hair (c, d) evolve toward a more erect posture. (a) Paracas Necropolis 38–39, Museo Nacional de Arqueología, Antropología, y Historia del Perú, Lima, s/n, border; (b) PN 258–5, MNAAHP 2652, mantle; (c) Royal Ontario Museum, Toronto, 916.7.3, fragment of Boston Museum of Fine Arts, 21.2556, mantle; (d) PN 451–8, MNAAHP 1661, mantle.

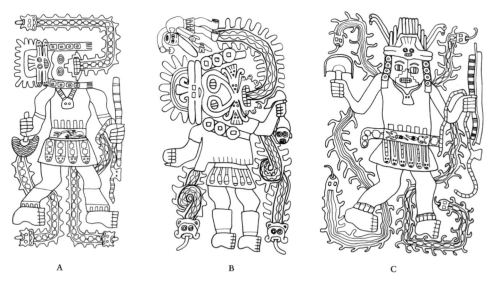

A   B   C

FIGURE 4.10. The skirted figure progresses to wearing a corona headdress (a, b) and to walking in an upright posture (c): (a) Brooklyn Museum, 34.1542, mantle; (b) Paracas Necropolis 451–29, Museo Nacional de Arqueología, Antropología, y Historia del Perú, Lima, 3071, mantle; (c) PN 310–3, MNAAHP 3167, mantle.

The pair of figures alternates in having a dented chest (Figure 4.10a) and a swollen chest, an alternation that connects them thematically with the backbent figures with chest wounds. One figure evolves to a fully upright posture (Figure 4.10c), while continuing to wear the skirt and carry the fan and baton. The baton of the backbent figure has subtly evolved into a larger staff in this and other figures (Figures 4.8c; 4.9b, c, d; 4.10a, c), a staff similar to those that occur as offerings exterior to the bundles (Tello and Mejía 1979: 336). Another figure wearing a corona headdress and the skirt (Figure 4.10b) exhibits animal attributes in its whiskered mouth mask and tunic with a tail. The streamer that sprouts from its mouth ends in a complete backbent figure that wears almost the same clothes in the same colors. The streamer now appears like a metaphorical umbilicus, connecting the more elaborately dressed large figure to its progeny, the more acutely bent, small figure. An umbilical cord, as conduit to the fetus, is a logical extension of the association of streamers with blood and bodily fluids already discussed. The progression of figures on the ends of streamers, from heads to half-formed and fully formed figures, also suggests the umbilical cord and is another level of reference in the streamers.

The cycle of the backbent figure to this point has evolved on a number of trajectories: from an acutely bent posture to upright; from long, loose hair to short, then covered hair and corona headdress; from wearing only the skirt to wearing a tunic as well; from unadorned to having wristlets, anklets, pendants, and adornments on the face and head. Many retain references to wounds in the chest or neck and continue to carry the fan and baton/staff, while a few now carry severed heads and ornaments in their hands. Some have acquired animal traits, such as foot form, mouth mask, or a tunic with a tail, and others exhibit sprouting streamers with animal heads or even full bodies attached. The overlapping attributes of the figures suggest that they are related, but their differences indicate that they do not belong to a static figure type. Each figure appears to have been composed from circumscribed sets of evolving attributes in posture, hair length, dress, ornaments, and animal traits.

FERTILITY AND THE PLANT METAPHOR

Before proceeding with the illustration of transformations to animal counterparts, the theme of fertility and regeneration and its metaphoric line require some introduction. References to fertility or rebirth in the embroideries are often couched in the metaphor of sprouting seeds and plant growth, a widespread practice in Andean mortuary complexes.[16] Human figures, for instance, sprout corn and beans from their heads and mouth, and shootlike

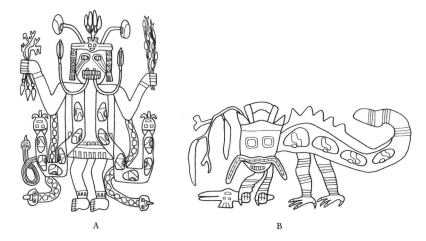

A   B

FIGURE 4.11. The vegetative metaphor is pervasive in the embroideries, and figures with human (a) and feline (b) traits are shown with plants sprouting from their heads: (a) Paracas Necropolis 310-2, Museo Nacional de Arqueología, Antropología, y Historia del Perú, Lima, 3142, mantle; (b) PN 310-31, MNAAHP 3860, poncho.

streamers filled with beans emanate from the chest (Figure 4.11a). Transforming cat figures, who walk on two feet, sprout beans from their heads and have beans for pelage markings (Figure 4.11b).

Monkey figures sprout tubers from their chests, the site of a major wound in some backbent figures. The body is sometimes represented as a spotted seed casing (Figure 4.12a) and sometimes clothed in human garments (Figure 4.12b). The figures carry beans, and the streamers that sprout from the neck may be filled with beans and/or disembodied heads. Seeds, particularly beans, substitute metaphorically for heads, an association noted by other researchers (Sawyer 1961: 289; 1966: 122). Like the bony skull, beans are roughly ovoid in shape and are hard and durable, at least until planted.

The metaphor appears to run two ways, with representations of animals with plant/seed traits and seeds with animal traits. The ovoid body of a sprouting seed is central to some figures that have sprouting shoots terminating in various plants (Figure 4.12c). The softened seed, with emerging sprout on its back, is represented with head and limbs. The legs have fuzz on them, possibly equating plant roots with legs.

Many figures sprout shoots from heads, necks, and orifices, and the sprouting streamers terminate in new heads or even full bodies, albeit smaller ones than the main figure. Such figures seem to be producing small figures on the ends of umbilicus-like shoots after the manner of plants that have underground edible parts (Figure 4.13). This visual metaphor may be borrowed from the growth habits of tubers, which sprout from multiple eyes, or from peanuts, where the nuts develop on the ends of underground shoots. Peanuts and tubers (although not potatoes), as well as beans and corn, are among the most numerous of the food offerings that accompany the Necropolis bundles. A relationship, possibly kinship between mythic ancestor figures, is implied by the shoots that connect the small figures with the main figure.

Agricultural practice is mimicked in a generalized way at the Necropolis site, where the seed-shaped bundles are buried in the ground, a conceptual association noted in contemporary Andean mortuary practice.[17] Some of the bundles may have received "fertilizing" libations at certain points in their construction, based on the pattern of textile deterioration within layers.[18] One of the bundles, replete with textile offerings, had a twelve-kilo sack of black beans at its center, instead of the expected corpse (Tello

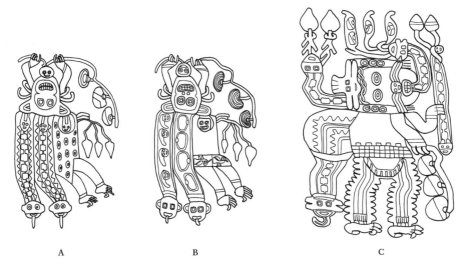

A   B   C

FIGURE 4.12. The metaphoric lines of plant growth and of wounds and blood interchange in the monkeylike figures (a, b). The bodies of some figures are shown as seeds (a, c). (a) Museo Arqueológico de la Universidad Nacional de San Marcos, Lima, 4.34 1247T 0915, border; (b) Paracas Necropolis 38–46, Museo Nacional de Arqueología, Antropología, y Historia del Perú, Lima, 2699, mantle border; (c) PN 38–4, MNAAHP 1559, mantle.

FIGURE 4.13. Figures sprout like plants, with streamers emanating from orifices or the sites of wounds on other figures. Paracas Necropolis 319-13, Museo Nacional de Arqueología, Antropología, y Historia del Perú, Lima, 1682, mantle.

and Mejía 1979: 489–492). The plant references in the bundles and the embroidered textiles sometimes point to specific cultigens but, at other times, appear to be generic, as in planting, sprouting, and reproducing, or even categoric, as in above-ground and below-ground.[19]

The metaphoric line of plant growth often parallels and sometimes interchanges with the metaphoric line of wounds, blood, and bodily fluids. The metaphoric lines intermingle in figures where plants or streamers with beans sprout from the sites of wounds or where severed heads and seeds substitute for each other. The coherence of the interchanging metaphors likely turns on the association of water and blood as fertile fluids, necessary for regeneration in the agricultural and mythic cycles.

TRANSFORMATION TO FALCON AND CONDOR COUNTERPARTS
The transformation sequence that begins with the backbent figures and evolves toward richly adorned ancestor figures with mouth mask and streamers (Figure 4.10b) continues in a number of directions with figures adopting progressively more animal traits. The embroidered animal figures appear to be on an equal footing with the human figures as they transform. When predation is represented, the animals generally have the upper hand over humans. Many animal figures are clearly supernatural, indicated by the improbable or impossible combinations of species and postures and the use of human weapons or ornaments. The representation of animals in the embroideries could refer to a particular origin myth, perhaps one in which the animals have roles as the first ancestors. This tentative suggestion is based on the direction in the transformation sequences and on the ascendancy of

the animal figures when predation is represented. The mythic transformation cycle appears to progress from young, then mature, human ancestors toward the animal counterparts.

Many figures take on traits of the falcon, such as the pronged marking beneath the eye and the patterned wing and tail feathers. One is shown with a complete falcon lying along its back (Figure 4.14a), but it retains references to the backbent figure in the angle of its head, the tiny skirted figure above the mouth mask, and the shoot that sprouts from the chest, site of a major wound in backbent figures. Another figure with patterned wings shows the falcon head emerging from the mouth, as if the human body were interpenetrated by that of the falcon at the moment of transformation (Figure 4.14b). One winged figure with bird claws for hands adopts the posture of a falcon in its upper body, while remaining standing on its two human legs (Figure 4.14c).

Some figures preserve human arms and head and an upright posture while having a predominantly falcon body (Figure 4.15a). An example near

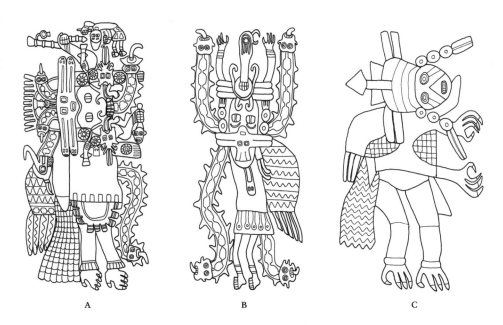

A   B   C

FIGURE 4.14. Three variants illustrate the transformation toward falcon counterpart from human ancestor figure: (a) American Museum of Natural History, New York, 41.0/1501, mantle; (b) Paracas Necropolis 319-84, Museo Nacional de Arqueología, Antropología, y Historia del Perú, Lima, 3120, mantle; (c) PN 421-64, MNAAHP 2411, poncho.

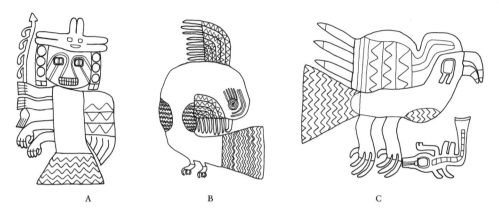

FIGURE 4.15. Figures with predominantly falcon traits retain references to mythic transformation: (a) Paracas Necropolis 27-5, Museo Arqueológico de la Universidad Nacional de San Antonio Abad, Cuzco, mantle; (b) Brooklyn Museum, 34.1558, mantle; (c) PN 310-32, Museo Nacional de Arqueología, Antropología, y Historia del Perú, Lima, 3552, poncho.

FIGURE 4.16. Three variants illustrate progressive stages in the transformation continuum toward condor counterpart: (a) Paracas Necropolis 319-56, Museo Nacional de Arqueología, Antropología, y Historia del Perú, Lima, 1012, mantle; (b) PN 318-8, MNAAHP 1684, mantle; (c) Royal Ontario Museum, Toronto, 916.8.2, mantle.

the completed transformation to falcon has only the residue of the backbent figure in the backward thrust of its neck (Figure 4.15b). Depictions that have been considered "naturalistic" may represent the completed transformation to falcon counterpart in the mythic cycle. One falcon is shown uncharacteristically as a sea-hunter, and its supernatural fish-prey has a human arm (Figure 4.15c). The range of figures suggests that a transformation narrative underlies the varied representations of figures with human and falcon traits and links them together.

A similar series of transforming condors can be assembled. The fleshy caruncle above the beak, the rolls of skin on the head and neck, the neck ruff, the long flight feathers, and the plain tail feathers are some traits that identify condors. Clothed, bipedal figures may be represented with a complete condor, or distinctive parts of one, attached or clasped to their body (Figure 4.16a, b). They may have the head or forward-bent posture of the condor while retaining arms, legs, and human clothing (Figure 4.16b, c). A number are represented almost entirely in condor guise, often with vestiges of the human-ancestor carried in details (Figure 4.17a–d). One wears a shell pendant (Figure 4.17a), another feeds on a severed head of conveniently small size (Figure 4.17b), while one has its beak driven into its own chest (Figure 4.17d), echoing the autosacrificial act of the backbent figure. Condor figures without direct references to transformation (Figure 4.17c) are so closely comparable to the others that it seems likely they represent the animal endpoint of the transformation continuum.

These examples of the transformation of richly adorned ancestor figures to the falcon and condor counterparts illustrate staged sequences of change in the acquisition of animal traits. The clothing worn by the figures and the treatment of the hair have also undergone orderly changes from the scanty skirt and long hair associated with the backbent figure.

Most of the ancestor figures with significant animal attributes wear a loincloth, although a few retain the skirt (Figure 4.14b). They generally have their hair hidden by a headdress or turban (Figures 4.13, 4.14, 4.16). The changes in clothing and headgear may be associated with maturation stages. Like Inca boys who donned loincloths when they became knights (Cobo 1990 [1653]: 126–132), these figures may be "mature" ancestors as they transform to animal counterparts.

Clothing is one of the trajectories of change in the transformation of the embroidered figures. As already discussed, the backbent figure acquires a torso-covering garment, along with various adornments. The changes in the hair treatment and in the garments worn by figures may be modeled on daily-life customs of signifying life stages through dress and grooming, a

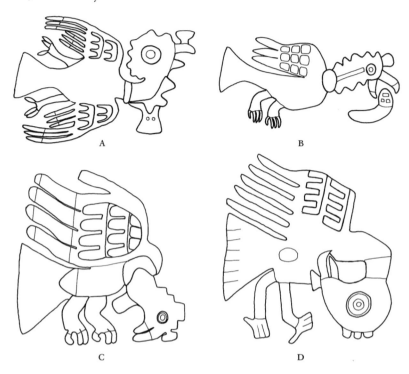

FIGURE 4.17. Figures with predominantly condor traits can be seen as part of the transformation continuum toward condor counterpart: (a) Göteborgs Etnografiska Museum, Sweden, 35.32.188, poncho; (b) Paracas Necropolis 243-33, Museo Nacional de Arqueología, Antropología, y Historia del Perú, Lima, 3185, border; (c) PN 157-10, MNAAHP 0683, mantle; (d) PN 421-102, MNAAHP 2789, poncho.

deep-seated Andean practice that endures to the present. The scanty skirt worn by the backbent figure could be a representation of a flared, wrap-around skirt that is worn by very young boys before they are toilet-trained in villages like Taquile (Frame 1989: Fig. 31). The backbent figure, if it is a representation of the recent dead as I contend, is at an immature stage of ancestorhood and so might logically wear the skirt of an immature boy. The long, loose hair of the backbent figure may also refer to an immature stage of ancestorhood. In the Andes, a child's hair is not cut in infancy, and, when it is cut, it is the focus of a significant ceremony. Hair length and headgear often reflect age and status, among other things, in Andean villages.

TRANSFORMATION TO PREDATORS OF THE SEA AND EARTH

The transformation to marine animals is well represented in the embroideries. However, the distinction between sharks and killer whales is often blurred, or perhaps purposefully generalized. Both are fierce predators of the ocean and share traits of fins, tail, and prominent teeth. Gill markings behind the eye, when this area is depicted, will be taken to indicate shark, as killer whales have no gills.

So far, the transformation to animal counterparts has been illustrated largely through ordering figures that mix distinctive traits of animals and humans in varying proportions corresponding to successive stages. In the following examples (Figure 4.18), an instantaneous and complete transformation is engineered by the artist, who uses a startling perceptual phenomenon to capture the transformation from humanlike ancestor to shark counterpart. Seen right side up, the figure has essentially human traits: it is bipedal and wears clothes and an elaborate headdress with eye surrounds composed of shark bodies (Figure 4.18a). The figure alternates in orientation on the mantle field, and, when it is glimpsed upside down, a fearsome face oscillates into view (Figure 4.18b). The jagged negative space between the fins and tails of the eye surrounds coalesces as a toothy jaw. Suddenly a shark is coming straight at us, trailing a human body behind. A similarly composed figure repeats on a mantle in Bundle 310 (Figure 18c, d). The transformation from humanlike ancestor to animal counterpart is compressed into a single outline in these examples, and the figure perceptually transforms when seen in another orientation. Richard Burger has noted this phenomenon in the Raimondi stela and uses Kubler's term "anatropic" to describe it (1992: 147, 175).

A number of embroidered figures use this phenomenon to some degree. A figure's headdress and mouth mask sometimes perceptually interchange functions, giving fleeting glimpses of a figure with a more fearsome mouth in a head oriented in the opposite direction (Lavalle and Lang 1983: 108, 118–119). Another example actually alternates two figures, one with head erect and the other with head inverted, which visually fixes the perceptual oscillation of the previous examples (Peters 1991: Fig. 7.49).

Different stages in the transformation to shark counterpart also occur on different textiles. Complete attributes of human and shark can be integrated in an anatropic figure (Figure 4.19a). Others may have the head and body of a shark, but retain the limbs, posture, and sometimes clothes of a human (Figure 4.19b, c). A number of almost completely sharklike figures still retain a human arm and hand (Figure 4.19d). One figure has exagger-

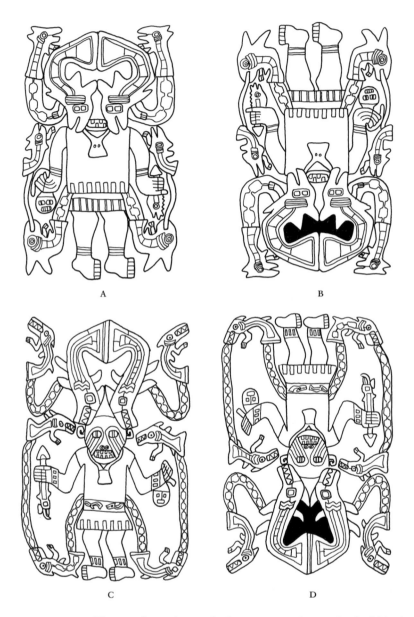

FIGURE 4.18. The transformation to shark counterpart is contained within the outline of human ancestor figures (a, c). The negative space in the headdress, shown shaded (b, d), becomes the mouth of the shark. (a, b) Paracas Necropolis 319–9, Museo Nacional de Arqueología, Antropología, y Historia del Perú, Lima, 1444, mantle; (c, d) PN 310–1, MNAAHP 1480, mantle.

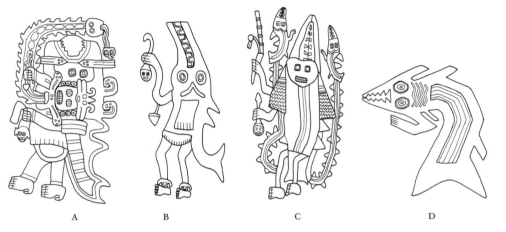

A   B   C   D

FIGURE 4.19. Figures representing the transformation to shark counterpart combine human and shark traits in various admixtures: (a) Paracas Necropolis 253–8, Museo Nacional de Arqueología, Antropología, y Historia del Perú, Lima, 3229, mantle; (b) PN 378–19, MNAAHP 2695, mantle; (c) PN 38–48, MNAAHP 3129, mantle; (d) PN 94–9, MNAAHP 1460, mantle.

ated fins that may be bird wings (Figure 4.19c). Some figures exhibit traits of more than one animal, as noted by Peters (1991).

A number of figures with fishy traits do not depict gills, or the area where gills would be found is obscured. These denizens of the deep may be killer whales or they may be a mythical composite that has been referred to as the "Master of Fishes" (Yacovleff 1932b), as those in Figure 4.19 may also be. Fishy figures without gills exhibit a similar series of stages in the transformation toward the animal counterpart (Figure 4.20a–e). Bipedal figures with clothing evolve toward the horizontal alignment of a swimmer (Figure 4.20a–c), and the swimming figures retain human appendages (Figure 4.20d, e). Several examples combine traits of the "Master of Fishes" with those of humans, condors, and felines in a figure with a forward-bent posture (Peters 1991: Fig. 7.6; Anton 1987: Fig. 69). All have a predatory/sacrificial interest in the backbent figure, or in its abbreviated form of a severed head with long hair. The transformation to "Master of Fishes" occurs in modeled form in an early Nasca ceramic that is incised and slip-decorated (Lapiner 1976: Fig. 469), as well as in one that is entirely slip-decorated (*Museums of the Andes* 1981: 68).

Among the stages in the transformation to animal counterpart are forward-bent figures (Figures 4.14c; 4.16c; 4.20b, c). This posture mimics the anatomy or locomotion of the animal counterparts whose bodies

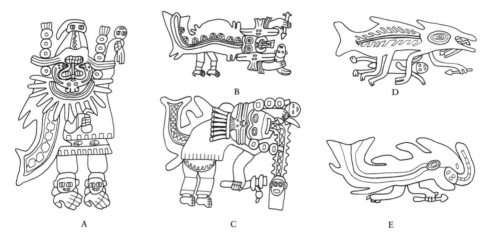

FIGURE 4.20. Fishy figures without gill markings may represent the mythical "Master of Fishes." Standing figures (a–c) evolve into swimmers (d, e), but retain human limbs and weapons: (a) University Museum, Philadelphia, SA 4603, mantle; (b) Paracas Necropolis 89–16, Museo Nacional de Arqueología, Antropología, y Historia del Perú, Lima, 1546, mantle; (c) Royal Ontario Museum, Toronto, 916.8.1, mantle; (d) Boston Museum of Fine Arts, 21.2558, loincloth; (e) PN 378–34, MNAAHP 2738, border.

parallel the earth as they move. The figures illustrate the opposite end of the trajectory of posture change that begins with the backward-bent posture. This trajectory seems to span references from prey to predator and victim to sacrificer among many animal-like and humanlike figures. The scantily clad figure with skeletal ribs so often represented as victim in the backbent posture also occurs in the forward-bent posture, but usually with the fan held over the lower part of the face, as if concealing a frightening mouth (Figure 4.21a–c). These figures have evolved substantially and have acquired animal feet, sprouting streamers, wigs and headdresses, weapons, and severed heads. The latter attributes also suggest that they are changing from the role of victim toward that of aggressor or sacrificer/predator. The figure with the most bestial demeanor has evolved the furthest in the acquisition of clothing, headdress, adornments, streamers, and progeny (Figure 4.21d). It lowers the fan to reveal a large, whiskered mouth mask and bared teeth.

The correspondence in posture between prey and victim and between predator and sacrificer suggests that these are parallel mythic roles for animals and humans. In the transforming figures, where animal and human traits meld, the means for drawing blood also cross over. Predominantly animal figures can also brandish weapons, and predominantly human figures can feed on victims.

The feline is the animal counterpart that is central in some elaborate figure groupings that depict feeding on victims or prey. A series illustrates a progressive adoption of feline traits by the main figures (Figure 4.22a–c).

A

B

C

D

FIGURE 4.21. The skirted figures also occur in the forward-bent posture of animal predators, but usually with the mouth hidden behind a fan (a–c). When the fan is lowered, an animal-mouth mask is revealed (d). (a) Paracas Necropolis 89-17, Museo Nacional de Arqueología, Antropología, y Historia del Perú, Lima, 1609, mantle; (b) PN 290-16, MNAAHP 1087, mantle; (c) Indianapolis Museum of Art, mantle fragment (Gilfoy 1983: 62); (d) American Museum of Natural History, New York, 41.0/1507, mantle.

The first is a predominantly human figure, with animal feet and a cat-pelt on its head or back. The second has fur, ears, whiskers, and claws of a cat but wears human clothes and stands upright. The third has the body and posture of a stalking cat. All three have sprouting streamers, but the most catlike has procreated complete figures on the ends of streamers, suggesting that it is at the most advanced stage of transformation (Figure 4.22c). The three figures feed on the backbent figure, assisted in two cases (Figure 4.22a, c) by carrion-eaters who clean the bones. These complex images might imply that the recent dead, in the form of the backbent figure, are food and drink for the mature ancestors in mythic terms. They might also imply that carrion-eaters have mythic roles in reducing the recent dead to the enduring, bony essence, after the major bloodletting of the predator/sacrificer.

Figures that have transformed almost entirely to felines often preserve traces of their human counterpart in an upright posture or bipedal stance (Figures 4.11b; 4.23a, b) or in the wearing of human ornaments (Figure

A   B   C

FIGURE 4.22. Figures with progressively more feline traits feed on the backbent figure: (a) Paracas Necropolis 319–46, Museo Nacional de Arqueología, Antropología, y Historia del Perú, Lima, 1700, mantle; (b) PN 319-10, private collection, Houston, mantle; (c) PN 188–9, American Museum of Natural History, New York, 41.2/8870, mantle.

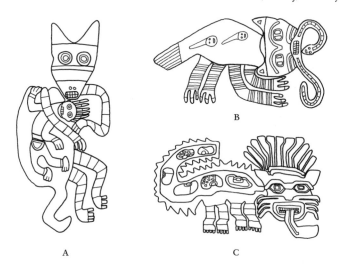

A   B   C

FIGURE 4.23. Figures that are predominantly feline retain traits of the humanlike ancestor: (a) Paracas Necropolis 262-43, Museo Nacional de Arqueología, Antropología, y Historia del Perú, Lima, 2663, border; (b) PN 378-28, MNAAHP 3040, poncho; (c) PN 421-116, MNAAHP 1770, skirt tie cover.

4.23c). An early Nasca ceramic, incised and slip-painted, shows a feline figure sitting like a human, with forepaws on its flexed knees (Townsend 1985: Fig. 12). Many transforming feline figures are shown feeding on the backbent figure or the severed head (Figures 4.22a-c and 4.23a; Paul 1990: Plates 13 and 24), or feeding on birds (Peters 1991: Figs. 7.22 and 7.23; Lavalle and Lang 1983: 122).

PREDATION, SACRIFICE, AND FEEDING

Ann Peters has commented previously on "the relations of predation" that inform a number of embroidered images (1991: 309-311). While figures with predominantly animal traits are sometimes shown devouring their natural prey, many figures are engaged in feeding or drinking on a mythic level with their tongues planted in human heads or bodies. Predation in the natural world is undoubtedly an important, underlying model for relations between figures in the embroideries. The rending that predatory animals do with their beaks, fangs, and claws, humans also do, but with weapons. Sacrifice, or cutting with human weapons, and predation are shown as parallel activities in the embroideries, and they are carried out by transforming figures with human and animal traits. Both activities result in torn flesh and

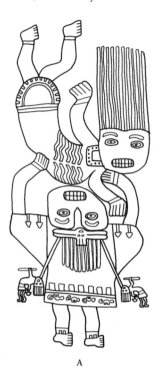
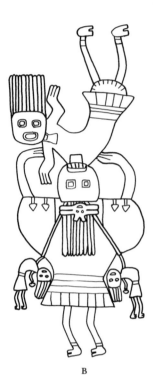

A   B

FIGURE 4.24. Ancestor figures feed/drink at the chest of the less mature backbent figures: (a) Paracas Necropolis 262–15, Museo Nacional de Arqueología, Antropología, y Historia del Perú, Lima, 2541, mantle fragment; (b) PN 262–34, MNAAHP 3045, skirt.

copious blood flow. However, the emphasis in the embroideries is perhaps not so much on the hierarchical "alimentary pyramid" (1991: 310–311) that Peters refers to as on the circulation of food and fertilizing liquids, particularly to the ancestors.[20] The cycling of food and drink to the ancestors, and to all parts of a mythic universe, may underlie the many references in the embroideries to predation and wounding/sacrifice. The depictions of feeding are not entirely restricted to predation, as in the case of hummingbirds and flowers (Lavalle and Lang 1983: 60–62) or llamas nursing their young (Peters 1991: Fig. 7.51). These depictions suggest an interest in the wider circulation of food and drink, encompassing all parts of a mythic universe.

Humanlike ancestor figures with midlength hair, tunics, and ornaments feed on the less mature backbent figures who exhibit longer hair, fewer clothes, and a smaller size (Figure 4.24a, b). The eater and the eaten in these depictions appear related, as if at different stages in the continuum of ancestor growth, with the backbent figure providing sustenance for the more mature ancestor figure. The relationship in the embroidered figures could refer, in part, to the offertory nature of human burials and the inevitable decomposition that follows. In a circulatory universe (Allen 1988), the corpse in the bundle would, like manure, occupy a positive and fertilizing position in the mythic food chain. The decomposing soft tissues and fluids of the recent dead feed the earth, the plants, and the ancestors already buried in the earth. The embroidered depiction of a more mature ancestor feeding on the recent dead in the form of the backbent figure may encapsulate such a linkage in the circulatory chain.

Feeding the effigy bundles at the Necropolis site was certainly an important concern, as indicated by the double-spouted bottles, presumably containing liquids, and the plates, baskets, and gourds containing food that surrounded some bundles (Tello and Mejía 1979: 336–338). Food offerings are also included inside most bundles, in a gourd placed near the chin of the recent dead, in the basket it sits in, or interleaved among the cloth layers (Yacovleff and Muelle 1934; Tello and Mejía 1979; Towle 1952). Libations may have been poured onto the bundle during construction, as noted earlier. While these acts of feeding during the construction of the bundle appear to be aimed at promoting the growth and transformation of the recent dead to an ancestor, the recent dead actively reciprocates and, through its decomposing body, provides food and fertilizing liquids for the earth and those buried in the earth.

A three-dimensional version of the action in Figure 4.24 is represented on a monumental jar of the early Nasca style (Figure 4.25a). The richly adorned personage appears to drink through its arching tongue at the neck of the backbent figure, whose modeled head lolls backward. The forward-hunching posture of the predator/sacrificer contrasts with the backward-bent posture of the victim in this and other cases (Figure 4.25b). Variations of this theme occur on a number of the large ceramics of the early Nasca style, where the larger figure, who wears the standard adornments of the embroidered ancestor figures, grasps a backbent figure in one hand and sometimes another figure, a head, or a plant in the other (J. Tello 1959: Figs. 84–87; Larco Hoyle 1966: Fig. 90; Sawyer 1968: 57). Many of the large Nasca ceramics use the same visual vocabulary encountered in the Necropolis embroideries to recombine references to blood, fertility, and transformation.

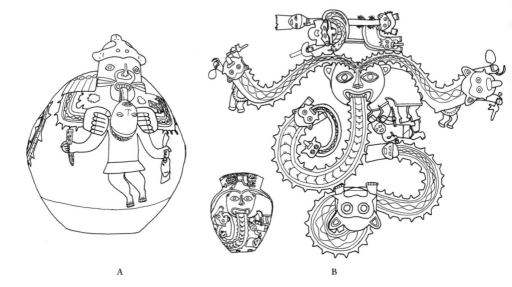

A   B

FIGURE 4.25. The forward-bent posture is associated with animal predators and with human bloodletting. A modeled ceramic (a) and a painted urn (b) of the early Nasca style contrast the postures of aggressor and victim: (a) after Sotheby's (1981: 47); (b) after J. Tello 1959: Plate LXXXII.

SUMMARY AND CONCLUSIONS

Only a small percentage of the Necropolis embroideries in the block-color style have been illustrated here. There are many figures that do not fit directly into the sequences I have sketched,[21] although they may share the conventions and metaphors discussed. They include figures with traits of other animal species, for instance, human and insect attributes (Figure 4.26), an identification made by Ann Peters. The inclusion of winged-insect imagery may seem obscure until one thinks of the metamorphosis in the chrysalis that transforms a wormlike creature into a moth or butterfly after a period of dormancy.[22] The transformation sequences in the embroideries and the construction of an ancestor effigy around the corpse of the recent dead are no more dramatic than metamorphosis and are, in some ways, quite parallel.

This chapter is concerned with describing pervasive themes and interconnections between figures in the Necropolis embroideries. Figures from different textiles and different bundles are arranged in sequences to illustrate the gradual evolution that links disparate figures together. The general trend and direction of the figure sequences is arrived at through examining related figures with clustered, overlapping, and divergent attributes. Figures no doubt have a wealth of particular associations and mythic roles beyond those suggested here.

Transformation is an overarching theme referred to in many of the block-color-style embroideries from the Necropolis. Series of related figures, gradually changing along a number of trajectories, are ordered to illustrate sequences of transition and transformation. Instantaneous transformation of anatropic figures is also illustrated. The transformation appears to be mythic in nature, starting with the backbent figures, who are animated despite grievous wounds, and who evolve toward richly dressed ancestor figures. These figures continue transforming by adopting progressively more animal traits until they become animals or composites of animals, notably the major predators: feline, falcon, condor, and shark/killer whale. The major actions center on the bloody activities of predation, wounding, scavenging, and autosacrifice.

The mythic transformation is interwoven with the regeneration theme, carried in the metaphor of plant growth, and many mature ancestor figures sprout like seeds and reproduce progeny on the ends of shoots. Wounds, blood, and bodily fluids parallel and interchange with the metaphoric line of plant growth, layering multiple allusions in the streamers that sprout

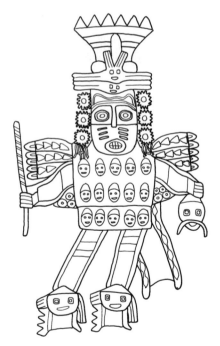

FIGURE 4.26. Figures transforming toward winged insects may relate to funerary themes, because they undergo a transformation parallel to that of the recent dead in the bundle. This figure has traits that suggest the swallowtail butterfly. Paracas Necropolis 382–10, Museo Nacional de Arqueología, Antropología, y Historia del Perú, Lima, 5904, mantle.

from bodies. Both metaphoric lines may supplicate for fertility and agricultural abundance through references to the coming of the waters and the growth of plants. Visual puns, such as fan-heart-knife, wound–sprouting plant, and bean-head mix metaphoric lines freely and signal interconnected meanings.

The natural order of earthly life is incorporated into the cosmic order of the mythic web. The ancestor figures feed regularly, grow and mature, and reproduce. The maturation of the ancestor figures is reflected in changes in hair treatment, clothing, posture, adornments, and the acquisition of weapons and handheld objects and, finally, in the transformation toward the animal counterparts. The ancestor figures reproduce on the ends of umbilicus-like streamers. The recent dead, in the figure of the backbent victim of autosacrifice, is both food and progeny of the ancestor figures, and eventually evolves into an ancestor figure. The mythic web encompasses animal species of the sea, sky, and earth, who are shown feeding, bleeding, reproducing, and transforming from human counterparts. Plant species that produce edible parts above- and below-ground sprout from animal bodies or are animated with limbs and faces. Plants and animals, including humans and ancestors, are intimately connected through their shared cycles of growth, maturation, reproduction, and death. Crafted objects, made from animal, vegetable, and mineral sources, are animated in the mythic world depicted in the embroideries. The panoramic inclusivity of the mythic web reflects an interconnected and animated universe, one that is fueled by the circulation of food and fertile fluids such as blood.

Most of the figures used to illustrate this study have their closest ceramic correlates in vessels of the Nasca style, phases 1 and 2. None of the Nasca ceramics was, however, found at the Necropolis, where Topará-style ceramics predominate. Many of the illustrated embroideries come from bundles that Dwyer (1971: 233a) and Paul (1990: 60) place in phase 2 of the Early Intermediate Period, although others are from bundles they place in phase 1 (A and B) and even phase 10B of the Early Horizon.[23]

The phase 2 bundles have a greater (but not complete) stylistic and iconographic consistency than the bundles of the preceding phase and more completely coincide with the figures, themes, metaphors, and conventions discussed here. Only some textiles in the phase 1A and phase 1B bundles coincide, as these bundles contain embroideries in the linear and broad-line styles, as well as hybrids of styles that have not yet been described. The linear and broad-line embroidery styles share some of the figures and themes illustrated here, such as the backbent figure and the transforming figures that combine human and animal traits, but they are distinct enough to suggest that they were made by different groups of people, probably inhabiting the area between the Cañete Valley and the Nasca drainage. If this were the case, then the differences in textile styles, basic to the seriation of the bundles, might represent differences through space instead of, or in addition to, through time.[24]

The mixture of textile styles in some bundles and the order in which they were placed in the bundles suggest to me that the Necropolis was the site of a regional cult, drawing textile tribute from various groups for the construction of the effigy bundles. According to Richard Burger (1992: 190–195, 220), who cites the Chavín cult, Pachacamac, and the Yaya Mama cult from around Lake Titicaca, regional cults are more likely to have doctrines of universality and theism, transcending the politico-jural focus of local cults. The emphasis on bloodletting, fertility, and the mythic transformation of ancestor figures in many of the Necropolis embroideries fits this description of a regional cult.

Acknowledgments

I would like to thank the staff, past and present, in the Textile Department at the Museo Nacional de Arqueología, Antropología, y Historia in Lima who assisted in my study of the Necropolis textiles during eight visits between 1979 and 1996, in particular, the late Eduardo Versteylen, and also Elba Manrique de Bellota, María Medina Castro, and Rossana Mendoza Neyra. I would also like to thank Vuka Roussakis, Anahid Akasheh, and Barbara Conklin at the American Museum of Natural History, New York, for their assistance in studying the Necropolis textiles and documentation there. A Summer Fellowship at Dumbarton Oaks (1993) gave me sustained access to the Necropolis slide archive of Anne Paul, which is housed there, and an opportunity for discussions with Ann Rowe and Anne Paul. Working with Julie Jones on the 1995 exhibition at the Metropolitan Museum of Art, New York (Ancient Peruvian Mantles, 300 B.C.–A.D.200) provided the stimulus to develop the research on the backward-bent figure. Sue Bergh acted as sounding board during the research period, and the editors of this volume, Elizabeth Benson and Anita Cook, made helpful suggestions for clarifications in the final manuscript. I deeply appreciate the encouragement I received from Eduardo Versteylen, Nobuko Kajitani, and Alan Sawyer, who generously allowed me to use their slides and other materials pertaining to Necropolis textiles.

Earlier versions of this chapter were presented as a paper in August 1996 at the Coloquio sobre Arqueología de la Costa Sur Peruana, Museo Regional de Ica, Peru, and in January 1997 at the Thirty-seventh Annual Meeting of The Institute of Andean Studies, Berkeley, California.

Notes

1. Peters (1991) has offered a synthetic treatment of the Necropolis "block-color" style imagery. Although we link and interpret the imagery in quite different ways, I would like to acknowledge a debt to her work for stimulating and enlarging the ways in which I view the imagery. Early identification studies on the plants and animals represented in Paracas and Nasca iconography include Valcárcel 1932; Yacovleff 1931, 1932a, 1932b, 1933a, 1933b; Yacovleff and Herrera 1934; Yacovleff and Muelle 1934.

2. The "block-color" style is one of three embroidery styles from the Necropolis that have been described in print, along with the "linear" style (Dwyer 1979: 109) and the "broad-line" style (Paul 1982: 263). The seriation of the opened bundles from the Necropolis extends from phase 10 of the Early Horizon to phase 2 of the Early Intermediate Period, according to Dwyer (1971; 1979) and Paul (1990: 60). The absolute dates for these phases proposed by Paul (1991a: 22) are 100 B.C.–A.D. 200.

3. Reichel-Dolmatoff (1978: 10) uses the term "metaphoric lines" to describe messages on different levels of conceptualization encoded in artifacts, anatomy, physiology, topography, etc. I am applying it to different levels of reference that converge in the Necropolis embroidered figures.

4. Paracas Necropolis (PN) signifies a textile from a bundle excavated at the Paracas Necropolis of Wari Kayan. The following number refers to the bundle number assigned by Tello's excavators, and the number after the dash is the specimen number assigned consecutively as the bundle was unwrapped. These numbers are followed by the name of the museum collection and the current registration number, where available.

5. Carrión Cachot (1931: 75–85) identifies garment types, as well as noting average sizes and a representative range of garment dimensions from ten bundles studied prior to 1931. Skirts range from 147 cm. to 340 cm. in length, while headcloths or turbans range from 120 cm. to 300 cm. in length by 25 cm. to 75 cm. in width. Ponchos vary by at least four times the area, for example, from 39 cm. × 30 cm. (Paul 1991b: 199, Specimen 28 of Bundle 89) to 81 cm. × 61 cm. (Tello and Mejía 1979: 373, Specimen 31 of Bundle 310). The variability in sizes, the uneven distribution of garment types, and the evident newness of the garments led Carrión Cachot to consider the garments as offerings, and not the wardrobe of the deceased during life. See Paul (1990: 63–64, note 5) for the contrary point of view.

6. Carrión Cachot (1931: 48–49; 1949: 23, 35); Bennett and Bird (1949: 180).

7. See comparative tables in Carrión Cachot (1931: 48) and in Paul (1990: 60) for occurrences of garment types in ten and forty bundles, respectively. Although their figures are not in complete agreement, Bundles 89 and 91 have almost all the loincloths of those bundles tabulated, Bundles 421 and 243 have over one-third of the ponchos, and Bundles 421 and 157 have over one-third of the skirts.

8. Daggett (1994) provides the most comprehensive bibliography on the opening of the Necropolis bundles. My generalized statements on the construction of the bundles are drawn from those sources plus unpublished reports and registration sheets on four bundles opened at the American Museum of Natural History and lists of bundle contents at the Museo Nacional de Arqueología, Antropología,

y Historia, Lima. Daggett also clarifies conflicting information on the number and size of bundles, and his summary indicates that the published reports cover about 10 percent of the Necropolis bundles, mainly large and midsized ones.

9. I have adopted the words "recent dead" and "ancestors" from Salomon (1995) for talking about the dead, who are very much alive in myth, art, and mortuary ritual and who evolve through stages in a cycle that roughly reflects the life cycle of the living.

10. Bird and Bellinger 1952: Plate VI (falling); Yacovleff 1933b: 154 (dancing); Paul and Turpin 1986 (trance, ecstatic shaman, magical flight); Anton 1987: Figs. 58, 59 (diving, falling, dancing); Sawyer 1962, Fig. 5 (drowned).

11. I am grateful to Katharina Schreiber (personal correspondence, 1996) for this suggestion and for the photograph of a head from a Nasca cemetery that has protruding cervical vertebrae.

12. This cast has been published (Bennett 1946, vol. II, Plate 20c) and is presumed to be a cast of an authentic incised and slip-painted vessel. The catalogue says, "from the Valley of Nasca" and gives the donor as Myron I. Granger. Handwritten on the cast is "Cahuachi, Nasca. P. Soldi—broken when found."

13. Margaret Young-Sanchez provided me with detailed photographs of the spearthrower (Cleveland Museum of Art, 40.507) and a copy of her unpublished paper (1993). She interprets the figure with the cut throat as a victim of sacrifice.

14. Baraybar (1987: 7) has found evidence in Nasca trophy heads of spectacular bleeding from cuts made shortly before death and suggests that bloodletting was part of the rituals associated with human sacrifice. Decapitated bodies and severed heads are common in Nasca burials (Carmichael 1994: 84), including a case of decapitation after natural mummification.

15. Published sources record that a few of the Necropolis bundles had corpses with evidence of wounds or contained incomplete skeletons (Tello and Mejía 1979: 330, 444, 447–448, 451–453, 488). Most of the corpses described were mature males, between fifty and sixty years of age, without evident wounds. Controversy surrounds Tello's initial claim that corpses had been eviscerated and artificially mummified (1929: 131–135).

16. According to Salomon (1995: 340–341), the "vegetative metaphor certainly pervades Andean mortuary complexes," and it is "one of the most durable elements in Andean cosmology." Among the contemporary Laymi of Bolivia, human fertility in mortuary practice is "metaphorically transposed into the key of vegetation," with the most common symbol being flowers (Harris 1982: 48).

17. In Laymi, Bolivia, the burial of the dead is conceptually likened to the acts of cultivation and planting (Harris 1982: 52). Allen (1982) presents a modern Andean case where the dried and shriveled seeds and tubers, from which new growth will come, are metaphorically compared to dead people. Carmichael (1994: 83–84) reviews ethnographic and iconographic studies linking death and fertility concepts in Nasca art.

18. An example occurs in the group of plain cloths in the second layer of Bundle 310, Specimens 8–33 (Tello and Mejía 1979: 370–371). The conservation state varies from good to regular, semicarbonized to very carbonized in groups of adjacent cloths. The large size of these wrapping cloths, which would span all sides of the bundle, seems to preclude the possibility that the deterioration was all on the under-

side and due to the decomposing corpse. The authors note the good condition of only some of the cloths.

19. The dichotomy of plants with edible parts above- and below-ground has been noted in relation to the imagery on the Tello Obelisk (Lathrap 1973).

20. Allen (1988: 50–54, 170–171, 226) discusses the model of a circulatory universe in the food, drink, and coca rituals involving the living and the dead in the community of Sonqo, Peru. The critical place occupied by manure in the ritual cycling of food, drink, and coca is interesting in light of the number of figures with streamers emanating from hindquarters (Figs. 4.8b, 4.14b, 4.16 a–c, and 4.21d).

21. For example, several embroidered mantles have eight or more different figures wearing human garb of various types (Lumbreras 1974: 91, Fig. 102 top; Dwyer and Dwyer 1975: 158–159, Figs. 9, 10).

22. The wing form and patterning on this figure (Figure 4.26) suggest the venation and scales of butterfly wings rather than bird wings, a point made to me by Robert Eckhardt. Bird wings are consistently represented as being jointed, and usually the long flight feathers are distinguished from secondary feathers. The figure's tail element resembles the rear wings of a swallowtail butterfly in flight when the two wings draw together (see Brackenbury 1992: Plate 85c). Another possibility for the inclusion of winged-insect imagery in funerary art is contained in Salomon's generalization on the theory of life and death gleaned from motifs in colonial documents (1995: 329): "a human being consisted of perishable soft parts . . . ; a durable skeleton and hide, which became the lasting person or mummy; and a volatile personal shade or spirit, sometimes visualized as a flying insect."

23. The illustrated figures are from the following bundles, with phase attributions according to Paul (1990: 60): phase 2 (38, 253, 258, 318, 319, 451); phase 1B (27, 89, 262, 290, 310, 378, 382); phase 1A (49, 91, 94, 243, 421); phase 10B (157). Bundle 188, housed at the American Museum of Natural History, was not included in the seriation. Dwyer's seriation (1971: 233a) includes fewer Necropolis bundles and places Bundle 27 in phase 2 and Bundle 258 in phase 1B.

24. The seriation as now constructed (Paul 1990: 60; Dwyer 1971: 233a) lines up complete bundles on a single timeline, and anomalies exist. Among those illustrated here, for example, there are similar figures in bundles dated to different phases (Figs. 4.2, 4.3, and 4.8b; Fig. 4.18a, c), and some stylistically later pieces occur in bundles of earlier phases (Figs. 4.8c, 4.17c, and 4.23c). Bundle 89, the only complete bundle published and tested against the seriation, has textiles that correspond stylistically to both phase 1B and 2 (Paul 1991b: 220–221, note 3). Bundle 310, seriated as a 1B bundle, has mantles (Figs. 4.10c, 4.11a, 4.18c) closely related to ones in phase 2 bundles (Figs. 9d, 10b). Further anomalies in the seriation exist among textiles not illustrated here (Ann Rowe, personal communication, 1993). John Rowe observes that some bundles have stylistically more advanced textiles in the outer layers and some have more conservative ones (1995: 37–38). He suggests that the mummy bundles at the Necropolis, aside from those dated to phase 2, may "represent one, two, or at most three" depositions from other locations and that there is no reason to assume that those buried at the Necropolis "lived in the desert on the Paracas Peninsula."

CHAPTER 5 *Children and Ancestors:*
Ritual Practices at the Moche Site of
Huaca de la Luna, North Coast of Peru

STEVE
BOURGET
Sainsbury Research Unit,
University of East Anglia,
United Kingdom

INTRODUCTION

The massive sacrificial precinct recently discovered and studied at the Moche site of Huaca de la Luna, in the Moche Valley of the Peruvian north coast (Bourget 1997a), is one of the rare Moche sites to provide evidence of organized sacrificial practices outside of mortuary contexts. The only other examples now known are at Dos Cabezas (Cordy-Collins, "Decapitation," this volume) and Huanchaco (Donnan and Foote 1978). At the end of our 1996 field season at Huaca de la Luna, the remains of two headless children were found buried in this sacrificial precinct. They were located beneath a series of male individuals captured in combat, brought there, and sacrificed during at least two spells of torrential rains.

In the first part of this chapter, the general context of the site and of these peculiar rituals will be presented. I will then discuss in more detail the presence of the children in the precinct and explore the representations of children, ritual hunting, and sacrifices in the iconography in order to propose some interpretations concerning this exceptional ritual. It will be suggested that the young individuals found at the base of the sacrificial site are conceptually linked to the ancestors and to the practice of ritual warfare, capture, and human sacrifice. Furthermore, it will be proposed that sacrificial practices and funerary rituals were the building blocks of Moche liturgy and that the priests of Platform II, as sacrificers, and the individuals of Plaza 3A, as their sacrificed victims, were inextricably linked together in a system of symbolic duality.

THE HUACA DE LA LUNA

The Huaca de la Luna, one of the principal ceremonial centers of the Moche, is composed of three platforms connected by a series of terraces, corridors, and plazas (Figure 5.1). The temple has been constructed at the

FIGURE 5.1. Huaca de la Luna. Photo by Steve Bourget.

foot of a conical hill called the Cerro Blanco. It is not a unique pattern, for at least two other Moche sites, somewhat similar in their architecture, were built at the foot of a small mountain. To the north, Mocollope in the Chicama Valley is situated at the base of Cerro Mocollope, while, immediately to the south, Huancaco in the Virú Valley nestles against Cerro Compositán.

Platform I of the Huaca de la Luna, the first one constructed and by far the most complex, is currently being investigated by Santiago Uceda and his team (Uceda, Mujica, and Morales 1997). Their work has shown that this platform has been transformed and enlarged at least six times (Uceda and Canziani 1993; Uceda and Mujica 1997). Our research has concentrated on the second platform, Platform II, and its associated plaza, Plaza 3A. Platform III is probably the latest structure in the building sequence of the Huaca de la Luna complex. Apart from extensive looting, this platform has received little attention in the past (Kroeber 1930; Seler 1915). Although some mapping was recently completed, Platform III has not been systematically studied by the Huaca de la Luna Archaeological Project.

Platform II and Plaza 3A constitute an elongation of the Huaca de la Luna main platform toward Cerro Blanco during one of its last phases of reorganization (Figure 5.1). More research is needed to determine which construction phase is associated with this new addition, but it seems for the moment that its principal access was from Platform I through Plaza 3B.

This late extension represents a single architectural project constructed in the sixth and seventh centuries, during the Moche IV stylistic phase. It is formed by an open plaza and a rectangular structure bisecting a rocky outcrop (Figure 5.2). The platform and the plaza cover an area of 840 square meters and 1,100 square meters, respectively.

The presence of the rocky outcrop in the center of the site led us to excavate in the plaza. Indeed, similar outcrops surrounded by walls have been noted also at the Moche sites of Mocollope (Chicama Valley), Huancaco

Figure 2: Platform-II, Plaza-3a

◎	Posthole
T1	Tomb
S1	Trench
106, 02	Altitude (meters)
– · – · ·	Excavation limit
97	Excavation season
0 _____ 5 m	

FIGURE 5.2. Plaza 3A and Platform II. Map by Steve Bourget.

(Virú Valley), and Pañamarca (Nepeña Valley). As a research hypothesis, it was proposed that these rocks were considered sacred by the Moche priesthood and that human sacrifices may have been realized in front of these "natural altars." This theoretical approach has been fruitful, and it is in the northwest corner of the plaza, just in front of the rocky outcrop, that a number of sacrificial rituals were first discovered in 1995 (Bourget 1997b). During the last three seasons, fifteen strata of human remains representing at least six distinct rituals were excavated. Given the complexity of the site and the extent of the sacrifices performed, the exact number of individuals has not been determined. Nevertheless, it can be estimated that the remains of at least seventy persons were found in the plaza.

In the meantime, excavations were also carried out on Platform II, and four tombs were recovered. It is important to note that these tombs were situated exclusively in the northern part of the structure, just above the sacrificial site (Figure 5.2: T1–T4). Unfortunately, evidence of colonial and modern looting was noted in each of them.[1] Nevertheless, it has been possible to determine that two of these elaborate burials, Tomb 1 and Tomb 3, were those of old men who probably occupied important positions in the Huaca de la Luna priesthood. Stylistically, all the ceramics found in these burials belong to the Moche IV period, and a calibrated date of 540–655 A.D. (1 sigma) has been obtained from a wooden post situated in the center of Tomb 2. I will come back to some of the discoveries made in these burial chambers later on.

Construction of the Site

Study of the construction of the platform and the plaza indicates that both structures were built with rectangular towers of adobes, also called construction blocks, set one against the other and measuring about seven meters high (Figure 5.3). On the average, a construction block measures 2 m. × 1.5 m. and is formed of about 1,800 adobes. The different angles taken by these construction blocks seem to indicate that they were not set in sequence, one after the other, row after row. To the contrary, it appears that many of them were built standing alone, here and there, then joined together with adjacent construction blocks. In fact, it is quite possible that many groups were involved in the construction of the building and that they could have been working at the same time but in different parts of the site. Thus, with fewer than two hundred workers the platform could have been constructed, fairly rapidly, in a matter of a few months.

For example, it took about 750,000 adobes to construct Platform II at

FIGURE 5.3. Construction blocks on Platform II. Photo by Steve Bourget.

its present size. If ten groups of bricklayers (*adoberos*), working at the same time, could have laid down 500 adobes per day each, it would have taken only 150 days to create the existing structure. Of course, we will never know the number of people involved nor the exact time needed to build it, but the point is that the construction of this temple and its plaza may not necessarily have been the product of a long and organized project but the outcome of a sudden decision taken in very specific circumstances.

The north and south walls and part of the west wall of the plaza were also constructed with two series of construction blocks set one against the other. The north and south walls are the highest-standing walls of the Huaca de la Luna, and they are still between six and seven meters high. These walls were constructed directly on the same yellowish sand that contained the children's burials.

In order to build this site behind the Huaca de la Luna main platform, the Moche had to displace part of a Moche III cemetery. Remains of some of the tombs were found along the north wall of the platform. The rest of the cemetery is still in place between this platform and Cerro Blanco. Interestingly, fragments of Moche III ceramics, probably from this displaced cemetery, were thrown in the sacrificial plaza during the rituals. Was it to propitiate the ancestors disturbed by the removing of the tombs?

THE RITUALS IN THE PLAZA

After the completion of this extension of the Huaca de la Luna, one of the first rituals performed in the plaza was the burial of three children. The body of one of them was complete, but the two others were headless. Although postburial disturbances cannot be ruled out, the fact that their cervical vertebrae were still in anatomical position seems to indicate that they could have had their heads removed before their burial. As I mentioned earlier, they were discovered in the same layer of yellowish sand on which the walls of the plaza were later constructed.

The Children

The first child was found some 60 cm. below the surface of this layer of sand. The child was resting on its back, oriented on a north-south axis, with the head to the south. Like the two others, its arms rested alongside the body, and the ankles were side by side. It was between two and one-half and three and one-half years old at the time of death. Although there is some evidence of periostitis, some porosity, and swelling, these conditions do not appear severe enough to have been the single cause of death. No other indicators of trauma were noted.

The second child was also resting on its back, some 15 cm. below the sand surface, in an east-west axis with the shoulder to the east. The head was missing, and the decayed remains of a big seashell were found alongside the body. This child was about twelve months of age, and clear bone deformations were noted. The preliminary analysis indicates that the child would have suffered from an acute case of periostitis or osteomyelitis. This illness could have been congenital and would have been severe enough to have been the cause of the child's death.

The third child was, like the others, in a fully extended position and lying on its back. It was found only 10 cm. below the surface with the feet very close to the north wall and the body on a north-south axis (Figure 5.4). This child was about three years of age, and the head was also missing. The child was covered with decayed remains of textiles, and it was holding a whistle in each hand. The close proximity of this child both to the base of the north wall and to the surface indicates that it must have been buried after the construction of the plaza and not before, otherwise its burial would certainly have been disturbed by the building activities.

Shortly after the completion of the walls and the burial of the children, a first episode of rain left a deposit of clay in the northwest corner of the plaza. Immediately afterward, two retaining walls, delimiting a space of about 21 square meters (Figure 5.2), were constructed. The east wall, com-

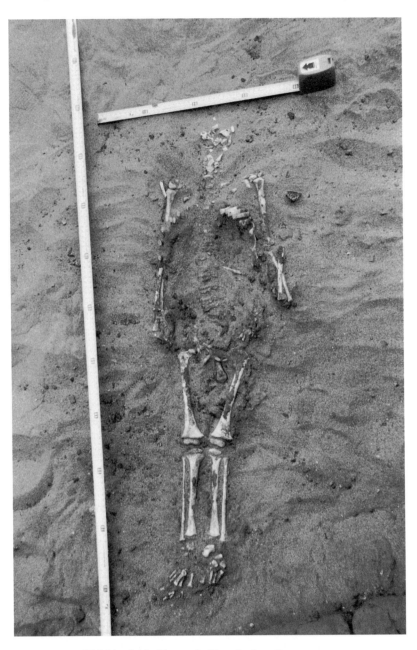

FIGURE 5.4. Child burial in Plaza 3A. Photo by Steve Bourget.

posed of a single row of eight adobes, connected the north wall to a fallen boulder from the rocky outcrop. The second wall was built with four rows of adobes and linked the same rock to the west wall. Not only did this walled space form a rectangular area around the children, it was also inside this special precinct that the first two sacrificial rituals took place.

The Sacrificial Rituals

The first sacrifice was carried out during the second spell of torrential rains that brought the clay from the north and west walls of the plaza in the rectangular pit. Judging by the physical evidence, it seems that during this first sacrificial ritual only five or six individuals were killed in this pool of mud. Some time after the rains, a second ritual took place just on top of the first one, directly on the dried and hardened clay surface. Although most of the sacrifices were restricted to the same area, the sacrificial practices were much more extensive than in the first ritual, and many more individuals were then dispatched to the ancestors.

At some point during this ritual, a pit some 4 meters square was dug at the foot of the west wall, and a hole was carved into the wall itself. These depressions were then filled more than a meter thick with human remains, and dozens of clay statuettes were thrown in from the summit of the west wall. Other statuettes were placed between the victims and smashed in situ with rocks from the outcrop. The clay effigies, measuring between 35 and 60 cm., represent nude males, each with a rope around his neck (Figure 5.5). They are generally represented seated cross-legged, and their hands, painted in black, are usually resting on their knees. Their bodies and their faces are literally covered with complex representations of anthropozoomorphic beings, animals, symbols, and intricate designs.

Later, after an undetermined period of time, other torrential rains fell in the Moche Valley. This time the deposit of clay in the plaza was much more extensive and the sacrifices covered a surface of about 60 square meters. The clay and the corpses covered completely the small rectangular space in the northwest corner of the plaza. Exactly as in the previous ritual sequence, individuals were killed in the soft clay, probably during the rainfalls. Subsequently, another group was sacrificed right above the previous one, some time after the precipitation had stopped.

Indeed, the close proximity of the corpses, some resting directly on top of the others, indicates that this fourth series of sacrifices must have taken place shortly after the rains and the solidification of the clay (Figure 5.6). The main difference between the first set of sacrificial rituals and this one is not quality but quantity; many more people were killed, decapitated,

FIGURE 5.5. Clay statuette from Plaza 3A. Photo by Steve Bourget.

FIGURE 5.6. Victims of sacrifice in Plaza 3A. Photo by Steve Bourget.

and dismembered. This ritual represented the last sacrificial ceremony performed in the plaza. The numerous pupal cases of muscoid flies, the weathering of the bones, and the sun-dried layer of mud indicate that, as in the previous rituals, the last human remains were left exposed to the natural elements and were eventually covered with eolian sand and layers of clay.[2]

Although excavations were carried out also in the center and the southern parts of the plaza, no other evidence of activities or occupation during this period of time was detected. Thus, given the present evidence, it seemed that only 5 percent of the plaza, concentrated in the northwest corner and right at the foot of the rocky outcrop, was used for the ritual activities. It also tends to confirm the hypothesis that the rocky outcrop was indeed imbued with a certain sacredness and that the sacrificial acts had to be performed just in front of it. Furthermore, more than one hundred rock fragments of this small mound were used as projectiles against the human beings and their clay counterparts.

Preliminary study by John Verano and his colleagues suggests that all the victims were aged between fifteen and thirty-five years. Much physical evidence indicates that they were once warriors and that they were captured during violent encounters. Also, indices of trauma are extensive, and many tools were used for the sacrifices: ropes, maces, lances, knives, and rocks (Verano, this volume).

The question is: what are the children doing underneath this series of sacrificed men captured during warfare? Are these children in any way linked to the series of sacrifices? Since they were buried just after the construction of the plaza, the problem is to know if, indeed, this structure was purposely built for the performance of these sacrificial rituals.

THE CHILD AND THE WHISTLERS

Not only was the child at the base of the north wall headless, it also had a small whistle in either hand (Figure 5.4). The left hand probably fell inside the funerary bundle sometime before the burial, and its whistle was thus found just below the pelvis, but the child's right hand was still holding firmly the musical instrument. The two whistles were almost identical, as was the high-pitched note they produced (Figure 5.7).[3] The slight disarticulation of a part of the body indicates that some soft tissue decomposition had taken place and that the child was probably not immediately buried after its death.

A look at Moche iconography is needed in order to document further the meaning of whistling and the ritual use of children. The ritual system of representation frequently shows children being carried by diverse individu-

FIGURE 5.7. Whistles found with the child in Plaza 3A. Photo by Steve Bourget.

als. For example, a whistling bottle (Figure 5.8) shows a person whistling and carrying a child under her arm. Recognizing the feminine sex in Moche iconography is a difficult undertaking, but, in this case, I would propose that the shawl worn by this actor is a marker of this gender. A second whistler also carries a child (Figure 5.9). This ceramic was found in an elaborate burial at the foot of Huaca de la Luna in 1899 by Max Uhle. I would like also to draw attention to the presence of wrinkles on their cheeks. I will come back to these facial features later on.[4]

Children are carried not only by human beings but also by other entities, such as a skeletonized individual wearing the distinctive shawl (Figure 5.10). Interestingly, this ceramic vessel is also a musical instrument, and the air chamber of the whistle is situated inside the head of the cadaver. The sound is thus produced through the eyes and the mouth of the dead person. The child is wrapped in a textile or a blanket and is being carried on its back, which is somewhat similar to the position adopted by the corpse in a Moche burial.

Children are carried also by anthropomorphized bats of both sexes. For example, the bat-being in Figure 5.11 carries a child under one arm and a warrior mace under the other. Another example (not represented here), depicts a bat-individual wearing a shawl and carrying a child under her right arm (see Berrin 1997: Fig. 87). These bat-beings have often been linked to ritual bleeding and sacrifice by decapitation (Bourget 1994; Donnan 1978). When the face of the child is clearly depicted, the eyes are often closed. This could well be a sign that the child is dead.

Thus, the young individual in the plaza and the act of carrying a child in the iconography are not only closely associated with real whistles or with individuals whistling but also with the feminine gender, death, and sacrifi-

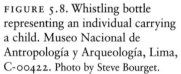

FIGURE 5.8. Whistling bottle representing an individual carrying a child. Museo Nacional de Antropología y Arqueología, Lima, C-00422. Photo by Steve Bourget.

FIGURE 5.9. Ceramic bottle representing an individual carrying a child. Phoebe A. Hearst Museum of Anthropology, University of California, Berkeley, PAH-2938. Photo by Steve Bourget.

cial beings such as bats. But could it also be linked to the war of capture, El Niño events, and, in sum, to the whole ritual program of the plaza?

HUNTING, WARFARE, AND SACRIFICE

In order to bridge the gap between the two distinct ritual systems of the plaza, a rare ceramic from a Peruvian museum will be used (Figure 5.12a, b, c). It brings together two sets of information that are usually depicted separately. The first one is a figure modeled on top of the bottle, which represents a whistling woman carrying a child. The second is painted all around the chamber of the bottle. It shows two individuals carrying an intricate bundle on their backs and holding a bulbous mace in their hands. A bundle is also shown as a discrete object between the two individuals.

Ritual Hunting

The peculiar mace that they carry is a special weapon used in certain scenes of warfare and in the ritual hunts of deer (*Odocoileus virginianus*), sea lions (*Otaria* spp.), and foxes (*Lycalopex sechurae*). In this chapter, I will deal only with the first two hunting activities. The fox hunts are usually simpler and in many respects very similar to the hunting of deer. Both animals, as a related pair, warrant more concentrated research than that presented here.

The first hunt (Figure 5.13) involves humans wearing elaborate head-dresses and tunics in pursuit of deer. The smaller figures are hitting the deer with the clubs while the larger ones, armed with spearthrowers, are giving them the coup de grâce. It is a theme that has already been studied

FIGURE 5.10. Skeletonized person carrying a child. Museo Nacional de Antropología y Arqueología, Lima, C-01025. Photo by Steve Bourget.

FIGURE 5.11. Bat-being carrying a child. American Museum of Natural History, New York, 41.2/8566. Photo by Steve Bourget.

FIGURE 5.12A–C.
Person holding a child
and individuals carrying
a bundle. Museo
Nacional de
Antropología y
Arqueología, Lima,
C-54577. Photo by Steve
Bourget.

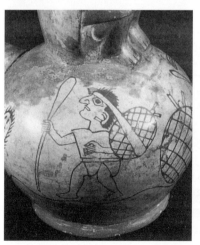

FIGURE 5.13. Deer hunt. Drawn from Donnan 1997: Fig. 7.

by Christopher Donnan and successfully linked to ritual warfare and the capture of prisoners:

> The many parallels between deer hunting and warfare strongly suggest that these were related activities in the Moche world. The similarities in dress, ornament, body paint, and weapons used in these two activities indicate that the same class of adult males, and perhaps even the same individuals, were participating in both. The purpose of combat was not the conquest of enemy territory, but the capture of opponents for ritual sacrifice. Similarly, the purpose of deer hunting was not to obtain food but to capture deer for ritual sacrifice. (1997: 58–59)

Indeed, in anthropomorphized form, the deer is often depicted either as a warrior holding the very same war mace or as a nude male seated cross-legged with both hands clasped and wearing a rope around his neck. As we saw a short while ago, many clay statuettes representing nude men in the same position and with a similar tie were recovered from the sacrificial site.

The bundles transported by the two individuals on the ceramic vessel in Figure 5.12 are often represented carried by other whistlers or placed between priests engaged in complex rituals (see Berrin 1997: Fig. 79). In the Moche V style, similar objects are consistently depicted attached to each extremity of totora boats (see McClelland 1990: 81). In 1972, Alana Cordy-Collins was probably the first person to try to identify these things, and she proposed that they could have been some type of special net bag used to catch crabs (1972: 8). Although I do agree that they may be nets of some sort, I would tend to see them in fact as bundles of hunting and/or fishing nets.

In ritual deer-hunting scenes (Figure 5.13), long nets are represented on the lower register. Moreover, the small figures attending these nets are similar to those painted on the previous ceramic (Figure 5.12). In the deer-hunting scene in Figure 5.13, the second attendant, on the right, has a bulbous mace lying just behind him. He also wears a similar headdress and tubular ear ornaments identical to those of the individual situated on the right side of the net bundle (Figure 5.12c). This would tend to confirm that these big bundles represent long hunting nets rolled up.

Interestingly, the individuals that we just saw attending the hunting nets or carrying the net bundles are the same actors who perform the second type of hunt, the killing of sea lions (Figure 5.14). These sea-lion hunters wear the same tunics, headdresses, and ear ornaments. They also have a special bag tied around their waists like those worn by the net attendants of the deer-hunt scene. The sea-lion hunt is also practiced with the same type of wooden mace. It is important to note the presence of a woman wearing a shawl on the left side of the scene. Sitting in front of a house, she is in the process of preparing a stirrup-spout bottle. Just behind her, three other funerary offerings have already been prepared. In at least two other similar examples of sea-lion killings, women preparing jars are also depicted.

In certain deer-hunting scenes (Figure 5.15), similar individuals are shown carrying these jars with branches tied around their necks. Thus, these pairs of recurring actors in both scenes, the attendants with the clubs and the women with the jars, seem to confirm that both ritual hunts are conceptually related, although this apparent congruity does not necessarily

FIGURE 5.14. Sea-lion hunt. Drawn from Kutscher 1983: Abb. 89.

FIGURE 5.15. Deer hunt. Drawn from Donnan 1997: Fig. 8.

mean that both rituals are in essence identical. Also, in this deer-hunt scene, the branches around the jars are very similar to those on the trees. This might indicate their provenance. Furthermore, these peculiar branches are depicted on the chest of a clay statuette (Figure 5.5) and also on the shawl of one of the women (Figure 5.9). In the latter case, the branches terminate with bird heads.

In a previous study, I proposed that there was a sexual dichotomy of the ritual activities and that women were closely associated with the preparation of the cadaver, the funerary offerings, and the victims of sacrifice just before the ritual (Bourget 1994). The carrying of children would be an extension of these actions. Thus, each one of these activities would correspond to a transitional stage of the ritual leading eventually to a burial, a sacrifice, or an offering. I would thus propose that the woman in front of the house is in the process of preparing four funerary offerings: a stirrup-spout bottle, two jars, and a gourd container (Figure 5.14). Although Christopher Donnan has proposed that the jars in the deer-hunting scene (Figure 5.15) "may have contained blood and been conceptualized as the equivalent of prisoners with ropes around their necks" (1997: 58), I would tend to see them as part of the funerary paraphernalia. These two interpretations are not necessarily mutually exclusive, and funerary and sacrificial rituals are probably closely related. After all, all these scenes are depicted on funerary offerings! It is a complex subject, and more research will have to be done in order to understand better the complex relationships between gender and funerary and sacrificial rituals.

Warfare, Capture, and Sacrifice

I would tend to see the deer hunt and the killing of sea lions as closely associated with the war of capture and the sacrifice of warriors. The relationship
of sea-lion hunting is made even clearer by showing, in some cases, sea-
lion hunters carrying not only the special mace, but shields of warriors (see
Berrin 1997: 113). In this regard, Elizabeth Benson was probably the first
person to realize the relationship between sea-lion hunts and a certain form
of sacrifice: "Another type of sacrifice—and a possible calendrical one—
was the hunting of otaries" (1995: 258). Indeed, in the sacrificial plaza, a
sea lion was painted on the body of a clay statuette, and the canine of a very
young sea lion was resting on the chest of a victim. Moreover, a sea-lion
vertebra was found in a small recess at the bottom of a posthole on Platform II. It is very revealing to discover the representation of a victim tied
inside a sacrificial rack adorned with the heads of sea lions (see Donnan
1978: Fig. 148). Moreover, this victim has the same haircut as the statuettes
of the plaza.

Following somewhat the same logic as that pertaining to the sacrificial
rack, the bulbous head of the mace of a warrior can take the shape of a sea-
lion head (Figure 5.16). The implement becomes the victim and reiterates
the fact that this object is symbolically linked to the killing of these marine
mammals. In the tomb of the first priest discovered on Platform II, a very
similar bottle was found with a warrior in the same position holding the
very same mace (Figure 5.17). Thus, it seems that the individual resting in
this burial, a man in his sixties, might have been closely linked to this ritual.
Although this tomb was seriously looted, a well-preserved wooden mace
was fortunately found (Figure 5.18). The black residue covering this club
has recently been examined by Margaret Newman using immunological
analysis; the sample has shown a strong positive reaction to human anti-
serum only (1996). This means that this artifact is literally caked from head
to shaft with human blood. This club could strongly indicate that the individual buried in Tomb 1 was one of the sacrificers working in the plaza
down below.

In 1946, at Huaca de la Cruz in the Virú Valley, a bulbous-shaped mace
was found in the tomb of a Moche priest. The scene sculpted around the
mace is complex and represents a fight and the eventual capture of three
prisoners. Interestingly, a series of ceramics found in this tomb is closely
related to the themes just discussed: a jar in the form of a sea lion, a deer-
hunting scene, an individual wearing the headdress of the sea-lion hunters,
two almost-identical drinking cups in the form of bat heads, and another
vessel almost identical to the warrior with the conical helmet found in

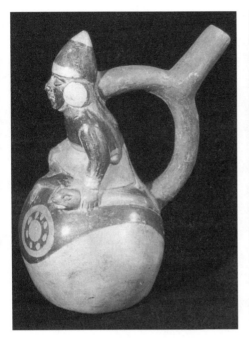

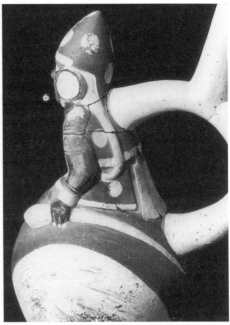

FIGURE 5.16. Warrior holding a mace. Museo Nacional de Antropología y Arqueología, Lima, C-03244. Photo by Steve Bourget.

FIGURE 5.17. Ceramic vessel from Tomb 1 representing a warrior holding a mace. Huaca de la Luna, PII-833. Photo by Steve Bourget.

FIGURE 5.18. Wooden mace from Tomb 1, Huaca de la Luna. Photo by Steve Bourget.

FIGURE 5.19. Sea lion holding its offspring. Museo Nacional de Antropología y Arqueología, Lima, C-01500. Photo by Steve Bourget.

Tomb 1 of Platform II (Figure 5.17; Strong and Evans 1952: Plates XXVII B; XXVIII F, B, D). Other ceramic vessels at the Huaca de la Cruz also matched those discovered on Platform II, suggesting that this priest was possibly a sacrificer.

The use of the same maces in warfare and hunting is certainly not fortuitous, and it strongly suggests homologous meanings between these activities. Ritual warfare and ritual hunting are so closely related to one another that the war of capture can, in fact, signify metaphorically the ritual hunting of sacrificial victims. This depersonalization process of the Moche warrior is further exacerbated by the representations of combatants or sacrificial victims in the guise of anthropomorphized deer.

Before I conclude, I would like to come back to a few other scenes related to the children, the act of whistling, and the concept of duality. As I have said, the offering of children could be associated with the ritual hunting of sea lions and deer. It is thus not surprising to see a deer and a sea lion holding their young "as a human mother would," as has been said by Elizabeth Benson (1972: 54) (Figure 5.19).

Whistling and Sacrifice

The act of whistling is associated not only with the offering of children but also with sacrificial victims. One bottle represents, on its top, a victim tied to a sacrificial rack and in the act of whistling (Donnan and McClelland 1999: Fig. 4.85), indicating that whistling is performed by a sacrificial victim. Painted on the chamber of a similar vessel (Figure 5.20), the same victim is being held on either side by a woman. Cut-off arms and cut-off legs are also represented in the scene. In another scene of sacrifice, it has been proposed that these are women closely related to those carrying the jars in the deer-hunt scene (Figure 5.15; Donnan 1997: 58). Also, a woman preparing funerary pots inside a house is depicted on the side of the bottle in Figure 5.20. On the chamber of the bottle, the women holding the victim prior to his sacrifice are associated with the preparation of the funerary offerings prior to the burial ritual itself. As I said earlier, these are two events that precede the resolution of their respective ceremonies, namely, the sacrifice and the burial. It is also worth noting that a small whistle in the form of a bird was found among the sacrificed warriors of the plaza.

I would like to propose that the act of whistling is linked with the crucial moment of a ritual just before the offering of a child, the sacrifice of a victim, or the burial itself. In fact, one ceramic vessel depicts a whistling man transporting the funerary offerings (see Donnan 1978: Fig. 237). Whistling is possibly a sound produced to warn the ancestors of the human

FIGURE 5.20. Sacrificial victim (Kutscher 1983: Abb. 120–1). Courtesy of Kommission für Allgemeine und Vergleichende Archäologie, Bonn.

offerings to come. Indeed, the victim who is standing above the painted scene of Figure 5.20 (for a similar figure, see Donnan and McClelland 1999: Fig. 4.85) has the same wrinkles on its cheeks as the women in Figures 5.8 and 5.9. Similar wrinkles are usually depicted in the faces of very important actors in the iconography, often supernatural sacrificers. I would thus tend to see these facial attributes as a definite symbol of ancientness and ancestorship.

If whistling, which takes place at the moment of the offering of a child or during a sacrifice, serves to "warn" the ancestors, then the act of receiving these "gifts" might also have been depicted in the iconography. In such a case, it would be plausible that a certain mythical sequence is represented in these three scenes: the whistling women offering a child (Figures 5.8, 5.9) or two women holding a sacrifice-to-be, who may be whistling (Figure 5.20; Donnan and McClelland 1999: Fig. 4.85); a whistling skeletonized individual transporting a dead child (Figure 5.10); and, finally, a representative of the ancestors in the guise of an anthropomorphized bat (Figure 5.11) collecting the child. It is thus not surprising to see that the bat-being, which has been summoned, is not whistling.

SYMBOLIC DUALITY
Another theme linking the tombs on Platform II and the ceremonial system of Plaza 3A is the concept of symbolic duality. This concept has already been recognized in Moche funerary systems, particularly at Sipán (Alva and Donnan 1993). In the overall study at Huaca de la Luna, the duality system seems to go much further and appears to encompass the whole ritual program, including the buildings, the murals, the burials, and the sacrificial site itself.

Platform II is a solid structure towering above the open space of Plaza 3A. Both structures are physically linked by the same wall to the north and to the south, while a sacred rock joins them. The platform was used for funerary rituals, while the plaza was the place of sacrifices. The pairing of the platform and the plaza and the placement of the tombs of the sacrificial priests just above the sacrificed people would suggest a form of asymmetric symbolic duality and also a certain shared importance between funerary rituals and sacrificial practices. It is a complex subject that would warrant a separate study, but as a research hypothesis, I would venture to say that funerary and sacrificial rituals are the two principal tenets of Moche religion.

Other examples of duality abound both in the plaza and in the tombs of the platform. First of all, in the plaza there were two children with their heads missing. One of them had two whistles, one in each hand. During the sacrificial rituals, the pairing of human bodies or body parts was also common (Figure 5.21). In the second priest's tomb in the platform, fifteen pairs of offerings were found. A double duality is represented by two jars (Figure 5.22), by the repetition of the same vessel representing a skeletonized face, and, also, by the fact that one of them is ceramic and the other one is unfired clay.

CONCLUSION

To conclude, I would suggest that Platform II and Plaza 3A were built rapidly sometime during the Moche IV stylistic period. It is not known if this architectural project was undertaken because of the presence of a massive El Niño or because ecological markers such as new marine species or the appearance of strange *lomas* were announcing an impending disaster.[5] Nevertheless, I would propose that these structures were created specifically for the performance of sacrificial rituals during spells of torrential rains.

Shortly after the completion of the plaza, dedicatory offerings of children were made. It is not possible to say if they were sacrificed, decapitated, or simply offered to the Huaca and the ancestors after their natural death. Given the nature of the representation of children in the iconography and their numerous links with other subjects such as skeletonized individuals, bats, deer, and sea lions, these young individuals form part of the whole sacrificial and ritual liturgy of the Moche. They are, in a manner which is still difficult to document completely, associated with the ritual hunt and killing of deer and sea lions.

In return, the sacrificial victims of the plaza are closely linked not only with El Niño phenomena but also with the world of the sea and especially the killing of sea lions. One of the principal reasons for choosing these marine mammals as surrogate victims might be because of the transformation of their predatory activities during El Niño events. In effect, during this period, sea lions are deprived of their main sources of protein, the sardines and the anchovies. They have to plunge deeper and deeper to get their food, and they become extremely hungry and angry. They will frequently destroy the fishing nets of the fishermen in order to get their food (Schweigger 1947: 209). So, during difficult periods of El Niño events, the Moche and the sea lions had to compete for the same resources. The sight of big sea lions attacking their fishing nets must have been impressive just as much for the Moche as it is for the present-day fishermen. For example, Thor Heyerdahl said that during a short El Niño–like period at the beginning of

FIGURE 5.21.
Sacrificial victims in
Plaza 3A. Photo by Steve
Bourget.

FIGURE 5.22.
Funerary jars from
Tomb 2, PII-798, 799.
Photo by Steve Bourget.

the 1990s, the fishermen of Lambayeque had "to cease fishing due to the numbers of huge sea lions which destroyed their nets and gathered on the beaches" (Heyerdahl, Sandweiss, and Narváez 1995: 209).

Other evidence would have to be presented, but, as a research hypothesis, I would like to propose that rituals of warfare and capture could have led to other forms of sacrifice. In this perspective, the ritual hunting of deer and foxes could well have been associated with other activities of ritualized warfare leading eventually to other sacrificial rituals. For example, young deer and foxes are carried like children by certain individuals in the mountain sacrifice scene (see Donnan 1978: Fig. 225). Recently, I proposed that the sacrifice in the mountains was regulative in nature and was celebrated at the beginning of the humid season. The young mammals and the numerous land snails (*Scutalus* spp.) present in these scenes would then act as ecological markers and signal the advent of the new growing season. It would thus have been an annual ritual for agricultural renewal and fertility as a whole (Bourget 1994).[6]

In the case that we have just been discussing, the offering of children, which has a long tradition in the Andean world (Benson, this volume), would have been special burials dedicated to the completion of the sacrificial plaza, to the calamitous rains to come, and, above all, to the Almighty Ancestors.

Acknowledgments

The Plaza 3A and Platform II Project was made possible by the generous support of The British Academy, The Leverhulme Trust, and the Sainsbury Research Unit. I am also very grateful to Dr. Santiago Uceda, who has permitted me to join the Huaca de la Luna Project as a research associate, and to all the people in Peru, Canada, England, and the United States who have participated in this project. I want also to extend my gratitude to the specialists who conducted the osteological analysis: Laurel S. Anderson, Florencia Bracamonte, Linda Neilson, John Verano, and Bonnie Yoshida.

Notes

1. We can differentiate between these two periods of looting in the following manner. During the colonial times, looters employed by the Spaniards only took metal (gold, silver, copper) objects and disregarded other remains. This has led to some startling discoveries in the Huaca de la Luna main platform (R. Tello 1997). During modern times, everything that has any commercial value (metal, ceramic, textile, wood, etc.) is collected.

2. Muscoid flies are among the first sarcosaprophagous flies to arrive and to lay eggs on putrefying flesh. The numerous empty pupal cases, found in the plaza, indicate that the victims were left exposed. For a detailed discussion about this subject, see Faulkner 1986.

3. These musical instruments are quite rare, and, to my knowledge, whistles are not part of Moche funerary artifacts.

4. Anne Marie Hocquenghem considers that these are old men offering children at the beginning of a new season or a new reign (1980; 1987). In these two publications, she associates the offering of children in Moche iconography with a *rite de passage* between two solstices and especially with the beginning of the humid season. Her interpretations are essentially based on an analogy between the Moche representations and the recorded information on Inca and Quechua rituals.

5. *Lomas* are bands of fog vegetation appearing on certain slopes exposed to the prevailing winds.

6. For a detailed analysis of the mountain sacrifice theme see Zighelboim 1995.

CHAPTER 6   *Ritual Uses of Trophy Heads in Ancient Nasca Society*

DONALD A.
PROULX
*Department of
Anthropology,
University of Massachusetts*

INTRODUCTION

Centered in the Ica and Nasca Valleys of south coastal Peru, the ancient culture known as Nasca dominated a wide area of southern Peru between 100 B.C. and A.D. 700. Here the Nasca people practiced intensive agriculture in one of the driest and most formidable environments in the world. The vast desert that covers the coastal plain of Peru and northern Chile is bisected by over forty river valleys that carry rain from the higher Andes across the landscape, emptying into the Pacific Ocean. It was in these narrow valleys and their tributaries that the ancient populations eked out their precarious existence, exploited the maritime resources of the ocean, and planted their crops in those parts of the valleys where sufficient water and adequate soils could be found. Survival in this harsh environment was of utmost concern, and many activities, both secular and sacred, revolved around providing for adequate food and water as well as appeasing the spiritual powers that controlled the forces of nature.

The Nasca culture developed directly out of the earlier Paracas culture, from which it derived many of its characteristic attributes. Archaeologists use the introduction of slip-painted pottery to mark the beginning of the Nasca culture, although many other cultural changes were occurring simultaneously. Elaborately decorated textiles with rich religious iconography are found in both the late Paracas and early Nasca cultures, but within several generations of the beginning of the Nasca culture, this complex iconography shifts from textiles to ceramics, representing another major difference between the two cultures. However, many Paracas traditions continue well into the Nasca sequence, including the ritual use of trophy heads and many of the fundamental religious icons.

Recent evidence suggests that politically the Nasca people did not have a unified central government or a capital city, which are characteristics of state-level societies, but rather were divided into a series of chiefdoms, each with its own leader, yet sharing in a common cultural tradition (see Silverman 1993: 337ff.). The centers of these chiefdoms have yet to be determined, although the multiple tributaries of the Río Grande de Nasca system may have formed the natural boundaries for such a division. The huge site of Cahuachi, covering 150 hectares in the Nasca River drainage, was once thought to be the capital, but has now been identified as an empty ceremonial center—a place of pilgrimage and burial used only for ritual purposes (Silverman 1993). Habitation sites, most of them small to moderate in size, are situated on the flanks of the rivers close to the primary centers of cultivation. Like those constructed by contemporary farmers in the region, many of these houses were made of poles and cane matting or of wattle and daub, although stone and adobe were used where the resources permitted. Excavation of these settlements is now just beginning, and as of now we know little of the daily life of the people.

The Nasca buried their dead in shallow graves dug approximately six to eight feet into the sand and roofed over with wooden beams derived from the local huarango tree. Sometimes adobes were used to line the tombs or to cover the roofing beams. Bodies were placed in a seated position in the tomb and were accompanied by ceramic vessels, gourd containers with food, weapons, weaving implements, and ornaments. Although museum and private collections contain examples of golden mouth masks and ornaments along with elaborate textiles that are thought to be Nasca, no elite tomb containing the remains of an individual that could be singled out as a leader has yet been scientifically excavated. Because there are no absolute or exclusive differences among the more than two hundred Nasca burials that have been scientifically recorded, but rather a graded continuum from simple to more elaborate graves, the mortuary evidence supports the presence of a ranked rather than a stratified society (Carmichael 1988: 399–400). Thus, politically and socially the Nasca were quite different from their Moche contemporaries on the north coast, who had a highly stratified society and royal tombs with many elite goods (Alva and Donnan 1993).

The Nasca were skilled craftsmen who wove exquisite textiles from both cotton and wool, fashioned ornaments from imported shell and stone, produced elaborate featherwork, decorated gourd containers with pyroengraved designs, carved objects from wood and stone, and made metal ornaments from gold. The Nasca are best known for their beautiful polychrome painted pottery, which displayed an amazing array of naturalistic and religious motifs. While painting was the primary means of decoration, modeled vessels in the form of humans and animals were common. The iconography displayed on these vessels forms the basis for much of what we know about Nasca society and religion. In addition, the Nasca possessed medical skills that included primitive skull surgery (trepanation), which probably was undertaken to repair damage to the skull caused by battle wounds. For social and cosmetic reasons, some members of the society also deformed their skulls and practiced tattooing on various body parts.

Also associated with the Nasca are the giant drawings known as geoglyphs, or more popularly as the "Nasca Lines," located on the desert near their settlements (see, inter alia, Aveni 1990b; Silverman 1990; Reiche 1968). Produced by removing or sweeping away the small darkened rocks on the desert surface, revealing the lighter-colored sand beneath, the Nasca Lines have survived the centuries due to the lack of rainfall and blowing winds in this arid region. The geoglyphs exist in two main varieties: lines, trapezoids, triangles, and other geometric forms extending for miles across the pampa, as well as giant representations of birds, animals, and other naturalistic motifs similar to those portrayed on Nasca pottery and textiles. The function of these lines has been disputed, and several different roles have been proposed, including their use as: ritual pathways leading to sacred sites (Silverman 1990: 453); ceque lines, produced over time as an enactment of sacred social rites (Urton 1990; Aveni 1990b); or a calendrical system (Reiche 1968, 1974; Kosok 1965). Recent evidence suggests that at least some of the geometric lines point to sources of subterranean water, implying that the ancients had developed a profound knowledge of the geology and hydrology of the region (Johnson 1997). Whatever their function, the lines reflect a pattern of cooperative labor directed by the secular or religious leaders of the society.

TROPHY HEADS AND DECAPITATION

Ritual sacrifice has a long history in the central Andes beginning in the Pre-Ceramic Period (prior to 1800 B.C.) and continuing through Inca times (see other chapters in this volume). Almost every major culture in the long sequence for this area, including Chavín, Cupisnique, Moche, Paracas, Nasca, Huari, Chimú, and Inca, practiced the tradition of taking heads for ritual use, although each of these cultures had its own unique ceremonies and different ritual context in conjunction with head-taking. The Nasca culture was no exception, deriving its impetus from the earlier Paracas culture from which it was born. One of the most distinctive features of the Nasca culture is the frequent depiction of severed human heads in the ceramic and textile art. Referred to in the literature as "trophy heads," these objects can be either displayed as single elements, held in the hands or attached to the belts of warriors or shamans, or associated with a wide range

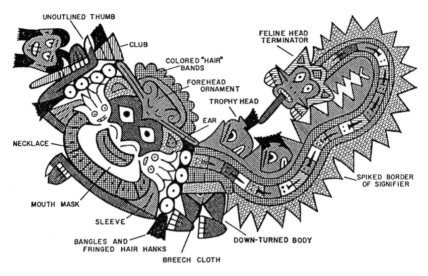

FIGURE 6.1. Anthropomorphic Mythical Being holding trophy head and club in its hand, with additional trophy heads appended to the cloak or signifier (after Proulx 1968: Fig. 19).

of "mythical creatures" who represent spiritual forces in the society. The most frequently portrayed creature in early Nasca art is the Anthropomorphic Mythical Being, which is displayed in a number of variations (Proulx 1968: 16ff.; 1983: 95ff.). In one manifestation, the creature carries a club and trophy head in its hand and is wearing a long cloak, probably derived from the animal skins once worn by religious leaders in the society (Figure 6.1). Trophy heads are often attached to this cloak. Another type is represented by a masked, standing figure, holding trophy heads in its hands with still others attached to its belt (Figure 6.2). A third type, the "Trophy Head Taster" (see Wolfe 1981: 19), has wings like a falcon and has its tongue protruding into a severed head (Figure 6.3). Other mythical beings with direct trophy-head associations are the Mythical Killer Whale, representing the powerful forces of the sea (Proulx 1968: 19; 1983: 96), and the Horrible Bird, a condorlike creature, representing the forces of the sky (Proulx 1968: 19; 1983: 97–98).

Of all the cultures that practiced head-taking in ancient Peru, only Nasca and Paracas are known to have meticulously prepared severed heads for ritual use. Over one hundred examples of naturally mummified trophy heads have been recorded by archaeologists (Figure 6.4). Each was produced in much the same manner. The head was cut from the body with

FIGURE 6.2. Standing Anthropomorphic Mythical Being holding severed trophy head and club. Trophy heads are also appended to the belt and loincloth (after Seler 1923: Fig. 27a).

FIGURE 6.3. Trophy Head Taster—a winged version of the Anthropomorphic Mythical Being with its tongue extending on to a trophy head (after Seler 1923: Fig. 74).

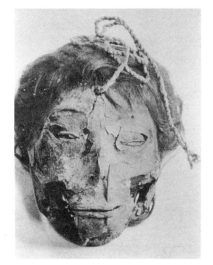

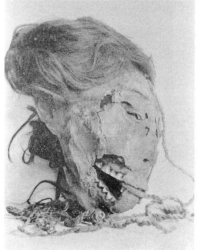

FIGURE 6.4. Three views of a Nasca trophy head excavated by Julio C. Tello at the cemetery of Las Salinas near Coyungo in the lower Río Grande de Nasca Valley (after Tello 1918: Láms. III, IV, V).

a sharp obsidian knife by slicing through the neck and separating the cervical vertebrae. Then the base of the skull, including the foramen magnum and portions of the occipital bone, was broken away (Figure 6.5). The evidence suggests that this was done with a club or similar instrument (see Coelho 1972; J. Tello 1918; Browne, Silverman, and García 1993). The brain was then removed through this opening. Next, a hole was punched or drilled through the center of the forehead for insertion of a carrying rope (Figure 6.6), which was secured inside the head by a wooden toggle (Figure 6.7). Finally, the lips were pinned shut using one or two long thorns from the local huarango tree (Figure 6.8). The cavity within the skull was stuffed with cloth, which in the case of specimens excavated at Chaviña in the Acarí Valley, contained traces of vegetable matter, including maize, mani, pacae, and cactus skins.

MILITARY ASPECTS OF NASCA SOCIETY

Before discussing the implications of head-taking and the ritual uses of trophy heads in Nasca society, it would be useful to discuss the general nature of warfare in this group. Some scholars argue that the Nasca were an aggressive society constantly at war over rights to water and land and access to other resources (Proulx 1989; Verano 1995; Roark 1965; Rydén 1930; J. Tello 1918; Tuya 1949; Uhle 1901, 1908; Weiss 1958). Others suggest that the warfare was strictly ritual, carried out simply to obtain heads (Coelho 1972; Neira and Coelho 1972–1973) or for ritual sacrifice of victims after capture (Baraybar 1987–1988; Kauffmann Doig 1966). I have addressed this question in detail in a previous work (Proulx 1989), but the main points need to be reiterated in order to understand the nature of warfare as opposed to the ritual uses the trophy heads were put to.

The importance of warfare in Nasca society is clearly seen in both the ceramic iconography and the artifacts discovered in archaeological sites. Nasca warriors holding clubs, spears, spearthrowers, and slings are portrayed on some of the earliest Nasca pottery, often in association with human trophy heads (Figure 6.9). Although some of these earliest manifestations of armed men might be interpreted as hunting scenes, the presence of trophy heads held in the hands or attached to the belt indicates the true meaning. Front-facing warriors are most prevalent in the early Nasca phases, but by Middle Nasca times they are depicted in profile. Representations of weapons, especially spears, but also bloody clubs, become more numerous in Middle Nasca (Phase 5), and one could argue for an increase in warfare at this time (which coincidentally correlates with periods of drought and subsequent relocation of people within the tributaries of the Río Grande de Nasca dating to A.D. 540 to 560 and 570 to 610; Schreiber and Lancho 1995: 251). The Late Nasca Period (Phases 6 and 7) witnessed a continuation of military themes in Nasca ceramic art, including painted warriors holding elaborate feather staffs (Blasco and Ramos 1991: Fig. 385) or dressed in special clothing and headdresses (*Museums of the Andes* 1981: 67), as well as modeled vessels of warriors holding trophy heads in their hands (*Museums of the Andes* 1981: 64). Silverman (1993: 339–340) suggests

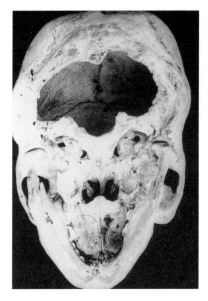

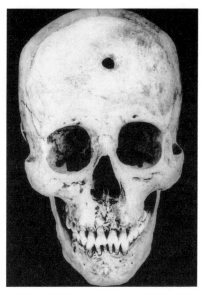

FIGURE 6.5. Broken base of a Nasca trophy head from Cerro Carapo in the Ingenio tributary of the Río Grande de Nasca drainage. Photo by Helaine Silverman and David Brown, courtesy of Helaine Silverman.

FIGURE 6.6. Nasca trophy head, illustrating a hole drilled through the forehead for insertion of a carrying rope. Cerro Carapo, Ingenio Valley, Río Grande de Nasca drainage. Photo by Helaine Silverman and David Brown, courtesy of Helaine Silverman.

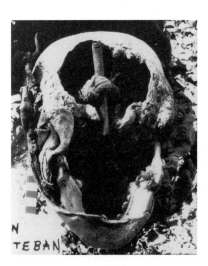

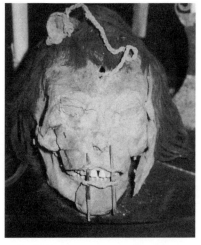

FIGURE 6.7. The base of a Nasca trophy head from the site of Cahuachi, showing the terminus of a woven carrying rope which has been secured inside the head by a wooden toggle. Photo by Helaine Silverman and David Brown, courtesy of Helaine Silverman.

FIGURE 6.8. Nasca trophy head on display at the Museo Nacional de Antropología y Arqueología, Lima. Photo by Donald A. Proulx.

FIGURE 6.9. Nasca warriors with captive and trophy head (after Seler 1923: Fig. 137).

that increasing pressure from highland groups in the late Nasca phases may have led to an increase in warfare and head-taking.

Supplementing the iconographic evidence are many archaeological examples of weapons, which include woven slings, metal and stone mace heads, wooden clubs, obsidian knives, spears, and spearthrowers. Slings are the most common weapon, being easily made and transported by even the most humble person. Looted Nasca graves often have large numbers of slings left behind by the *huaqueros,* who see little value in them. Pottery often depicts a male with a sling wrapped around his headdress when not in use. Slings could be used equally for hunting, repelling predators, and warfare, and they appear to have been a normal adjunct to a man's costume. Clubs, on the other hand, were probably used primarily for hand-to-hand combat. When used in conjunction with a stone or metal star-shaped head, such a weapon could produce severe trauma, including the type of wounds that would require trepanation, or skull surgery.

Spears are frequently seen in the art, although archaeological examples are rare. Constructed of huarango wood or perhaps heavy cane, they appear to have been tipped with obsidian points according to William Farabee, who found eight to ten spears with such points, along with a spearthrower in his Tomb 61 at Cahuachi in 1922 (cited in Carmichael 1988: 484). Spearthrowers, or atlatls, have been found in numerous Nasca graves and are also made of huarango wood, with bone or metal "hooks," which are often shaped in the form of birds or animals. These spearthrowers are frequently seen in the hands of warriors painted on the late pottery, often with a parrot perched on them for some symbolic reason.

Although the Nasca have few motifs on their pottery depicting events of everyday life, especially those implying movement or action, battle scenes are an exception. There are many examples of men engaged in hand-to-

FIGURE 6.10.
Nasca battle scene,
illustrating
decapitation with
an obsidian knife.
The dots
surrounding the
figures represent
blood (Amano
Museum, Lima,
specimen
MAR-037).

hand combat, where clubs or obsidian knives are the principal weapon. Decapitation scenes are vividly depicted on a few choice vessels, and it is clear that one of the objectives of battle was to obtain the heads of the enemy. One of the best examples of a battle scene can be seen on a unique vessel now in the collections of the Amano Museum in Lima. Elaborately dressed warriors are holding their victims by the hair with one hand while cutting the neck with a knife held in the other (Figure 6.10). To ensure that the viewer knows exactly what is transpiring, red dots, representing blood, fill the background. The iconography clearly portrays decapitation during battle, not as a separate ritual sacrifice following capture of an enemy. There are no depictions on the pottery of prisoners of war, torture of victims, or decapitation other than on the battlefield—again in contrast to Moche pottery, where such scenes are quite common. Battle scenes also include headless corpses lying on the ground, warriors with wounds, and a few rare vessels displaying trophy heads hanging from banners or poles following a battle. The fact that warriors were wounded in battle and that skull surgery was performed to save their lives further supports a secular motivation for warfare with subsequent use of trophy heads for ritual purposes. John Verano's analysis of eighty-four Nasca trophy heads has demonstrated that 85 percent of these specimens are males between the ages of twenty and fifty, while females make up only 6 percent of the sample (1995: 214). Children and adolescents are represented by a similar small percentage (6 percent). These data suggest a model of combat between groups of adult males rather than rituals whose main purpose would be the taking of heads. If the acquisition of heads was the main objective of such rituals, one would expect to see a more balanced ratio of specimens from both sexes and all age groups.

Who were the Nasca fighting? Under the old model which visualized Nasca as a primitive state with a central government emanating from the capital of Cahuachi, it was easy to argue that the Nasca were expanding through military means, thrusting into neighboring valleys and imposing their culture on the inhabitants, much like the current model for the Moche culture on the north coast. With the reevaluation of Cahuachi as an empty ceremonial center, and the lack of good archaeological evidence for expansion and centralized control over outposts in Pisco and Acarí (Carmichael 1992), it seems most likely that the various Nasca chiefdoms were fighting amongst themselves for access to resources, particularly water and additional land for agriculture. In the battle scenes portrayed on the pottery, little difference in dress, weaponry, and bodily depiction is shown among the combatants, although one or two vessels depict the "enemy" painted in a different color (Carmichael 1988: Illustration 19). This theory of inter-valley secular warfare needs to be further tested in the future by examining the settlement patterns revealed by the various, but as yet unpublished, surveys which have recently been undertaken in the Nasca drainage (e.g., Schreiber's work in the Taruga, Las Trancas, Tierras Blancas, and Aja tributaries, Silverman's work in the Ingenio Valley, Browne's survey of the Palpa region, and Carmichael's work in the lower Río Grande). The presence of fortifications or strategically positioned sites in critical locations could add to our understanding of the nature of Nasca warfare.

RITUAL USES OF TROPHY HEADS IN NASCA SOCIETY

The careful preparation of the trophy heads, described above, was only the first step in the ultimate ritual use and disposition of these remains. The

main practitioner in such rituals was the shaman, who acted as an inter-
mediary between the spirit world and the everyday world. Judging from the
archaeological evidence and the ceramic iconography, the major compo-
nents of many Nasca rituals were: (1) music provided by clay panpipes, clay
trumpets, drums, and rattles; (2) ritual drinks, which may have included
chicha (corn beer), but also involved the ingestion of hallucinogenic drugs
derived from the San Pedro cactus (Sharon 1972: 119; Dobkin del Rios
1980); (3) the use of trophy heads; and (4) processions to sacred places such
as Cahuachi. Among the ritual ceremonies depicted in the iconography are
many portraying a musician/shaman playing panpipes (Figure 6.11), surrounded by images of cacti, large storage containers holding some type of
beverage, and participants drinking from small cups (Figure 6.12). It seems
clear that the cacti are deliberately displayed to indicate their role in providing the connection to the spirit world by means of the mind-altering drug
they contain.

Trophy heads were also used in ceremonies in honor of the dead. Several
vessels depict a mummy bundle being honored by a figure playing panpipes
and holding a trophy head (Figure 6.13). Ceramic jars modeled in the form
of a trophy head are common in the collections and may have been used
in such ceremonies as well (Figure 6.14). In 1926 Alfred Kroeber found
the body of a beheaded corpse in a cemetery in the Nasca Valley (Kroeber
1956: 357). A ceramic vessel in the shape of a head had been placed in the
tomb as if to serve as a substitute. Nasca "head jars" come in a wide range
of sizes and forms. Some are clearly modeled with the intention of depicting all the salient aspects of a real trophy head: pinned lips, carrying rope,
bloody foramen magnum, skin flaps, etc. (Lavalle 1986: 130). Others appear
more lifelike and may have been fashioned to replace the missing heads of
decapitated victims (Blasco and Ramos 1991: Figs. 472–493).

Following any individual usage that trophy heads may have had, many
were ritually interred in caches in numbers ranging from three or four up
to groups of forty or more. One of the most impressive recent discoveries
of a cache of trophy heads was made by David Browne, Helaine Silverman,
and Rubén García (1993) at the site of Cerro Carapo in the Palpa Valley in
the Río Grande de Nasca drainage. Forty-eight trophy heads, virtually all
males between the ages of twenty and forty-five, were grouped together in
a single offering (Figure 6.15). Other caches have been found at Chaviña
(Coelho 1972; Lothrop and Mahler 1957) and at Tambo Viejo (Riddell and
Belin 1987) in the Acarí Valley, and at Cahuachi (Silverman 1993: Chapter 15) and Jumana (Pezzia 1969) in the Río Nasca Valley (see Verano 1995:
210–212 for a complete inventory). The specimens from Tambo Viejo were

FIGURE 6.11. Musicians playing panpipes in a ritual. The figures have symbols of a cactus on their torsos representing the hallucinogenic drink used in these ceremonies (after Ubbelohde-Doering 1931: Tafel XV).

FIGURE 6.12. Nasca ritual scene, illustrating small cups used in the drinking of a hallucinogenic beverage obtained from the San Pedro cactus. Also shown in the scene are the actual cactus and the large storage jars containing the brew. Museo Nacional de Antropología y Arqueología, Lima, specimen C-65296; photo courtesy of Patrick Carmichael.

FIGURE 6.13. Burial scene depicting a shaman holding a trophy head and playing panpipes in front of a mummy bundle. Courtesy of Patrick Carmichael.

FIGURE 6.14. Trophy-head jar with pinned lips and closed eyes (after Seler 1923: Fig. 157).

buried in pottery jars. One of the most interesting vessels I have studied, from the collections of the Museo Nacional de Antropología y Arqueología in Lima, portrays the ritual entombment of a group of trophy heads beneath a pyramid-shaped mound (Figure 6.16). A masked shaman, holding staffs in his hands and surrounded by small drinking cups, flanks one side of the mound, while an unmasked individual, also holding staffs, is found on the opposite side. A feline of unknown type floats over the mound, having some unspecified symbolic meaning. A number of pottery vessels displaying piles of severed heads may also symbolize ritual entombment.

FIGURE 6.15. Part of a cache of forty-eight Nasca trophy heads discovered at Cerro Carapo in the Ingenio tributary of the Río Grande de Nasca drainage by Helaine Silverman, David Browne, and Rubén García. Photo by Helaine Silverman and David Brown, courtesy of Helaine Silverman.

FIGURE 6.16. Drawing of a ritual scene on a Nasca double-spout bottle portraying the ritual entombment of a cache of trophy heads by a masked shaman holding staffs. Museo Nacional de Antropología y Arqueología, Lima, specimen C-13466; drawing after Uhle 1959: Abb. 1.

THE SIGNIFICANCE OF TROPHY HEADS IN NASCA RELIGION
In order to understand the role of trophy heads in Nasca society, a brief discussion of the nature of Nasca religion is necessary. Unlike the theocratic state religions of cultures like the Egyptians, Sumerians, Aztec, or Inca, Nasca religion existed at a more primitive level, incorporating the concept of animism, or belief in spirit beings. I agree with Richard Townsend, who noted that

> the Nazca, like other Indian Peoples of the Americas, believed that there was an active, sacred relationship between man and nature. According to this mode of thought, the divine order of the universe was reflected in the organization of society and in all important activities of human life. Thus, the control of water, planting of fields, harvesting of crops, preparations and celebrations of war, inauguration of rulers, and similar communal events had symbolic meaning and were bound, in a ramifying network of connections, to the forces and phenomena of the surrounding land and sky. This connection of cosmological ideas and social processes is the central point of inquiry in approaching the Nazca world. (Townsend 1985: 122)

The spirit world of the Nasca included the most powerful creatures of the air (condor and falcon), earth (jaguar and puma), and water (killer whale and shark). Although naturalistic representations of each of these animals and birds appear in the art, they are more often represented in symbolic form—killer-whale jaws and fins; falcon tails, wings, and eye markings; feline whiskers and body markings—in myriad combinations which often included human or anthropomorphic elements. Mythical beings, including the Horrible Bird, the Mythical Killer Whale, the Anthropomorphic Mythical Being, the Mythical Spotted Cat, etc., should be viewed as symbolic representations of either the nature spirits themselves or the spiritual power (*huaca*) that they emit. Most are combinations of several powerful elements.

The religious practitioners in Nasca society were shamans, intermediaries between the spirit world and the everyday world, who used various means to contact the spirits, including hallucinogenic drugs to induce visions and to gain control over supernatural forces. Most of the ceremonial scenes in the ceramic iconography, described above, were conducted by these individuals. It is likely that sacred places, such as certain mountains, as well as paraphernalia including panpipes, mouth masks, animal-

FIGURE 6.17. Plants growing from the mouths of Nasca trophy heads. Photo by Donald A. Proulx.

skin cloaks, and Spondylus-shell necklaces, were part of this religious complex. Therefore, Nasca religion incorporated elements of magic rather than prayer, and took place at sacred sites and locations rather than in formal temples.

The taking of trophy heads and their ritual burial in caches can best be understood in this context. In the environmentally hostile world of the Nasca, many of the rituals carried out by the shamans related to propitiating and controlling the forces of nature, especially those responsible for adequate water, good soils, and a sufficient harvest. The prime purpose for taking heads was magical in nature—to ensure the continued abundance of the food crops. The trophy heads were symbolic of, or a metaphor for, regeneration and rebirth. This concept can be seen iconographically in various scenes where plants are growing from the mouths of trophy heads (Figure 6.17). In the same vein, trophy heads often substitute visually and metaphorically for plants or parts of plants. In their view of the world, the Nasca people must have placed great importance on the human head as a source of power. The burial of caches of trophy heads must have resulted in the concentration of a great amount of ritual power.

Although Carmichael (1994: 84) has suggested that in some instances trophy heads may represent revered ancestors, I find this inference unconvincing. There is no evidence that the heads were taken from honored dead relatives, but rather were the trophies of warfare collected for ritual purposes. John Verano agrees, noting that

> it is clear that Nasca trophy heads are not a random sampling of a living population, nor do they fit the profile of revered elders; with few exceptions they are young adult males. Such an age and sex distribution is consistent with the hypothesis that Nasca trophy heads were collected from enemy combatants rather than from revered ancestors. (1995: 214)

Trophy heads can also be seen as offerings to the spiritual forces represented by the mythical beings painted on the pottery. Some scholars argue that these mythical beings are actually costumed shamans in the process of carrying out rituals or perhaps transforming themselves into spirit beings. While this may be true for some images of the Anthropomorphic Mythical Being, I believe that the majority of these representations are visualizations of the powerful spirits themselves, whom the Nasca believed controlled their destiny. The trophy heads symbolize not only the most precious offerings to these creatures, but also symbolize the relationship between head-taking, blood, regeneration, and fertility.

The religion of the Nasca people is complex and their ideology and worldview quite foreign to that of today's complex societies. We can only begin to understand it by recognizing the unity the Nasca felt between nature and everyday events, and the role that magic played in this process. Trophy heads, perhaps more than any other symbol, exemplify these attributes and the attempt to control the supernatural forces which affected their lives.

CHAPTER 7

Huari D-Shaped Structures, Sacrificial Offerings, and Divine Rulership

ANITA G. COOK

Department of Anthropology, The Catholic University of America, Washington, D.C.

"They didn't do it out of cruelty, but because they were very devout," he explained, "It was their way of showing respect for the spirits of the mountains, of the earth, whom they were going to disturb. They did it to avoid reprisals and to assure their own survival. So there would be no landslides, no huaycos, so that lightning wouldn't strike them dead and their ponds wouldn't flood. You have to understand their thinking. For them, there were no natural catastrophes. Everything was decided by a higher power that had to be won over with sacrifices."
MARIO VARGAS LLOSA, Death in the Andes

INTRODUCTION

The Huari Empire coalesced in the Ayacucho Valley of Peru (Map 1) during the Middle Horizon (A.D. 650 to 1000). Its development ushered in new architectural forms, urban living on a scale unknown prior to this time in the central highlands, and new ritual practices such as the breaking of large and beautifully painted urns and jars as buried offerings. These vessels display the main images of Huari iconography that include an array of humans and Profile and Front View Staffed Figures (Menzel 1964, 1968; Cook 1987; W. H. Isbell and Cook 1987). Representational images in Huari art provide new insights into pre-Columbian lifeways, religion, ritual activity, human attire, social groupings, and even individual identities, but much lies ahead.

Huari iconography (found on ceramics, textiles, stone monoliths, architecture, semiprecious metal objects, carved and inlaid shell, and semiprecious stone, etc.) was the principal medium for conveying considerable amounts of visual information. However, with few exceptions, Andean modes of representation have been difficult to interpret, because the iconography has not been amenable to comparisons with archaeological remains. The interpretation of ancient Andean imagery and its relationship to material evidence of behavior has been practiced with considerable success only with the north-coast Moche culture of Peru (e.g., Alva and Donnan 1993; Benson 1972; Castillo 1989; Donnan 1978; Hocquenghem 1987; Quilter 1997). The problem is exacerbated by the fact that there was no known form of writing in the Andes prior to the Spanish contact.

In this study, the importance of a building type known only at Huari sites is emphasized, as are the activities that apparently took place within its walls, which include: special tombs, offerings, and human sacrifice. A motif on Huari offering pottery is identified as this building, and figures painted on the same vessels suggest that the structures included the practice of human sacrifice. These relationships highlight aspects of ancient politics and rituals that took place within a quintessentially Huari building that is replicated across the highlands as the empire expanded. Pre-Columbian evidence of ancient politics and religion in the Andes has been most success-fully studied through architecture, mausoleums, and associated sumptuary goods from elite contexts. In this study, the iconography made it possible to identify the sacrificial contexts of D-shaped structures.

RITUAL AND STATE ORIGINS

Huari imagery contains clues to interpreting recently discovered archaeo-logical remains at the capital of Huari and its provincial centers. Many of the issues raised in this chapter and in other contemporary debates that concern politics and ritual were discussed early in the twentieth century, particularly in the works of A. M. Hocart (1970 [1936]) and in similar pre-sentations by James Frazer (1981 [1890]), who serve as interesting examples that these ideas are not all new.

Hocart, for example, observed that small-scale societies have their own "king" or "ruler," who emerges when needed; a person prepared to as-sume the responsibility of regulating the lives of people or to be a supreme arbiter of justice. For Hocart, it is as if "nature had prepared the organiza-tion before it was needed, had anticipated the growth of the state" (Hocart 1970: 31–32). What was this organization about before it became govern-ment? For Hocart, it is an organization for ritual (Needham's introduction in Hocart 1970: xxvii).

> [It] is vastly older than government, for it exists where there is no gov-ernment and where none is needed. When however societies increase so much in complexity that a coordinating agency . . . is required, that ritual organization will gradually take over this task. (Hocart 1970: 35)

Hocart saw a ritual basis to state and imperial governments. He declared that "the first kings must have been dead kings" (Hocart 1954, cited in Hocart 1970: xxiii, in Needham's introduction). His ideas were soon superseded and largely abandoned by mainstream twentieth-century political theorists in anthropology (Gose 1993: 481). The contributions of Hocart and Frazer, however, continue to have more than a subtle appeal when we consider early Andean civilization; indeed, the seed of these concepts has reemerged in debates that reconsider the important role of ideology (e.g., Demarest and Conrad 1992; Moore 1996), as expressed in ritual and ceremony, in understanding the nature of early Andean statehood and imperialism. These early views emphasize issues relevant to understanding the Huari polity; they underscore how ritual organization is essential to and precedes the emergence of the state.

This study sheds light on Huari iconography as a key to understanding the organization of sacred space within the capital of Huari and at Huari sites outside the Ayacucho Valley. My specific objective is to explore the relationship between images of the Sacrificer in Huari iconography and a previously unidentified design on offering pottery (Figure 7.1), which I believe depicts a special-function circular structure with a flat side, known as a D-shaped structure. The importance of the D-shaped building is underscored by its depiction in Huari iconography, and it led to research that identified D-shaped structures throughout the empire.

RITUAL OFFERINGS AND THE ARCHAEOLOGICAL EVIDENCE OF RITUAL TRIBUTE

Huari offerings leave material expressions of ritual behavior in the form of subfloor caches (e.g., Cook 1985, 1987; Menzel 1964, 1968). For the Middle Horizon, there are numerous offering contexts, including caches of smashed, oversized, decorated ceramic vessels, such as the two offerings from Conchopata in Ayacucho, and others from Pacheco and Maymi on the south coast and from Ayapata in the highlands of Huancavelica (Cook 1987; W. H. Isbell and Cook 1987; Menzel 1964, 1968; Ravines 1977). Other types of offering deposits include nonceramic items such as the many finely carved miniature turquoise figurines from the Huari site of Pikillacta (Cook 1992) and individual figurines known from many other sites. In the context of politics, as exemplified in the emergence of Huari as the first Andean empire, these "ritual offerings" can be equated with "ritual tribute" by analogies drawn from ethnohistoric and ethnographic evidence. Offerings vary in context, size, and degree of elaboration, and their ultimate resting places contain large quantities of whole or broken objects. Some offerings are associated with mortuary remains that do not suggest a natural death. These variations indicate that many offering rituals await proper description, and that distinct offering episodes denote particular forms of

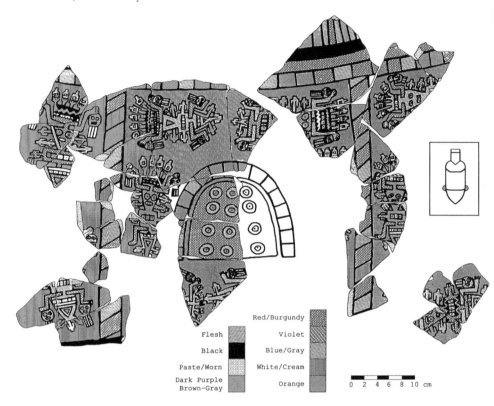

Flesh	Red/Burgundy
	Violet
Black	Blue/Gray
Paste/Worn	White/Cream
Dark Purple Brown-Gray	Orange

0 2 4 6 8 10 cm

FIGURE 7.1. Face-neck jar from the Conchopata 1977 offering with dome-shaped design that I interpret to be a D-shaped structure with Front View Sacrificers. Drawing by Anita G. Cook, with assistance from Jeffrey Splitstoser.

sacrifice that may be associated with the marking of status achievement, ruler rituals, and cults of the dead. This study elucidates ritual activity closely associated with the D-shaped building, and the offerings examined here will be limited to those that include sacrifice iconography.

In the buried cache in the offering recovered from Conchopata, in the city of Ayacucho, there were between twenty-two and twenty-five broken face-neck jars, most of which displayed the Front Face Staff Figure with Profile Staff Figures (Cook 1987: Figs. 21–26) in a theme closely resembling that found on the Gateway of the Sun at Tiahuanaco, and in abbreviated form in many other media, particularly ceramics and textiles at Huari sites. At least two or possibly three of these vessels (they were only partially reconstructed, making it difficult to determine the exact number) depict a different theme: a figure grasps a head in each hand and foot (Figures 7.1,

7.2; Cook 1987: Figs. 29–30), a design also found on earlier Nasca textiles from the south coast. Unlike the Profile Staff Figures that I have identified as Sacrificers (Cook 1983), these are drawn in front or top view and they do not hold an axe (Figures 7.1, 7.2). I am now convinced that these are Front View Sacrificers, perhaps individuals fulfilling a slightly different role than that of the Staff Profile Figures conveyed on the jars with the Front Face Staff Deity. The convergence of the altiplano Pucará/Tiahuanaco and coastal Paracas/Nasca/Moche practice of depicting sacrifice iconography is striking.

Numerous Front View Sacrificer figures fill most of the two or three vessel surfaces that have been reconstructed. They are interrupted by an unidentified dome-shaped motif. The dome is enclosed by an arch composed of a band of segmented rectangles painted in red, gray, and white (identi-

FIGURE 7.2. The Front View Sacrificer from the Conchopata 1977 offering. Drawn by Jeffrey Splitstoser from photo taken by Anita G. Cook.

0   2   4   6   8 cm

fied as cream on pottery in Figure 7.1). The shape is reminiscent of a rainbow (Figure 7.1). The dome-shaped design includes twelve repeated circles with circle-and-dot centers. This design has remained an enigma since 1977, when the offering was first studied.

To explore the archaeological correlates of the design in question, the archaeological evidence from the city of Huari is presented first. Second, the archaeological data from the provinces outside of Ayacucho are reviewed. With this background, the discussion returns to the iconography on offering pottery. The iconography reveals a key to the interpretation of Huari sacred space, architecture, and human sacrifice that is reinforced by relevant ethnographic and ethnohistoric information presented in the conclusions.

ARCHAEOLOGICAL EVIDENCE FOR D-SHAPED STRUCTURES, STONE-SLAB CHAMBERS, AND CYLINDRICAL CAPPED CISTS AT HUARI

In 1974, a road was cut through the architectural core of Huari that exposed numerous subsurface walls. Four of these zones were the focus of excavations and are important to this discussion. Each of the first three areas lies adjacent to the next, as one moves northwest to southeast along the road cut: they are known as Cheqo Wasi, Moraduchayoq, and Monjachayoq (see W. H. Isbell, Brewster-Wray, and Spickard 1991: Fig. 4). After 1980, another large-scale excavation, at Vegachayoq Moqo (Figure 7.3; ibid.), revealed large temple architecture with high-standing walls situated on tier terraces with trapezoidal niches (another interesting architectural feature at Huari that reemerges in Inca architecture). The niches contained burials that probably postdate the Huari occupation, suggesting that this area remained a ceremonial precinct for generations after Huari fell.

In 1977, Mario Benavides (1984), while excavating at Cheqo Wasi, revealed a ceremonial precinct with what he describes as a circular building, or D-shaped structure (Benavides 1991: Figs. 3, 11; W. H. Isbell and McEwan 1991: 11; W. H. Isbell, Brewster-Wray, and Spickard 1991: 46; W. H. Isbell 1991a: 296, 310), which I recently measured as 5.8 m. in diameter (Figure 7.4). This is now recognized as the first known D-shaped building to be discovered at Huari. In the center of the structure were five funerary chambers made of cut-stone slabs. Similar slab chambers were recovered in the 1930s by Julio C. Tello in the same area, just meters above where Benavides later excavated. Tello interpreted these as burial chambers because of their monumentality and shape, although they lacked human remains. The most direct evidence that the chambers functioned as funer-

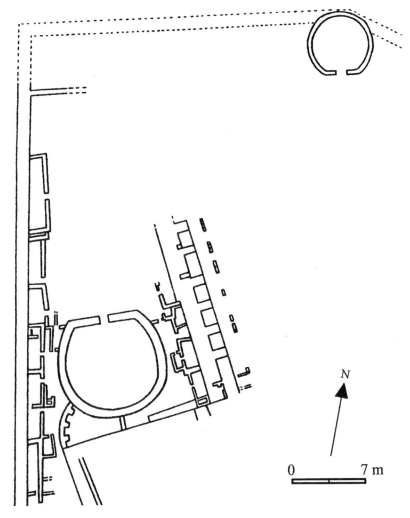

FIGURE 7.3. The D-shaped buildings in the Vegachayoq Moqo sector of Huari, also called the "Templo Mayor." Redrawn from González Carré et al. 1996: 42ff.

ary structures was provided by Benavides's excavations, which revealed the presence of human bone inside the structures (Benavides 1991: 65–66). The ceilings of these chambers are of large cut-stone slabs with holes drilled in their surface. Some of the holes are connected to small grooves or channels that served as conduits to the chamber interiors. These may have functioned as a means of removing the slab for postmortem secondary treatment of the

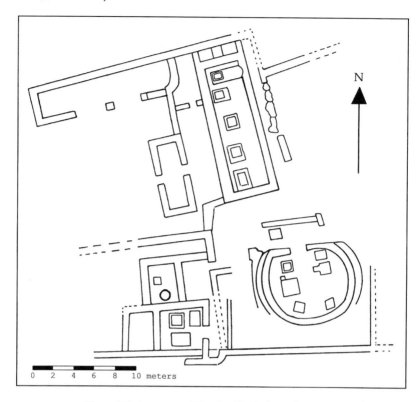

FIGURE 7.4. Cheqo Wasi sector at Huari with D-shaped structure in lower right and rectangular building in upper center. Redrawn from Benavides 1991: Fig. 2.

dead, for the addition of newly deceased individuals, for offering libations to the ancestors, or to allow the "ancient ones" to breathe.

In another long rectangular room, adjacent to the D-shaped temple, another five burial chambers were identified (Figure 7.4). These chambers contained human skulls and long bones with traces of cinnabar on them. Some of the chambers still had painted plaster evident in burgundy/red, white (cream in Figure 7.1), and blue. (Blue, gray, and even violet occur on Huari pottery and are very similar in color and at times indistinguishable.) Subfloor cists were also found in this sector. (These cists are cavities dug into the floor as shallow round or oval pits, or as deep, cylindrical, and stone-lined constructions, which may include an occasional niche or air vent, discussed below in greater detail.) A small statue was located at the entrance to the D-shaped structure, and another was recovered within the rectangular structure with slab-stone chambers (Benavides 1991: Fig. 13a).

All the cut-stone slab chambers at Cheqo Wasi are semisubterranean and multistoried (Figure 7.5). Cylindrical cists with perforated capstones are found on the first floor of the slab-stone funerary structures (González Carré et al. 1996: 21). In summary, at Cheqo Wasi, the slab-stone funerary chambers were located both within the D-shaped structure and within a rectangular building, and they share many architectural elements.

Between 1977 and 1980, William H. Isbell directed a series of excavations in the Moraduchayoq sector as part of the Huari Urban Prehistory Project. As a member of this project, I studied what is known as Cist Room 135, which contained three stone-lined cylindrical cists located under the plaster floor and sealed with one circular and two rectangular capstones (Cook 1994: 101–159, Lám. 5; W. H. Isbell, Brewster-Wray, and Spickard 1991). The dimensions of the room in which these cists were located measured 5.3 × 2 meters. The contents included regular-sized decorated pottery, two chrysocolla beads, and prestige items including Spondylus-shell artifacts. Human bone fragments were found in Cists 2 and 3; the skulls and long bones represent a minimum of two individuals. The walls of these cists were built with rough stones mortared with clay and covered with white plaster. The floor of Cist 1 consisted of large worked stone, while those in Cists 2 and 3 were of flagstone construction. Cist 1 was capped with a circular stone with two holes in its surface; the other two cists had rectangular capstones with a single hole through their centers.

Despite the extensive looting that occurred just after the site of Huari was abandoned, the ceramic pieces that were left in the cists could be re-

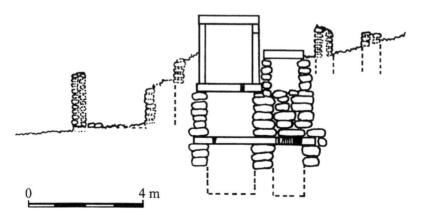

0   4 m

FIGURE 7.5. Capped cists at Cheqo Wasi, Huari, on the bottom floor within stone-slab funerary chambers. Redrawn from González Carré et al. 1996: 20ff.

assembled with those found outside. The contents of these capped cists were reconstructed, and I attributed relative dates to the pottery. The contents included some human bone fragments that were difficult to identify. As part of the analysis, the subfloor, capped cylindrical cists were defined as a new type of offering that had not been previously identified at Huari sites (Cook 1994).

At the center of Vegachayoq Moqo is a Middle Horizon Huari building that has been described as a D-shaped structure. Measurements recently taken by the author indicate an average diameter of 17.75 meters (Figure 7.3). It has been interpreted as the main temple (Bragayrac 1991; González Carré et al. 1996). Recent clearing of vegetation at Huari has revealed the tops of walls within this structure (Ismael Pérez, personal communication, 1998). Careful examination of the map of Huari architecture at Vegachayoq Moqo reveals as many as three D-shaped structures, and more than five additional ones can be identified at different locations within the city of Huari.

Small-scale excavations were carried out at Monjachayoq in 1977 by Abelardo Sandoval for the Instituto Nacional de Cultura. At that time there were large cut-stone blocks on the surface, and excavations revealed subterranean galleries filled with human bone. In 1997, archaeologist Ismael Pérez continued work at Monjachayoq, revealing a deep subterranean, multistoried mausoleum: the mazelike galleries at the base appear to be laid out in the shape of a llama and contained human bone (Pérez, personal communication, 1998). The exposed architecture includes a stone-lined circular pit very similar in shape and context to the capped cists mentioned above. Additionally, capstones found at Huari in several locations are cut in a D shape. Within Monjachayoq, more of these D-shaped capstones were found within the galleries. Remarkably, accesses to the galleries have cantilevered-lintel ceiling stones that are also D-shaped. Thus, within the largest mortuary monument yet excavated at Huari, capstones and ceiling lintels are built or carved to represent the same D shape, and a cylindrical stone-lined cist is in its midst.

Conchopata, located within the city limits of Ayacucho, just 12 km. from the city of Huari, has been known as an important Huari-period site since 1942. Tello excavated fragments of huge painted urns at this site. Subsequent work (Cook 1987; W. H. Isbell and Cook 1987; Lumbreras 1974; Menzel 1964, 1968; Pérez and Ochatoma 1999; Pozzi-Escot 1991) has revealed a large community with extensive architecture, evidence of ceramic production, subfloor capped burial cists, and areas dedicated to ritual activities that included the most important ritual offering events of the Middle

Horizon. These offerings included oversized urns and jars (Figure 7.1) with an elaborate iconography that we believe was conceived and elaborated at this site. Many of the residential zones and mortuary precincts (W. H. Isbell and Cook 1999) have yet to be fully appreciated (Figure 7.6a), particularly because the site is disappearing under urban sprawl. In 1997 José Ochatoma and his students excavated a well-preserved D-shaped structure (Figure 7.6b) in which were found broken oversized pottery, subfloor llama offerings, pits for the placement of oversized cone-based vessels, and a cache of human trophy heads (Ochatoma 1999). Denise Pozzi-Escot's map (Pozzi-Escot 1991) indicates that earlier, in 1982, half of another D-shaped structure (Figure 7.6a) was excavated but was in part destroyed by road construction leading to the airport. Indications of another earlier circular structure (possibly the remains of a third D-shaped building) were revealed during our 1999 excavations at Conchopata. No other site, except Huari itself, contains so many D-shaped structures. This site has the most direct evidence to connect the ritual significance of D-shaped buildings, as the locus of sacrifice, with sacrifice iconography on Middle Horizon offering vessels.

Ñawinpukio is situated above, within view and walking distance of Conchopata. This settlement was originally considered to be a Huarpa-period site that immediately predated the Middle Horizon. Recently, a large Huari component was identified, and an early D-shaped building, containing subfloor capped burials and camelid offerings (Machaca 1983), was excavated (another was only partially exposed). Not all the burials and offerings appear to be contemporaneous, which suggests that this D-shaped structure was used as a mortuary monument much like Cheqo Wasi.

Most recently, excavations at the site of Aqo Wayqo (Cabrera 1996; Ochatoma 1989), within the city limits of Ayacucho, revealed not only a Huari village of agriculturists, but small-scale craft production, including evidence of metallurgy, worked Spondylus, textile tools, chrysocolla, and turquoise artifacts. Many household foundations were identified and mapped.

At Aqo Wayqo an undisturbed, capped cylindrical cist was excavated. Its opening was circular in shape, and its diameter was identical to the one at Huari, both measuring 110 cm. The human remains were associated with ceramics, *tupus* (shawl pins), and lithics. The investigators believe that this is the tomb of an important local person in the community. Since the individual was no more than five years of age, the project director Martha Cabrera Romero suggests this may have been a human sacrifice. The bones were very fragile and in poor condition, making any additional observations

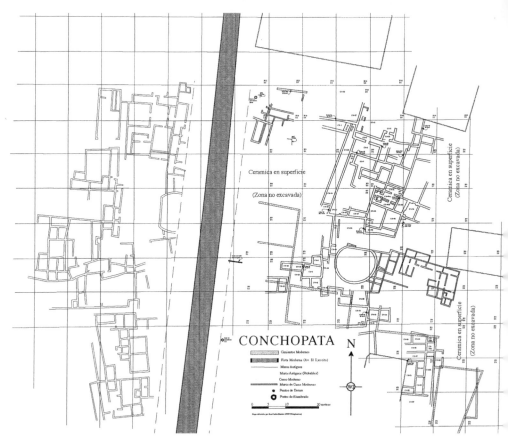

Ceramica en superficie

(Zona no excavada)

Ceramica en superficie
(Zona no excavada)

CONCHOPATA N

Ceramica en superficie
(Zona no excavada)

Cimientos Modernos

Pista Moderna (A+ El Ejercito)

Muro Antiguo

Muro Antiguo (Probables)

Cerco Moderno

Muros de Casas Modernas

Poztes de Durum

Poztes de Alumbrado

0   5   10   20 metros

FIGURE 7.6. (a) Map of Conchopata (Isbell and Cook 1999) (drawn by Juan Carlos Blacker); (b) D-shaped structure at Conchopata (photo by William Isbell).

difficult. Many subfloor cist offerings were identified during the course of excavations both at Aqo Wayqo and another nearby Huari settlement, known as Muyu Orqo (Berrocal 1991).

The cylindrical capped cists (Figures 7.5 and 7.9) have several relevant characteristics in common: (1) they are subterranean; (2) they are capped in a way that makes reentry and reuse possible; (3) they are lined with stone into which regular-sized offering ceramics, human bone, and semiprecious items were deposited; (4) they were situated within special-function rooms; and (5) they can be found on the first floor of the stone-slab burial chambers and in other room contexts, but all share the characteristic capstone with holes that served as perforations for offerings and libations and to facilitate reentry. In many respects, the shape and contents of these subfloor cists are reminiscent of what are today considered to be conduits to the underworld, or *pacarinas,* which are caves or springs, points of transition of time and space (Allen n.d.; B. J. Isbell 1978: 209–210).

The extent of looting at Huari caused us to doubt whether the cists had actually been used as burial places. I am now convinced that subfloor, capped cylindrical cists were a common Huari architectural feature and that the rituals associated with the objects found within them were a practice at Huari and were reproduced in agrarian villages within the Ayacucho area and in the provinces. At Huari the cists received special treatment and are also found within D-shaped structures as mortuary spaces.

These D-shaped structures, also known as temples, have been given far less attention than the orthogonal architectural plan so typical of Huari sites. By 1985, D-shaped structures were recognized at Huari within the Vegachayoq Moqo and Cheqo Wasi sectors and at Conchopata (W. H. Isbell and McEwan 1991: 11; W. H. Isbell, Brewster-Wray, and Spickard 1991: 46; Benavides 1991; Bragayrac 1991; Pozzi-Escot 1991). At that time they were known only in the Ayacucho Valley, and Isbell considered these an early architectural form indigenous to the area (W. H. Isbell 1991a; 1997), while round structures were noted at sites such as Cerro Baúl in Moquegua and Huaca del Loro (Paulsen 1983; Schreiber 1987) in the Nasca drainage.

Several more D-shaped structures are now known in Ayacucho (Cook 1999; W. H. Isbell and McEwan 1991; W. H. Isbell 1991a, 1991b, 1997; Williams 1997) within the urban core of Huari, and at Conchopata and Ñawinpukio, and they are known at an increasing number of Huari sites outside the Valley, including two very recent finds (see Map 1), at the site of Yako in the Chicha/Soras Valley, on the boundary between Ayacucho and Apurimac (Meddens, personal communication, 1999), and at the site of Tiqnay in the Department of Arequipa (Justin Jennings, personal communication, 1999).

ARCHAEOLOGICAL EVIDENCE FOR D-SHAPED
STRUCTURES, STONE-SLAB CHAMBERS, AND
CYLINDRICAL CAPPED CISTS AT PROVINCIAL
HUARI SITES OUTSIDE OF THE AYACUCHO VALLEY

As work progresses at Huari sites, some astounding similarities in temple architecture are emerging. William Isbell mapped the north highland Huari site of Honcopampa in 1987 (W. H. Isbell 1991b: Figs. 5, 8) and identified two D-shaped structures there, AC-13 and AC-14 (Figure 7.7; W. H. Isbell 1991b: Fig. 8). Small-scale excavations were conducted within several structures to determine the nature and length of Huari occupation at the site and to explore the function of the buildings, but unfortunately no excavations were conducted within the D-shaped units. Structure AC-13 (ca. 12.10 m. × 12.50 m.) still has standing walls of 5 m. in height. Isbell suggests that this may have originally been a multistoried towerlike building. AC-13 was probably the site of an old trench that Amat and Vescelius excavated in 1961. The cleaned trench wall contained ashy lenses and few artifacts; it was probably an area that had been cleaned frequently during its use (W. H. Isbell 1989: 105). Structure AC-14 is smaller (ca. 7.6 m. × 7.7 m.) and includes niches in its curved interior wall and has agglutinated architecture bonded to parts of its exterior wall. These structures will require careful excavation in the future to determine their use and overall morphology; at present we do not know if interior funerary chambers are present.

Cerro Baúl (Lumbreras, Mujica, and Vera 1982; Moseley et al. 1991; Feldman 1989; Williams 1997), one of several intrusive Huari sites that were identified in Moquegua by the Contisuyo Program in the early 1980s, has been the focus of several seasons of archaeological research. Most recently, Patrick Ryan Williams (1997) reported the results of excavations in a circular room, or D-shaped structure (Figure 7.8), which is identified as Unit 5 at the site. Agglutinated rectilinear rooms flank the exterior of the structure, and the door of the D-shaped building opens into a large patio, a layout similar to that at Vegachayoq Moqo at Huari (Figure 7.3). The short and long diameters of this structure are 9.1 m. × 10.2 m., similar to those at Honcopampa (Figure 7.7: Structure AC-14). The lack of occupational remains suggests to Williams that the structure was cleaned out just before its final use. Items associated with this structure and the agglutinated exterior rooms and plaza include: small amounts of the Huari-

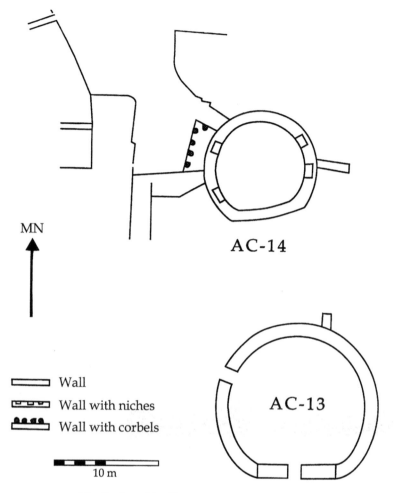

FIGURE 7.7. The D-shaped buildings at Honcopampa AC-13 and AC-14 (after W. H. Isbell 1989: Fig. 6).

style ceramics (specifically, Ocros and Chakipampa), grinding stones, llama bones, obsidian flakes and points, ceramic offerings situated around the exterior of the D-shaped structure, and a small gold-foil feline beneath the floor within the interior of the D-shaped building. (Another gold-foil feline was excavated on the earliest floor in Street 132 at Huari [Brewster-Wray 1990: Fig. 33].) The interior walls of the D-shaped Cerro Baúl structure (Figure 7.8) were of much higher quality and more finely finished than its exterior, a pattern observed also by Isbell (1991b) for D-shaped structures

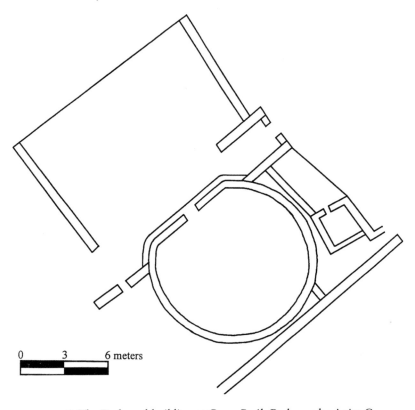

FIGURE 7.8. The D-shaped building at Cerro Baúl. Redrawn by Anita G. Cook from Patrick Ryan Williams, "The 1997 Cerro Baúl Excavation Project," Report to the G. A. Bruno Foundation, March 1, 1998, with permission of Williams.

at Honcopampa and by Benavides (1984) for the interior of the stone-slab burial chambers at Cheqo Wasi.

At Cerro Baúl (Figure 7.8), the interior walls of the D-shaped structure were covered by a layer of stucco and covered again by a fine grayish-white plaster (Williams 1997). The walls[1] were painted in white/cream, red, and gray, approximately the same colors described by Benavides (red, white/cream, and blue) on the slab burial chambers within the rectangular structure in the Cheqo Wasi sector at Huari (Figure 7.4). Clearly, there is a relationship between D-shaped structures, funerary stone-slab chambers with capstone cylindrical cists, and the red, white/cream, and blue paint that decorates both types of architecture. Although no D-shaped structures have yet been identified at Pikillacta, south of Cuzco, there are buildings with interior rounded corners. Gordon McEwan (1998) interprets these structures as the centers of ritual activity, and, in fact, these are the type of buildings that housed subfloor offerings such as the Pikillacta turquoise figurines (Cook 1992).

More interesting are the recent excavations near Cuzco that were conducted at the site of Batan Urqo in the Huaro Valley just south of Pikillacta. Julinho Zapata excavated similar cylindrical, stone-lined, and capped cists at Batan Urqo (Figure 7.9; Mary Glowacki, personal communication, 1996; Zapata 1997). The best reported example had been looted in the 1950s, and the contents that were recovered by the police in their investigations were given to the Museo Inka. These objects included: a small sculpture of a

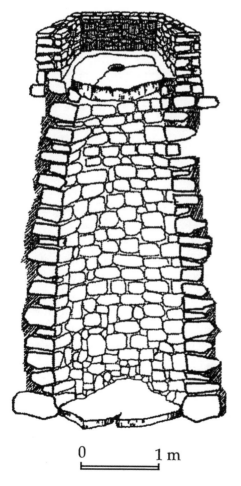

0   1 m

FIGURE 7.9. Capped cist at Batan Urqo, Huaro. Redrawn from Zapata 1997: Figs. 22 and 24.

llama in gold, four small gold disks, Spondylus fragments and other worked shell, turquoise beads, and a fragment of textile. Zapata noticed ash when he cleaned the cist in 1992. This capped cylindrical cist was located within the floor of the bottom level of a two-story structure and was clearly subterranean. Tombs of different types were excavated at the site, suggesting that the Huari cemetery had been used for generations previous to the Middle Horizon. Based on my interpretation of the role played by capped cylindrical cists, I would anticipate that the site housed a variety of ceremonial spaces, some of which were dedicated to mortuary rites. Batan Urqo is a large mound in the Huaro Valley, and it is a likely candidate for the recovery of D-shaped temple structures in the future.

Stone-slab funerary chambers within the Cheqo Wasi sector of Huari (Figure 7.5) and capped cists at Batan Urqo near Cuzco (Figure 7.9) are all subterranean features located in multistoried structures. Further, the Batan Urqo capped cists are practically identical to those in the Moraduchayoq and Cheqo Wasi sectors at Huari. Since, at Huari, the Moraduchayoq Cist Room 135 (Cook 1994: Lám. 5; W. H. Isbell, Brewster-Wray, and Spickard 1991: Fig. 18) contained cylindrical capped cists that look like those at Cheqo Wasi and Batan Urqo, it is likely that these also represent the lowest level of a former multistoried mortuary and offering structure.

The presence of D-shaped structures at the capital of Huari, at Conchopata, and at Ñawinpukio, and in the provinces at Honcopampa (Figure 7.7) in the north highlands, at Cerro Baúl (Figure 7.8) on the far south coast, and at the newly reported sites in the central and south highlands provides ample evidence that these structures were a major religious feature in Huari religion and integral to the politics of Huari expansion. The elite funerary architecture of stone-slab chambers that contain capped cists at Huari, and the more frequent occurrence of capped cist burials with offerings at other Huari sites in Ayacucho and at Huari provincial centers, indicate that mortuary behavior at the center was replicated at sites throughout the empire. The only place known to contain a D-shaped structure filled with stone-slab chambers and capped funerary cists is the Cheqo Wasi sector of Huari. It is likely that this area and Monjachayoq contained the most important Huari leaders: its kings, queens, and high priests.

D-SHAPED STRUCTURES DEPICTED ON OFFERING POTTERY WITH THE FRONT VIEW SACRIFICER

A close examination of D-shaped structures and the capped cists that contain offerings and burials at the site of Huari illustrates how offering spaces are represented in Huari iconography. The same relationship exists outside of the capital, for similar evidence is found at provincial Huari settlements. I recognized that the dome-shaped design, or "D" structure, on the face-neck jars of the Conchopata offering recovered in 1977 (Figure 7.1; Cook 1987) strongly resembles the D-shaped structures at Huari and that this seemed more than merely coincidental. Repeated around the painted dome-shaped design on the Conchopata jars is the newly defined Front View Sacrificer, with trophy heads dangling from its hands and feet (Figures 7.1, 7.2). I interpret the imagery on the face-neck jars to be Sacrificers associated with the D-shaped temples that are found at Huari and at nearby Huari sites in the Ayacucho Valley.

The close iconographic relationship between the painted D-shaped structure and the Front View Sacrificer (Figure 7.1) strongly suggests that the building was not only a sacred space but an area in which sacrifices were made. In fact, the D-shaped structure at Conchopata (Figure 7.6a) included a cache of human trophy heads. Furthermore, excavations in Cheqo Wasi (Figures 7.4, 7.5) revealed that these structures sometimes contained cut-stone funerary chambers. Within the dome-shaped design on the jars are twelve circles with circle-and-dot interiors (Figures 7.1, 7.2). These represent the perforations in the slab-stone roofs of the funerary chambers found within the D-shaped structures at Cheqo Wasi. The presence of statues, as guardians, at or close to the entrance of the two structures that contained funerary chambers in this sector of Huari, gives these contexts additional mortuary and ritual significance; it suggests a Huari ancestral cult. The identification of the dome-shaped design on the offering pottery as a D-shaped Huari temple is made even more convincing by the fact that both have the same colored paints: burgundy/red, white/cream, and blue/gray. In the architecture, these colors are used to cover the interior walls of structures, while, in the iconography, these colors fill the rectangles of the painted arch that encloses the dome-shaped design.

The offering iconography includes the D-shaped temple structure as identified in this essay. To date, it has been found only on the offering jars from the site of Conchopata associated with repeated Front View Sacrificers (Figures 7.1, 7.2) that grasp trophy heads in their hands and feet. The Sacrificer, as a core image in the Andes (Valcárcel 1959), is, in my estimation, more frequently represented than any other figure, including the Front Face Staff Figure, as seen within the Huari and Tiahuanaco polities. Unlike Luis Valcárcel, who described the *Degollador* (Decapitator) in the larger Andean context and through time, I have focused attention on the forms of representation and contexts that are particular to the second half of the first millennium A.D. and their immediate ancestry.

We now recognize at least two distinct forms of the Sacrificer: a "Profile Staff Sacrificer" (Cook 1983; 1987), seen in altiplano Pucará and Tiahuanaco iconography, on materials from burial contexts from the Chilean north coast, and from Huari sites in Ayacucho and its provinces, and a "Front View Sacrificer," with strong ties to Middle Nasca and to the north-coast Moche, and most likely part of a ritual tradition that was already fully developed in Paracas communities some five hundred years earlier, along the south coast in the Ica, Nasca, and Pisco Valleys. The Sacrificer and the behavior associated with this figure are undeniably important to understanding Huari religion and temple architecture. The sacrificial iconography is clearly reconfirmed in the archaeology by the trophy heads found with the D-shaped "temple" at Conchopata (Ochatoma 1999).

ANDEAN COSMOLOGY, RITUAL, AND SACRIFICE

Huari sacrifice iconography in the Conchopata offering, excavated in 1977, depicts Front View Sacrificers holding trophy heads that surround a D-shaped structure that has perforated cylindrical capped cists. There are archaeological counterparts, as discussed in the previous sections, and these are part of a larger Huari elite mortuary tradition that includes stone-slab chambers. Human sacrifice is implied in the iconography and documented in the archaeology of D-shaped structures. How then should we interpret these finds? I have summarized a selection of sources to illustrate that "sacrifice" in Central Andean contexts is materially expressed in "offerings" and that these offerings are, in fact, forms of payment. If more recent practices, as recorded in ethnographies and ethnohistory, serve us well, then "ritual offerings" are conceptualized as synonymous with "ritual payments." For example, when describing the contemporary community of Huaquirca in southern Peru, Gose writes: "mountain spirits generally take the human form of rich and powerful notables and are sacrificially 'fed' or 'paid' in the *t'inka* rites [libations and sacrificial rituals] that come to the fore during the phase of the year dedicated to private appropriation and consumption" (Gose 1994: 78). This conjunction of spatial, geographic, and sociopolitical hierarchy illustrates that "offerings" are, in fact, ritual payments or tribute to the mountain spirits to ensure healthy and abundant herds and crops. Indeed, the term used to describe these offerings is *pagapu* (e.g., Delgado 1984), meaning "payment to the mountain gods." In this capacity, ritual tribute ensures the economic and spiritual well-being of the community. The practice of making offerings appears to have been an organizational feature integral to the success of the Inca state, with youth or child sacrifice, known as *capac hucha* or *capacocha*, marking Inca imperial and sacred geography (see Benson, this volume; Verano, this volume). We may find the roots of this tradition and the locus of similar imperial strategies in the activities that took place within, and that necessitated the construction of, Huari D-shaped buildings.

Part of making sense of Andean cosmology is understanding that the natural landscape and Andean social organization are closely linked. For instance, both ethnography and early chronicles document that social and political hierarchies replicate the hierarchy used to describe sacred features on the landscape. Ethnographic descriptions of communities in Ayacucho and the south highlands near Cuzco reveal that geographic, religious, and sociopolitical hierarchies are similar and overlap (Allen 1988: 109; B. J. Isbell 1985: 151; Zuidema 1964). Mountains, or *apus* (also called *wamanis* in Ayacucho), are arranged hierarchically; the highest visible peak on the horizon is the most important local "place" (spirit, or god, for lack of a better translation). Even a small natural hillock on the valley floor does not escape attention and is often part of the local spatio-ritual landscape. Rituals are spread throughout the year and occur at specific places which are also organized hierarchically. Some involve local household rites, others include the community, and still others are regional in scope (Allen 1988; B. J. Isbell 1985; Gose 1994).

The Andean cosmos is understood, then, through this ritualized landscape, where acts of "sacrifice" are made that are described as impregnating the earth through food, liquids, materials, and occasionally human offerings. These circulate, usually along waterways, along rivers, to oceans, to the Milky Way (which is conceived as a river in the sky, Urton 1981), to mountain lakes, into the earth, and out of springs or *pacarinas* (origin places from which local groups first emerged in Andean origin myths) to regenerate the Andean universe. At Huari sites, the subterranean nature of the perforated capped cists, which are often housed within stone-slab superstructures with their own grooves that lead into the subterranean chambers, provides interesting material correlates for the circulatory nature of Andean cosmology. The stone chambers at Huari are understood to be elite mortuary architecture that housed the remains of the upper echelon of Huari society and even the heads of lineages and their families. In practice, the openings in capstones and stone chambers probably had both a functional and cosmological purpose: as orifices that served as conduits for libations and material offerings of various kinds, and as a means for reopening the cists for multiple interments.

To argue that divine rulership was operative during the Middle Horizon, in ways similar to those of the Inca, is premature at this stage, but there are tantalizing strands of evidence that point in this direction. In the following pages are some of the building blocks for this argument and a brief review of the evidence.

"SACRIFICE" AND THE SACRIFICER

A central and fearsome figure in prehistoric Andean iconography, the Sacrificer, is best known from north-coast cultures, particularly Cupisnique and Moche, which include several types that are illustrated over many hundreds of years (Cordy-Collins 1992 and this volume; Hocquenghem 1987). The image of a Sacrificer is simultaneously a metaphor for rulership in which sacrifice is construed as, or made equivalent to, tribute, and a metonym of cosmology, whereby sacrificial blood is understood to be a vital fluid that recreates and generates life. Despite the fact that the Sacrificer has received limited attention beyond the north coast (Valcárcel 1959, 1964; Cook 1983), anyone familiar with Andean imagery cannot avoid recognizing the frequency with which a figure with a knife in one hand and a human head in the other appears through time and across space both in the highlands and on the coast. In Ayacucho during precolonial times, the image of a Sacrificer occurs in various contexts, including pottery offerings (Cook 1987, 1994: Lám. 54; W. H. Isbell and Cook 1987). It consists of a profile figure with a knife in one hand and a severed human head in the other. The Sacrificer is depicted in Huari and in the southern altiplano region of Tiahuanaco; in the iconography of both of these polities, the Sacrificer is often associated with the Front Face Staff Figure[2] (also referred to as the Front Face Staff Deity, as in the 1942 offering recovered by Tello at the site of Conchopata; see Cook 1987; W. H. Isbell and Cook 1987) and can appear in other iconographic registers as well. The connection between the Front Face Staff Figure, the most important Middle Horizon Andean religious figure, and the Sacrificer simultaneously conveys notions of hierarchy and the ultimate offering, that of human sacrifice.

A new figure can be added to those identified as Sacrificers. As previously described, it occurs in an offering found at Conchopata in 1977 (Cook 1987: Figs. 29–30), along with the structure I identify as the D-shaped temple. This Front View Sacrificer is conveyed in a style similar to that of coastal Nasca textiles: it lacks a staff and holds bodiless heads in its hands and feet.

Not only does the Sacrificer have great antiquity as a visual image, it continues to play a role in Andean society. My interpretation relies on the nature of Andean cosmology drawn from early colonial descriptions of Inca and provincial rituals, and on information from contemporary ethnographies briefly described below.

José María Arguedas, using his ethnographic work in Ayacucho and Jauja (1953, cited in Ansión and Sifuentes 1989: 63, 65), makes two important statements regarding a creature called the *nakaq* or *nacac*.[3]

> La vinculación del *nacac* con el sacrificio cruento, la degollación como oficio religioso, aparece . . . como muy antiguo. . . . Es quizá este infausto personaje el mismo "nacac" de los antiguos sacrificios cruentos. El Degollador debió ser un personaje temido, pues no era un sacerdote propiamente dicho sino un individuo diestro en el oficio de seccionar el cuerpo de las víctimas, y deja visibles, palpitantes aún, las vísceras, para que el sacerdote iniciara los oficios.
>
> [The relationship between the *nacac* and cruel sacrifice, decapitation as a religious rite, appears . . . to be very ancient. This ill-famed figure is perhaps the "nacac" of those ancient cruel [human] sacrifices. The decapitator was probably a feared figure, since he was not technically a priest, but instead a person skilled in the practice of sectioning the body of the victims to expose the still palpitating organs, so the priest could initiate the ceremony.] (author's translation)

With reference to the definition of *nakaq* as a butcher of animals, which also occurs in the literature (e.g., Morote Best 1952: 69), Arguedas adds the following clarification:

> No se llama *nakaq* a los carniceros en los pueblos de Ayacucho y Apurimac donde he vivido, así como no se llama pishtacu a los de este mismo oficio en Jauja. Nakaq o pistacu son los degolladores de seres humanos. Y este terrible personaje del que se cuentan tan pavorosas historias ha dado a la palabra una limitación absoluta. *Nakaq* es sólo este degollador de seres humanos. (Arguedas 1953: 218–219, as cited in Ansión and Sifuentes 1989: 65; italics are author's emphasis.)
>
> [The butchers in the towns of Ayacucho and Apurimac where I lived are not called *nakaq*, nor is *pishtacu* a term used to refer to those of this profession in Jauja; *nakaq* or *pishtacu* are the decapitators of human beings. This horrible figure, about which such awful tales are told, has limited the definition of the term. *Nakaq* is exclusively the decapitator of human beings.] (author's translation)

Many ethnographic descriptions of the *nakaq* Sacrificer refer to white-bearded *hacendados,* or blue-eyed and blond-haired gringos (Vergara and Ferrúa 1989), who are said to kill peasants for commercial use in the West—literally, to grease the engines of capitalism and extract their fat and blood for medicinal uses, etc. But these descriptions are best understood if the processes of capitalism, terrorism, and violence in the Andes are addressed, issues elegantly handled by Gose (1986), Ansión and Sifuentes (1989), and Salomon (1987) and beyond the scope of the present study. The modern importance of the *nakaq* is a testimony to the power and endurance that this concept and image hold in many southern and central highland communities—its meaning has been adapted to new political circumstances. The Inca and subsequent Spanish empires represent two recent instances when outside exploitative forces gave increased significance to the fearsome folk image of the *nakaq* (Ansión and Sifuentes 1989: 62).

"Sacrificer," as I am using the term, is synonymous with the concepts associated with the *nakaq* as reported in early colonial sources and in later ethnographic accounts (e.g., Allen 1988: 111; B. J. Isbell 1985: 141, 144; Guaman Poma 1980: 251). Furthermore, the modern concepts and oral traditions associated with the *nakaq* have close parallels with examples of the Sacrificer known from prehistoric contexts:

1. the images are found in both urban and provincial areas;
2. they are assigned exclusively the function of human sacrifice for ritual purposes, mediating between humans and the world populated by the ancestors and gods (gods being the mountains, springs, caves, thunder, sacred stones, etc.).

During the Middle Horizon, well-being was ensured through sacrifice. We have already noted that the landscape today is viewed hierarchically from the highest peaks to the lesser ones, the highest receiving the most ritual attention; it is the *uma,* or the head *apu.* When this first appears in the archaeological record has yet to be determined. It is not a leap of faith, however, to suggest that as the Huari Empire coalesced, it relied on local practices and created some new ones. Today, the hierarchical nature of the landscape has the imprint of a hierarchical social system that was already set in motion before the Middle Horizon.

CONCLUSIONS

With the emergence of Huari, new offering patterns consonant with state interference appear. In instances of complex society, the rituals of politics can be traced in archaeologically excavated offering deposits, where these are considered equivalent to "ritual payments." I have equated the act of making an offering with the modern ethnographic concept of a *pagapu*, a payment that may have been transformed into ritual tribute with the emergence of Huari politics. Furthermore, an analogy can be drawn between the iconography and the archaeology, which suggests that the most important state rituals involving tribute (including the ultimate form: human sacrifice) took place within D-shaped structures.

The images tell a story that has been difficult to decipher. It is unlikely that we will ever know whether this behavior may be associated with the desire on the part of the supplicant to satisfy obligations to the state through ritual tribute of labor-intensive products, such as oversized painted ceramics, or whether these were state-mandated events. Iconography on the offering pottery includes beings holding staffs or trophy heads that are elevated to a semidivine or divine status. Are these tributary actions a means of payment to actual overlords? Or are they intended as tribute to deities, such as the powerful "places" (Allen 1988), or mountain deities, to ensure a productive agropastoral economy? Could Huari lords have absorbed these ritual practices and transformed them into a tribute-paying ritual event, and might this have been the road to divine kingship?

Concepts of rulership seem to pervade the images, yet there is also a concern with subterranean offerings, burial contexts, and the recycling of fluids, as suggested by the conduits and perforations in the slab-stone funerary chambers. Elements of death and regeneration that are reminiscent of ancestor cults also permeate the sacrifice iconography. Middle Horizon ritual offerings with sacrifice iconography share the following characteristics: (1) the offering cists are all subterranean regardless of where they are found; (2) their contents are mostly ceramics that were broken in situ and carefully buried, although some offerings were buried intact;[4] (3) the level of manufacture and overall care in design execution of cist contents leave little doubt that highly skilled artisans contributed their labor; and (4) the cists were usually found within walled rooms or larger plazas. Most of these features also characterize modern offerings that today are understood to connect the living to the ancestors, who are believed to reside both inside the earth and within mountains. The Nasca figures represent Sacrificers of coastal inspiration. Bodiless heads, with stylized blood dripping from the necks, are grasped in their hands and feet. The letting of blood is a central theme on the vessels, a theme connecting Ayacucho to related practices on the south coast and beyond.

Funerary and sacrificial rituals were closely connected in the Andes.

Huari sacrifice iconography and archaeology may also help us gain insights as to how the dead were treated. Secondary, disarticulated, and incomplete human remains were a common feature at Huari. In fact, there is no known formal Huari cemetery at the site, nor do we have a clear idea of how the urban residents disposed of their dead. Perhaps these data allude to particular patterns of disposal of the dead that we have not entertained. Hypothetically, the dead were probably buried in or near their village residences, and only administrators, elites, rulers, and captives were interred at the center. The stone-slab chambers at Cheqo Wasi (Figure 7.5) most likely contained the remains of the most important members of Huari society, if not its rulers. If so, then particular ways of disposing of members of different classes in Huari society merit future study.

Huari divine rulers and high-status individuals have been as difficult to identify as their residences and ultimate resting places. How the rulers were treated in life, how they were conveyed in images to the public, and how they were regarded after death remain obscure. Although only a few examples have been described, I have drawn on each to offer an interpretive "reading" of how the image of the Sacrificer, which appears in the iconography of offering pottery within particular architectural spaces and mortuary-ritual contexts, can be deciphered as a key symbol. There is also little doubt that the role of the Sacrificer in the Middle Horizon was widespread; its image was vividly portrayed in all areas that were affected by Huari or Tiahuanaco. Although the Sacrificer is a figure that predates the emergence of Middle Horizon polities, it ushers in changes from agrarian village life to a tribute-paying populace under state authority. The meaning of these events provides insights into the linking of sacrifice with Andean concepts of reciprocity and ancestor cults, in a tight web that is evident both in pre- or non-state political contexts and transformed, at least under Huari hegemony, to serve imperial needs and goals.

Acknowledgments

This chapter was presented as a paper as part of the fourth symposium sponsored by the Pre-Columbian Society of Washington, D.C., and its first on the Andes. I thank each and every member of the organizing committee and the enthusiastic members of the society for making these events possible, but I am especially thankful for my editor Elizabeth Benson's and Jeff Splitstoser's dedication to seeing this project to completion.

The interpretations offered in this study rely on archaeological excavations that were conducted by many scholars (Mario Benavides, Martha Cabrera, Enrique

González, W. H. Isbell, Justin Jennings, Luis Lumbreras, Frank Meddens, José Ochatoma, Ismael Pérez, Denise Pozzi-Escot, Katharina Schreiber, Julio C. Tello, Cirilio Vivanco, Patrick Ryan Williams, to mention a few) over the past twenty years and on the voluminous work that Dorothy Menzel has contributed to our understanding of the Middle Horizon. I obviously owe a great deal to William H. Isbell, who both introduced me to Huari studies and generously shared his ideas over the many years we have known each other. Without the rich information provided by these individuals and other Huari scholars and graduate students in my advanced seminars, my connections between iconography and human behavior could not have been made. I would also like to thank Joan Gero for her insights during our day at Huari in 1999. She observed that the lintel stones at access points of the Monja-chayoq galleries were also D-shaped. I would like to extend my gratitude to Elizabeth Benson, Katharina Schreiber, Jeff Splitstoser, Barbara Wolff, the anonymous reviewers of the University of Texas Press, and my colleagues in Ayacucho for their advice and comments on earlier drafts.

Special acknowledgments are owed to William H. Isbell for use of his Honco-pampa map and his slides, and to *Ñawpa Pacha* for use of Figure 7.1, which was previously published in 1987, volume 22–23, Fig. 29. Jeff Splitstoser's skills as a draftsperson and the many hours he generously gave to redrawing the photographs and completing the line drawings for publication are greatly appreciated.

Notes

1. The interior walls of the D-shaped structure at Cerro Baúl (Figure 7.8) had been replastered and repainted on several occasions. At one point, the walls had been whitewashed, and a red band was painted 15 to 25 centimeters above the surface of the floor (Williams 1997).

2. Known in Andean iconography since at least the first millennium B.C., the Front Face Staff Figure is given new meaning throughout the Andes during the expansion of Middle Horizon polities. The figure, although mostly seen in conjunction with profile figures, can also hold staffs with a variety of appendages at their base, for instance, full-bodied miniature captives, bodiless heads, or headless bodies. On the south coast, vessels with design panels that wrap around the circumference of a vessel often include severed limbs, symbolizing the act of sacrifice, and lack the full representation of the Sacrificer.

3. Also called *naq'aq, ñaqaq, ñaq'aq*, from the verb *naqay,* meaning "to behead or cut the throat of" in southern Quechua, and, in central and northern Quechua, known as *pishtakuq,* from the verb *pishtay,* with the same meaning. The Hispanized term in use today throughout the southern Andes is *pishtaco* or *pistaco,* which is used interchangeably with the translated Spanish term *degollador* (Ansión and Sifuentes 1989: 62–63).

4. Among the fanciest examples of the pottery included are decorated oversized urns and face-neck jars, although some cists include unpainted wares and a variety of vessel shapes, e.g., bowls, tumblers, and keros.

CHAPTER 8   *The Physical Evidence of*
            Human Sacrifice in Ancient Peru

JOHN W.
VERANO
Department of
Anthropology, Tulane
University

INTRODUCTION

Descriptions of human sacrifice by the Inca and other native peoples of Andean South America are scattered through many of the early colonial-period Spanish chronicles and histories (Figure 8.1). These are not eyewitness accounts, but are generally secondhand descriptions by native informants. Unlike accounts from Mexico, where human sacrifice was witnessed firsthand by Spanish soldiers and priests in the early sixteenth century, written accounts from Peru generally describe religious practices prior to the conquest of the Inca empire.

The secondhand nature of Andean accounts led, not unexpectedly, to differences of opinion as to the frequency with which, and context within which, human lives were offered by the Inca and other Andean peoples. At one extreme lie writers such as Garcilaso de la Vega, who claimed that the Inca banned the practice of human sacrifice. Reliable sources such as Fray Bernabé Cobo, however, described various rituals in which the Inca reportedly offered human lives (Rowe 1946). Sacrificial practices among the diverse peoples incorporated into the Inca empire are less known; such knowledge is limited for the most part to scattered references drawn from oral histories (Rowe 1948; Moseley and Cordy-Collins 1990).

Only during the twentieth century has archaeological evidence been brought to bear on the question of human sacrifice in pre-Hispanic Peru. Max Uhle was the first to uncover and systematically record archaeological evidence of human sacrifice by the Inca at the site of Pachacamac, on the central coast of Peru. Uhle excavated a cemetery that contained the bodies of numerous female sacrifices made by the Inca in the late fifteenth or early sixteenth century. Preservation was excellent, allowing him to make detailed observations of the bodies and their accompanying clothing and offerings. The bodies were naturally mummified, and tightly knotted cloth ligatures were still in place around their necks, indicating death by stran-

266

ÍDOLOS ÍVACAS
DEI OSCHIIACHAISV

FIGURE 8.1.
Offering a child
sacrifice to
Pachacamac (after
Guaman Poma de
Ayala 1980: 1:268
[266]).

gulation. Uhle compared this discovery with early colonial-period descriptions of Inca sacrifice, finding significant parallels with the written accounts (Uhle 1903). Uhle's work was important in providing evidence to refute Garcilaso de la Vega's claim that the Inca did not practice human sacrifice (Rowe 1995; Verano 1995).

It was not until the mid-twentieth century that additional evidence of Inca human sacrifice was documented archaeologically. The frozen body of a boy found on Cerro El Plomo in central Chile (Mostny 1957) has been joined in recent decades by a growing number of high-altitude Inca sacrifices found on mountain peaks in Chile, Argentina, and Peru (Schobinger 1991; Reinhard 1992). These mountain sacrifices correlate well in their context and associated offerings with early colonial-period accounts of the Inca sacrificial cycle known as *capac hucha,* in which children selected from different parts of the empire were brought to the Inca capital at Cuzco, then returned to their native region to be buried at high mountain shrines. The recent discovery of three such sacrifices atop the Nevado Ampato, near Arequipa, Peru, has drawn worldwide attention to this practice (Reinhard 1996; 1997).

Ethnohistorical accounts and archaeological evidence confirm that the Inca practiced human sacrifice. The offering of human lives appears to have been reserved for particularly important rituals and events, however, and was certainly not a daily occurrence in Inca times. Textiles, camelids, chicha, coca leaf, and other items were the offerings most frequently made to propitiate Andean deities (Rowe 1946; Murra 1962).

Certain Inca sacrificial practices can be reconstructed in substantial detail, given the availability of both ethnohistoric and archaeological evidence. Attempts to identify similar practices in pre-Inca societies are more difficult, due to a lack of ethnohistoric sources and the vagaries of archaeological preservation. Nevertheless, in recent decades important archaeological discoveries have been made that reveal evidence of a long tradition of human sacrifice in Andean South America. How human sacrifice can be identified from archaeological evidence, and the contribution physical anthropological analysis can make to interpreting these findings, are the subject of this chapter.

IDENTIFYING HUMAN SACRIFICE IN THE ARCHAEOLOGICAL RECORD

How is human sacrifice identified archaeologically? This is an important issue, because preconceived notions can lead to distinctly different interpretations of archaeological data. Human sacrifice implies the intentional offering of human life. The way in which sacrificial victims are dispatched may leave recognizable skeletal or soft-tissue evidence, but this is not always the case. Distinguishing between natural and induced death in archaeological remains is often difficult.

Disarticulated or partial human remains found in offering pits or within architecture are examples of archaeological finds that require careful evaluation. If complicating factors such as postburial disturbance can be ruled out, the key issue is whether the remains represent freshly sacrificed individuals or secondary offerings. The burial of skulls or other skeletal elements in ceremonial architecture is an ancient practice in the Andes, dating back at least to the Early Horizon at sites such as Chavín de Huántar (Burger 1984). Offerings of burned skeletal remains have also been documented (Lumbreras 1989; Cordy-Collins 1997). Complex mortuary practices involving the secondary burial of human remains and the removal of skeletal elements from tombs are also known (Menzel 1976; Buikstra 1995).

The offering of secondary remains is an activity quite different from the sacrifice of a living individual, and presumably carried distinct meanings for ancient Andean peoples. Confident diagnosis (or ruling out) of death by sacrifice becomes particularly important in interpreting such finds. The context in which the remains are found may provide important clues, for instance, as in the case of high-altitude Inca sacrifices, which generally do not show physical evidence of cause of death, but are found in mountaintop shrines far from human settlements or normal burial sites. On the other hand, the burial of selected skeletal elements may be identified by a lack of cut marks or other indications of intentional disarticulation of fleshed remains (Burger 1984; McEwan 1987).

The careful examination of remains, both in the field and in the laboratory, is essential for distinguishing between sacrificial victims and secondary offerings. The presence of cut marks, fractures, or other indications of trauma can suggest possible cause of death as well as record details of postmortem treatment of the remains. Careful examination can effectively distinguish a skull that was separated from the body in intentional decapitation from a skull that was collected from a tomb or other context and simply reburied. For example, Lumbreras (1981) identified a group of skulls buried in a Formative Period mound near Ayacucho as an offering of the heads of freshly decapitated individuals based on the presence of upper cervical vertebrae still articulated with the skulls. Cordy-Collins ("Decapitation," this volume) makes a similar interpretation for a cache of skulls found at the site of Dos Cabezas, based on both the presence of cervical vertebrae and cut marks consistent with decapitation.

Good archaeological preservation can play an important role in identifying sacrificial victims. Strangulation was a common method of dispatching sacrificial victims in Andean South America. It is described in various ethnohistoric sources and has been documented archaeologically as well. In Uhle's cemetery of sacrificed women at Pachacamac, all of the victims were strangled from behind with a cloth ligature. The excellent preservation of soft tissues and textiles allowed him to examine in detail the form of the knots and even the degree to which the victims' necks were constricted by the ligatures (Uhle 1903). Had preservation not been as good, and only skeletal remains been found, identification of death by strangulation probably would not have been possible. Modern forensic data show that while manual strangulation victims often show fracture of the hyoid bone, strangulation by ligature rarely leaves osteological evidence (Ubelaker 1992). Retainers in high-status tombs, such as a female found face down in Tomb 2 at Sipán (Alva and Donnan 1993; Verano 1995), may have been strangled

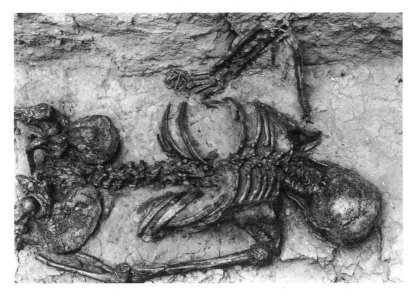

FIGURE 8.2. Female retainer burial from Tomb 2, Sipán. Photo by John W. Verano, courtesy of Walter Alva.

(Figure 8.2), but in the absence of clear indications of skeletal trauma, the specific cause of death cannot be determined.

Details such as the presence of a neck ligature can be crucial to the proper interpretation of a burial. Some years ago I was asked to examine a mummy that had been excavated at the Chimú administrative center of Manchan in the lower Casma River valley. Preliminary observations by the excavators suggested a high-status male burial. Status was inferred by the presence of elaborate textiles and grave goods; sex by the morphology of the mandible, which was judged to be "male" by the archaeologists. Subsequent study in the laboratory revealed the remains to be those of a female on the basis of pelvic morphology—a more reliable sex indicator. In addition, there was a cord tied tightly around the neck, suggesting death by strangulation. These findings changed the interpretation significantly— from the burial of a high-status male to a probable dedicatory sacrifice. In this case the fine textiles and other objects associated with the body apparently were not markers of the elite status of the individual in life, but of the ritual importance of the sacrifice itself.

The type of material used to construct a ligature may also indicate some difference in the way sacrificial victims were treated. Uhle's women at Pachacamac were strangled with cotton cloths. Two strangled females I have

FIGURE 8.3. Ligatures found around the necks of female sacrifices at El Brujo (photos by John W. Verano, courtesy of the El Brujo Archaeological Project): (a) (*above left*) Ligature from Sicán retainer burial. Some of the victim's hair is caught in the knot tied behind the neck (lower knot in photo). Diameter of opening: 7 cm.; (b) (*above right*) Moche sacrifice photographed during excavation; (c) (*left*) Lab photograph of ligature.

recently studied from the site of El Brujo in the Chicama River valley in northern Peru show cord ligatures constructed of distinct materials (Figure 8.3a–c). An adult female who was strangled and buried with a high-status male Lambayeque (Sicán) burial was dispatched with a fine cotton cord. A sacrificed Moche woman found in an isolated pit in a different area of the site was strangled with a coarse rope made of *cabuya* fiber, a strong plant fiber normally used for fishing nets and utilitarian cordage (Arabel Fernández, personal communication). The coarse fiber rope suggests a general lack of concern for the victim in this case. She was buried in a simple pit with a camelid, but with no other offerings.

FORMS OF SACRIFICE AND POSTMORTEM
TREATMENT OF REMAINS

The examples described above reflect some of the forms of human sacrifice for which we have archaeological evidence in the Andes. These include sacrifices of individuals or groups in ceremonial architecture, as well as the burial of retainers with high-status individuals. The demographic characteristics of sacrificial victims as well as the way their remains were treated may provide insight into the meaning and purpose of a particular sacrificial practice. For example, historic sources indicate that most Inca sacrifices were of children, who were "buried with gold and silver and other things and with special superstitions" (Cobo 1990 [1653]: 112). This corresponds well with what has been found in high-altitude shrines. However, the Inca were also reported to have sacrificed war prisoners following important military victories. While archaeological evidence of this has not yet been found, several sites on the north coast of Peru (discussed below) have produced impressive examples of prisoner sacrifice during pre-Inca times. A distinctive feature of these sacrifices is the way the bodies of the victims are treated. Rather than being carefully buried with rich offerings, the bodies were left to decompose on the surface, and many show signs of intentional mutilation (see Bourget, this volume). Such treatment, involving mutilation and the denial of proper burial, implies a sacrificial ritual and an attitude toward the victims that are quite distinct from those associated with the carefully buried Inca child sacrifices of the *capac hucha*.

TROPHIES AND COLLECTIBLES

There is evidence that selected human body parts such as heads, skulls, teeth, and long bones were occasionally collected and modified for ritual or personal use. The Inca were known to collect various trophies from their enemies (Rowe 1946: 279; Lastres 1951: 65), although only a few examples of these have been found archaeologically (e.g., J. Tello 1918). From pre-Inca times, the best-known examples of such trophies are mummified heads from the Paracas and Nasca cultures of southern coastal Peru, described by Proulx in this volume (see also Verano 1995). Proulx concludes that Nasca trophy heads were probably procured through warfare rather than sacrifice.

However, he notes the frequent association of trophy heads with super-naturals and with plant motifs and other symbols of fertility, and suggests that the heads had important ritual significance to the Nasca beyond their function as war trophies.

As is made clear in two other chapters in this volume (Cook; Cordy-Collins, "Decapitation"), Paracas and Nasca art had no monopoly on de-capitators holding human heads. This theme is found in many coastal and highland Andean art styles, dating from the Initial Period through the Late Horizon (ca. 1800 B.C.–A.D. 1530). Indeed, decapitation at the hands of supernatural beings seems to be the quintessential signifier of ritual death in the Andean world (Verano 1995). With the exception of those associated with the Paracas and Nasca cultures, however, very few heads of decapi-tated victims have been found archaeologically. It seems that the practice of collecting, preparing, and curating mummified human heads was a tra-dition that developed and flourished primarily on the south coast of Peru. Nevertheless, two discoveries of decapitated victims have been made at Moche sites on the north coast of Peru in just the past few years. The first, a cache of skulls, some with cervical vertebrae still articulated, is described by Cordy-Collins in this volume ("Decapitation"). The second find was made at the urban sector of the pyramids at Moche in 1996 (Verano 1998). It consists of two human crania modified into bowls by having the top of the vault cut away (Figure 8.4a, b). One of the crania has drilled holes for attachment of the lower jaw. Previously, such skull bowls were known only in the form of ceramic vessels (Figure 8.5), but it is now clear that actual skull vessels did exist. Both of these crania show cut marks on various sur-faces, indicating that they were prepared from fleshed heads (presumably of sacrificial victims) and not simply from dry skulls. Although some evidence of decapitation and the curation of skulls is now known for the Moche, the iconographic evidence suggests a greater interest in the collection of blood (see below) than a specific focus on collecting heads, as was the case in the Paracas and Nasca cultures.

PRISONER SACRIFICE

Although discoveries of high-altitude Inca sacrifices made in recent years are important in providing further evidence of the Inca practice of *capac hucha,* these finds are similar in most respects to earlier discoveries at high-altitude sites. As a result, they do not offer substantial new insight into sacrificial practices in the Andean world. What are perhaps more signifi-cant are two sacrificial sites recently discovered on the north coast of Peru. These provide the first well-documented archaeological evidence of pris-

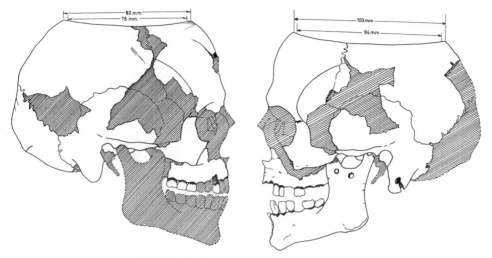

FIGURE 8.4. Modified skulls from the urban sector of the pyramids at Moche. Drawing by Gustavo Pérez.

oner sacrifice, an activity that previously was only inferred from depictions of combat, prisoner capture, and sacrifice in north-coast art. The discoveries were made in 1984 at the site of Pacatnamu in the Jequetepeque River valley, and in 1995 at the Huaca de la Luna (Pyramid of the Moon) in the Moche River valley.

THE PACATNAMU MASS BURIAL

In 1984, fourteen human skeletons were found at the bottom of a three-meter-deep defensive trench at the archaeological site of Pacatnamu in the lower Jequetepeque Valley (Figure 8.6; Verano 1986). They were found at the entrance to a major pyramid and architectural complex, known as Huaca 1, built during the later phase of occupation of the site, ca. A.D. 1100–1400 (Donnan 1986). The fourteen individuals were all adolescent and young adult males, ranging in age from approximately fifteen to thirty-five years (Verano 1986). They were found in three superimposed groups, separated from one another by a layer of sand and rubble. Surface weathering on some of the bones, as well as abundant remains of scavenging insects, indicates that the bodies were not promptly buried, but decomposed on the surface (Faulkner 1986). Rope fragments were found around the ankles of some individuals, and around the wrist of one, indicating that they were bound or hobbled. No traces of clothing other than a possible loincloth fragment were found with the skeletons.

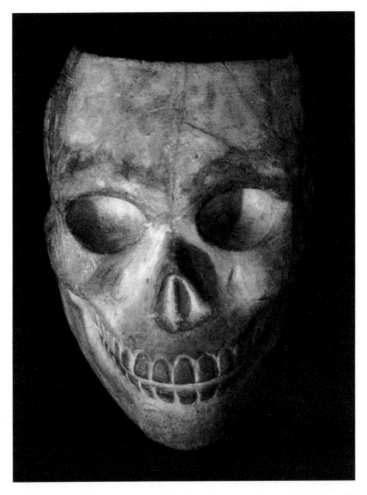

FIGURE 8.5. Moche ceramic vessel in the form of a skull (National Museum of Natural History, Smithsonian Institution, catalog number NMNH 148021. Height: 15 cm.). Photo by John W. Verano.

Laboratory study revealed evidence of multiple injuries, including stab wounds (two bone-point fragments were recovered in the excavation), cut marks, skull and long-bone fractures, and evidence of forced dismemberment. Two individuals show cut marks indicating that their throats were slit, two were decapitated, and five individuals appear to have had their chests cut open (Verano 1986). In addition, four individuals were missing their left radius, one of the bones of the forearm. Cut marks and fractures on bones that articulated with the missing radii indicate intentional removal from the victims. The radii may have been collected as trophies to be modified as flutes or other objects; there are descriptions of such practices in Inca times (Rowe 1946: 279).

The identity of the victims in the mass burial is unknown, although the ropes around their ankles and their age and sex distribution suggest that they were captives. Biometric comparisons of the victims' crania with samples from Pacatnamu and nearby coastal and highland sites were not conclusive in identifying them either as members of the local population

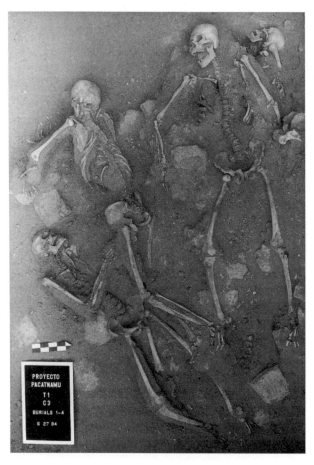

FIGURE 8.6. The uppermost layer of skeletons in the mass burial at Pacatnamu. Photo by John W. Verano.

FIGURE 8.7. Rollout drawing of a Moche IV vessel showing the arraignment and sacrifice of prisoners. Anthropomorphized vultures appear to be assisting in the sacrifice. Vessel from the collections of the American Museum of Natural History, New York. Drawing by Donna McClelland.

or as outsiders. Isotopic analysis of their bone collagen did indicate some dietary differences from the local population, however, suggesting that they were not locals (Verano and DeNiro 1993).

The pattern of wounds and postmortem treatment of the Pacatnamu victims show close parallels to Moche and Chimú artistic depictions of prisoner sacrifice (Figure 8.7). These scenes typically show the formal presentation and sacrifice of bound captives. Severed heads and limbs, splayed bodies, and vultures are commonly depicted in these scenes. The presence of vultures may be symbolic of their role as opportunistic carrion feeders, but there is some evidence they may have been active participants in the sacrifice of captives (Verano 1986; Rea 1986). In addition to artistic parallels, the Pacatnamu mass burial shows similarities to north-coast ethnohistoric accounts of punishments involving mutilation and exposure of the corpse to scavengers (Rowe 1948: 49). It thus provides important archaeological corroboration for events until recently inferred only from ethnohistoric accounts and iconography.

PRISONER SACRIFICE AT THE HUACA DE LA LUNA

In 1995, archaeologist Steve Bourget made a spectacular discovery at the Huaca de la Luna in the Moche River valley (Bourget 1997a; 1997b; this volume). In an enclosure (Plaza 3A) behind the main platform, he discovered a sacrificial site littered with the skeletal remains of Moche sacrificial victims. Excavations over three field seasons uncovered the remains of more than seventy individuals. An adjacent plaza, which to date has been only partially tested, contains additional skeletal remains. Careful excavation of Plaza 3A, and ongoing laboratory analysis of the osteological remains and associated ceramic offerings, permit a preliminary reconstruction of events which took place here ca. A.D. 550–650. An overview of the sacrificial site is presented by Steve Bourget in this volume. My discussion will focus on the analysis of the skeletal remains.

General Features of the Sample

Skeletal remains from Plaza 3A fall into four basic categories: (1) complete and articulated skeletons; (2) partial skeletons, missing the skull or one or more limbs; (3) isolated limbs, hands, feet, or other clusters of articulated elements; and (4) individual isolated bones. Complete skeletons are relatively rare, while partial skeletons, clusters of bones, or isolated elements are more common. The high frequency of disarticulation complicates estimating the number of individuals present in the deposit, but preliminary counts indicate at least seventy individuals. As at Pacatnamu, the bodies were not promptly buried, but were left exposed on the surface. Excavation revealed some fifteen superimposed layers of remains, imbedded in alternating layers of mud and sand (Bourget 1997a; 1997b; this volume). Some bones show extensive sun bleaching and surface weathering, while others show little evidence of exposure. Specific patterns of exposure have not been correlated with the stratigraphic position of the skeletons, but this is a subject of ongoing analysis.

Demographic Profile

All skeletal remains from Plaza 3A, with the exception of the two child burials found at a lower level (Bourget, this volume), are of adolescent and young adult males. No remains of females or children are present, nor are there any older adults (over forty-five years) present. Based on various skeletal and dental aging criteria, the mean age of the sample is twenty-three years, with a range of approximately fifteen to thirty-nine years. The demographic profile indicates a highly selected sample of individuals.

Physical Characteristics

The skeletal morphology of the Plaza 3A victims indicates that they were healthy and physically active individuals. In general, bones are large and show pronounced muscle attachment areas, and there is little evidence of anemias (porotic hyperostosis, cribra orbitalia) or other indicators of poor health (e.g., enamel hypoplasias). However, there is abundant evidence of previous skeletal trauma in this group. Healed fractures of ribs and long bones, as well as depressed fractures of the skull, were observed in eighteen individuals (Figure 8.8). Many of these fractures, especially of the skull and certain long bones, suggest interpersonal violence rather than accidental injury. Fracture incidence per individual and bone has not been calculated, but compared to other Moche skeletal samples I have studied (Verano 1994; 1997), Plaza 3A victims have an unusually high frequency of these injuries, which suggests that the Plaza 3A victims had a particularly active and violent lifestyle.

At the time of death, at least eleven individuals had injuries that were in the early stages of healing. These included fractures to ribs, scapula, long bones, and the margins of the nasal aperture (Figure 8.9). Estimates of post-injury intervals vary from several weeks to perhaps a month. These fractures presumably were sustained during combat or following capture and are important in suggesting that at least several weeks passed between the time of capture and sacrifice. What happened during this time is a subject for speculation, but Moche depictions of the arraignment of prisoners appear to show ceremonies involving the public display of captives (Franco, Gálvez, and Vásquez 1994; Donnan and McClelland 1979; Alva and Donnan 1993).

Perimortem Injuries in the Skeletons
Perimortem injuries can be defined as those that occur at or around the time of death, when bone is fresh and flexible. The two most common injuries of this kind in the Plaza 3A sample are cut marks on the cervical vertebrae and skull fractures. Although infrequent, cut marks were also seen on some crania, long bones, and bones of the hands and feet.

Cut marks were most commonly seen on the second and third cervical vertebrae, although examples were found on the first and fourth cervical vertebrae as well (Figure 8.10). In individuals with fully observable cervical spines, approximately 75 percent showed cut marks. They vary from one to more than nine distinct cuts, located on the anterior surface of the vertebral body and frequently on the transverse processes as well. The marks left on bone appear to be the result of cutting of the throat rather than an attempt to decapitate the victims. Many cases were observed of cut marks in individuals with the skull and vertebral column still fully articu-

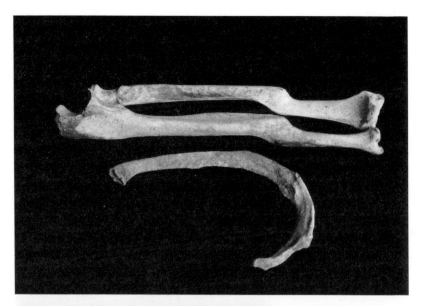

FIGURE 8.8. Healed fractures of the left radius, ulna, and second rib of one of the sacrificial victims at the Huaca de la Luna (Plaza 3A, Individual I). Photo by John W. Verano.

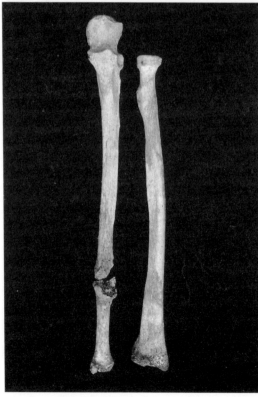

FIGURE 8.9. Fractured left ulna in the process of healing (Huaca de la Luna, Plaza 3A, HG96-102). Photo by John W. Verano.

FIGURE 8.10. Cut marks on the body of the second cervical vertebra (Huaca de la Luna, Plaza 3A, Individual XVIIIa). Photo by John W. Verano.

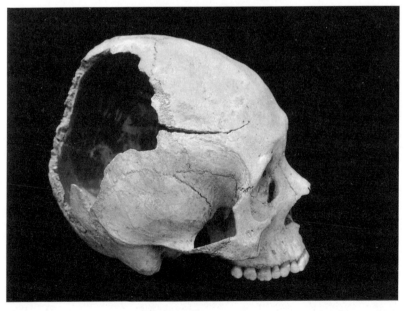

FIGURE 8.11. Perimortem skull fracture (Huaca de la Luna, Plaza 3A, HG96–102). Photo by John W. Verano.

lated. Moreover, cut marks were found primarily on the anterior and lateral surfaces of the vertebrae and not on the intervertebral joints or spinous processes, as would be expected in decapitation (Verano 1986). The cut marks present on the Plaza 3A victims correspond well to Moche artistic depictions of the slashing of the throat of captives to collect blood (Figure 8.7; Alva and Donnan 1993).

Skull fractures were generally massive, resulting in breakage of a large portion of the cranial vault (Figure 8.11). Most appear to have been produced by blows from blunt objects, although in a few cases the margins of broken areas suggest a more pointed weapon such as a star-headed mace. Based on preliminary examination of the fractured skulls, it is difficult to judge whether the blows were inflicted at the time of death or afterward, following some decomposition of soft tissues; the morphology of the fractures is ambiguous.

Other than skull fractures and cut marks on the cervical vertebrae, evidence of perimortem trauma is rare. Several crania show scattered cut marks on their external surfaces, but only a few examples of cut marks are present on postcranial bones. This is puzzling, given the high frequency of disarticulated remains in Plaza 3A. Isolated limbs, hands, and feet were common finds. In the laboratory these were carefully examined for cut marks or fractures suggesting forced disarticulation, but very little evidence was found to suggest this. The disarticulation and scattering of elements seen in Plaza 3A may be the result of natural decomposition of the bodies, perhaps assisted by vulture activity. Alternatively, the lack of cut marks might indicate that bodies and body parts were manipulated after sufficient decomposition had occurred to allow easy disarticulation. Bourget (1997a; 1997b) describes and illustrates examples from Plaza 3A of trunks, limbs, and other elements that he believes were intentionally arranged as opposed pairs.

Skeletal Remains in Plaza 3B

In 1996, limited excavations were conducted in an adjacent plaza, designated Plaza 3B (Montoya 1997). Partially articulated and disarticulated remains of at least seven individuals were found in several small excavation units. These remains are of particular interest because they clearly show cut marks indicating dismemberment and intentional defleshing (Figure 8.12). Cut marks were found on nearly all bones recovered from Plaza 3B. The locations of the cuts correspond to areas of muscle attachment, implying that the objective was not simply to disarticulate, but to *deflesh* the skeletons. The Plaza 3B excavations, although limited in extent, indicate that

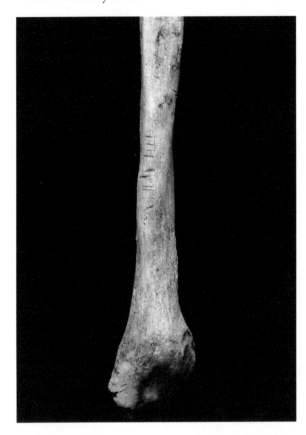

FIGURE 8.12. Cut marks on medial and posterior surfaces of distal left fibula (Huaca de la Luna, Plaza 3B, Entierro 1). Photo by John W. Verano.

some sacrificial victims at the Huaca de la Luna received more complex treatment than that observed in the remains deposited in Plaza 3A.

Ritual Behavior at the Huaca de la Luna

Evidence from Plaza 3A, and preliminary findings from limited excavation in Plaza 3B, suggest that activities involving the capture and sacrifice of prisoners played an important role in ritual practices at the Huaca de la Luna. The findings from Plaza 3B, in particular, indicate more complexity in the manipulation of the bodies of sacrificial victims than is seen in Plaza 3A. Evidence of defleshing of bodies raises the possibility of cannibalism at the Huaca de la Luna. Similar patterns of cut marks (corresponding to areas of muscle attachment) have been reported on disarticulated skeletal remains from archaeological sites in central Mexico by Carmen Pijoan and coworkers (Pijoan and Mansilla 1990; Pijoan, Mansilla, and Pastrana 1995). These workers interpret the cut marks and body processing as evidence of ritual cannibalism, a behavior frequently described in Mexican ethnohistoric sources. It is perhaps premature to conclude that ritual cannibalism was practiced by the Moche, given the limited osteological material excavated from Plaza 3B in 1996. Further excavation is needed to understand better the context of these remains.

CONCLUSION

Peruvian archaeology is a particularly dynamic field at present. It seems that each year brings the announcement of a significant new discovery. For those interested in ritual sacrifice in ancient Peru, the past decade has been a very productive one. Major advances have been made in interpreting the iconography of sacrificial practices and in linking art with archaeological evidence. Of all geographic areas, perhaps the north coast of Peru is where the greatest progress has been made in the archaeological documentation of sacrificial practices. Evidence of prisoner sacrifice and ritual decapitation has now been identified at multiple sites, and it is now clear that Moche depictions of ritual combat and the sacrifice of prisoners record actual events, and not simply mythological narrative. Sites such as Sipán and San José de Moro preserve the tombs of officials who presided over rituals involving the sacrifice of captives. The skeletal remains of their victims have now been identified at the Huaca de la Luna, and similar evidence can be expected to lie buried in ceremonial compounds at other Moche sites.

It is only in the past ten years that it has been possible to integrate the iconographic and archaeological evidence of human sacrifice in northern coastal Peru. Much of the new information coming out of sites such as Huaca de la Luna is still in the preliminary stages of analysis and interpretation. Other sacrificial sites remain to be discovered and excavated, and we can expect that current interpretations will need revision and refinement as new discoveries are made. It is the nature and pace of these discoveries that make Peruvian archaeology such a dynamic field of research today.

Acknowledgments

I am grateful to archaeologists Régulo Franco, César Gálvez, and Segundo Vásquez, codirectors of the Complejo El Brujo Archaeological Project, and to the late Dr. Guillermo Wiese de Osma of the Fundación Wiese for inviting me to study osteological and mummified materials at El Brujo, and to Steve Bourget and Santiago Uceda for their invitation to study the Huaca de la Luna skeletal material. Florencia Bracamonte and Laurel S. Anderson worked with me on data collection and analysis of the Plaza 3A material, and I am grateful for their assistance. Laboratory space and logistical support were kindly provided by Santiago Uceda and Enrique Vergara of the Archaeology Museum of the Universidad Nacional de Trujillo during the summers of 1996 and 1997, and by the El Brujo Project in 1997. My research was supported by a Tulane University Committee on Research Summer Fellowship (1995), a Fulbright Lectureship from the Council for the International Exchange of Scholars (1996), and a Tulane University Center for Latin American Studies Faculty Summer Research Grant (1997).

Bibliography

Allen, Catherine J. 1982. "Body and Soul in Quechua Thought." *Journal of Latin American Lore* 8 (2): 179–196.

———. 1988. *The Hold Life Has: Coca and Cultural Identity in an Andean Community*. Washington, D.C.: Smithsonian Institution Press.

———. n.d. *The Incas Have Gone Inside*. Ms. in Anita G. Cook's possession.

Alt Peru: Schätze aus Peru, von Chavin bis zum Inka. 1959. Exhibition catalogue, Rautenstrauch-Joest Museum, Cologne. Recklinghausen, Germany: Verlag Aurel Bongers.

Alva, Walter, and Christopher B. Donnan. 1993. *Royal Tombs of Sipán*. Los Angeles: Fowler Museum of Cultural History, University of California, Los Angeles.

Ansión, Juan, and Eudosio Sifuentes. 1989. "La imagen popular de la violencia a través de los relatos de degolladores." In *Pishtacos de verdugos a sacaojos*, ed. Juan Ansión, pp. 61–105. Lima: Tarea Asociación de Publicaciones Educativas.

Anton, Ferdinand. 1987. *Ancient Peruvian Textiles*. New York: Thames and Hudson.

Arguedas, José María. 1953. "Cuentos mágico-realistas y canciones de fiesta tradicionales; folklore del valle del Mantaro, provincias de Jauja y Concepción—Archivo del Instituto de Estudios Etnológicos." *Folklore Americano* 1 (1): 101–293. Lima.

Arnold, Denise Y. 1992. "La casa de adobes y piedras del Inka." In *Hacia un orden andino de las cosas,* ed. D. Y. Arnold, Domingo Jiménez Aruquipa, and Juan de Dios Yapita, pp. 31–108. La Paz: Hisbol/ILCA.

Arsenault, Daniel. 1994. "The 'Sacred Female Weaver' in a Moche Sacrificial Context: A Reappraisal of Some Images of Human Sacrifice in Moche Iconography." Paper presented at the Society for American Archaeology Annual Meetings, Anaheim, Calif.

Aveni, Anthony. 1990a. "An Assessment of Previous Studies of the Nazca Lines." In *The Lines of Nazca*, ed. Anthony Aveni, pp. 1–40. Memoirs of the American Philosophical Society, vol. 183. Philadelphia: American Philosophical Society.

———, ed. 1990b. *The Lines of Nazca*. Memoirs of the American Philosophical Society, vol. 183. Philadelphia: American Philosophical Society.

Baraybar, José Pablo. 1987. "Cabezas Trofeo Nasca: nuevas evidencias." *Gaceta Arqueológica Andina* 4 (15): 6–10.

———. 1987–1988. "Research Summary." In *Willay: Newsletter of the Andean Anthropological Research Group* 26/27: 4–5. Cambridge, Mass.

Benavides Calle, Mario. 1984. *Carácter del estado Wari*. Ayacucho, Peru: Universidad Nacional de San Cristóbal de Huamanga.

186 *Ritual Sacrifice in Ancient Peru*

———. 1991. "Cheqo Wasi, Huari." In *Huari Administrative Structure: Prehistoric Monumental Architecture and State Government*, ed. William Isbell and Gordon McEwan, pp. 55–69. Washington, D.C.: Dumbarton Oaks Research Library and Collection.

Bennett, Wendell C. 1938. "If You Died in Old Peru." *Natural History* 41 (2): 119–125.

———. 1946. "The Archeology of the Central Andes." In *Handbook of South American Indians*, vol. 2, ed. Julian H. Steward, pp. 61–147. Smithsonian Institution Bureau of American Ethnology, Bulletin 143. Washington, D.C.: Smithsonian Institution.

———, and Junius B. Bird. 1949. *Andean Culture History*. American Museum of Natural History Handbook No. 15. New York: American Museum of Natural History.

Benson, Elizabeth P. 1972. *The Mochica: A Culture of Peru*. London: Thames and Hudson.

———. 1985. "The Moche Moon." In *Recent Studies in Andean Prehistory and Protohistory. Papers from the Second Annual Conference on Andean Archaeology and Ethnohistory*, ed. D. P. Kvietok and D. H. Sandweiss, pp. 121–135. Ithaca, N.Y.: Latin American Studies Program, Cornell University.

———. 1988. "New World Deer-Hunt Rituals." In *Simpatías y diferencias, relaciones del arte mexicano con el de América Latina: X Coloquio Internacional de Historia del Arte del Instituto de Investigaciones Estéticas*, pp. 45–59. Mexico City: Universidad Nacional Autónoma de México.

———. 1989. "Women in Mochica Art." In *The Role of Gender in Pre-Columbian Art and Archaeology*, ed. Virginia E. Miller, pp. 63–74. Lanham, Md.: University Press of America.

———. 1991a. "The Chthonic Canine." *Latin American Indian Literatures Journal* 7 (1): 95–107.

———. 1991b. "Seven Human Figurines." In *Circa 1492: Art in the Age of Exploration*, ed. Jay C. Levinson, pp. 590–592. Washington, D.C.: National Gallery of Art.

———. 1995. "Art, Agriculture, Warfare and the Guano Islands." In *Andean Art: Visual Expression and Its Relation to Andean Beliefs and Values*, ed. Penny Dransart, pp. 245–264. Worldwide Archaeology Series, vol. 13. Aldershot, Hants., England: Avebury.

———. 1997. "Seated Anthropomorphic Stag Captive" and "Seated Anthropomorphic Stag." In *The Spirit of Ancient Peru: Treasures from the Museo Arqueológico Rafael Larco Herrera*, ed. K. Berrin, p. 160. New York and San Francisco: Thames and Hudson and the Fine Arts Museums of San Francisco.

Berrin, Kathleen, ed. 1997. *The Spirit of Ancient Peru: Treasures from the Museo Arqueológico Rafael Larco Herrera*. New York and San Francisco: Thames and Hudson and the Fine Arts Museums of San Francisco.

Berrocal, Marcelina. 1991. "Estudio arqueológico en Muyu Orqo, Ayacucho: Informe grado académico." Ayacucho, Peru: Universidad Nacional de San Cristóbal de Huamanga.

Betanzos, Juan de. 1996 [1557]. *Narrative of the Incas*. Translated and edited by Roland Hamilton and Dana Buchanan. Austin: University of Texas Press.

Bird, Junius B., and Louisa Bellinger. 1952. *Paracas Fabrics and Nazca Needlework: 3rd Century B.C.–3rd Century A.D.* Catalogue Raisonné. Washington, D.C.: Textile Museum.

Blasco Bosqued, Concepción, and Luis Ramos Gómez. 1991. *Catálogo de la cerámica Nazca del Museo de América*, vol. 2. Madrid: Ministerio de Cultura.

Bonavia, Duccio. 1994. *Arte e historia del Perú antiguo: Colección Enrico Poli Bianchi.* Lima: Banco del Sur.

Boone, Elizabeth Hill, ed. 1996. *Andean Art at Dumbarton Oaks*, 2 vols. Washington, D.C.: Dumbarton Oaks Research Library and Collection.

Bourget, Steve. 1994. "Los Sacerdotes a la Sombra del Cerro Blanco y del Arco Bicéfalo." *Revista del Museo de Arqueología, Anthropología e Historia* no. 5: 81–125. Facultad de Ciencias Sociales, Universidad Nacional de Trujillo, Trujillo, Peru.

———. 1997a. "La colére des ancêtres: découverte d'un site sacrificiel à la Huaca de la Luna, vallée de Moche." In *À l'ombre du Cerro Blanco: Nouvelles découvertes sur la culture Moche, côte nord du Pérou*, ed. C. Chapdelaine, pp. 83–99. Les Cahiers d'Anthropologie, no. 1. Montreal: Department of Anthropology, University of Montreal.

———. 1997b. "Las excavaciones en la Plaza 3A de la Huaca de la Luna." In *Investigaciones en la Huaca de la Luna 1995*, ed. Santiago Uceda, Elías Mujica, and Ricardo Morales, pp. 51–59. Trujillo, Peru: Facultad de Ciencias Sociales, Universidad Nacional de la Libertad.

Brackenbury, John. 1992. *Insects in Flight.* London: Blandford.

Bragayrac Dávila, Enrique. 1991. "Archaeological Investigations in the Vegachayoq Moqo Sector of Huari." In *Huari Administrative Structure: Prehistoric Monumental Architecture and State Government*, ed. William H. Isbell and Gordon McEwan, pp. 71–80. Washington, D.C.: Dumbarton Oaks Research Library and Collection.

Brewster-Wray, Christine. 1990. "Moraduchayoq: An Administrative Compound at the Site of Huari, Peru." Ph.D. dissertation, State University of Binghamton, Binghamton, New York.

Browne, David, Helaine Silverman, and Rubén García. 1993. "A Cache of 48 Nasca Trophy Heads from Cerro Carapo, Peru." *Latin American Antiquity* 4 (3): 274–294.

Buikstra, Jane E. 1995. "Tombs for the Living or for the Dead: The Osmore Ancestors." In *Tombs for the Living: Andean Mortuary Practices*, ed. Tom D. Dillehay, pp. 229–280. Washington, D.C.: Dumbarton Oaks Research Library and Collection.

Burger, Richard L. 1984. *The Prehistoric Occupation of Chavín de Huántar, Peru.* Berkeley: University of California Press.

———. 1992. *Chavín and the Origins of Andean Civilization.* New York: Thames and Hudson.

———, and Lucy Salazar-Burger. 1980. "Ritual and Religion at Huaricoto." *Archaeology* 36 (6): 26–32.

Cabrera Romero, Martha. 1996. "Unidades habitacionales, iconografía y rituales en un poblado rural de la Epoca Huari." Tesis para optar el Título de Licenciado en Arqueología, Facultad de Ciencias Sociales, Escuela de Formación Profesional de Arqueológia e Historia, Universidad Nacional de San Cristóbal de Huamanga, Ayacucho, Peru.

Carmichael, Patrick H. 1988. "Nasca Mortuary Customs: Death and Ancient Society on the South Coast of Peru." Ph.D. dissertation, Department of Archaeology, University of Calgary, Calgary, Alberta.

———. 1992. "Local Traditions on the South Coast of Peru during the Early Intermediate Period." *Willay: Newsletter of the Andean Anthropological Research Group* 37/38: 4–6. Cambridge, Mass.

———. 1994. "The Life from Death Continuum in Nasca Imagery." *Andean Past* 4: 81–90.

Carrión Cachot, Rebeca. 1931. "La indumentaria en la antigua cultura de Paracas." *Wira Kocha: Revista Peruana de Estudios Antropológicos* 1 (1): 37–86. Lima.

———. 1949. *Paracas: Cultural Elements*. Lima: Corporación Nacional de Turismo.

Castillo, Luis Jaime. 1989. *Personajes Míticos, escenas y narraciones en la iconografía mochica*. Lima: Pontificia Universidad Católica del Perú.

Cieza de León, Pedro. 1959 [1553?]. *The Incas*. Translated by Harriet de Onis; edited and introduced by Wolfgang von Hagen. Norman: University of Oklahoma Press.

Cobo, Bernabé. 1956 [1653]. *Historia de Nuevo Mundo,* lib. IV. Madrid: Biblioteca de Autores Españoles.

———. 1990 [1653]. *Inca Religion and Customs*. Translated and edited by Roland Hamilton. Austin: University of Texas Press.

Coelho, Vera Penteado. 1972. "Enterramentos de cabeças da cultura Nasca." Tese de Doutoramento apresentada ao Departamento de Comunicações e Artes da Universidade de São Paulo.

Conrad, Geoffrey W. 1982. "The Burial Platforms of Chan Chan." In *Chan Chan: Desert City*, ed. Michael E. Moseley and Kent C. Day, pp. 87–117. Albuquerque: A School of American Research Book, University of New Mexico Press.

Cook, Anita G. 1983. "Aspects of State Ideology in Huari and Tiahuanaco Iconography: The Central Deity and Sacrificer." In *Investigations of the Andean Past: Papers from the First Annual Northeast Conference on Andean Archaeology and Ethnohistory*, ed. Daniel H. Sandweiss, pp. 161–185. Ithaca, N.Y.: Cornell Latin American Studies Program.

———. 1985. "The Politico-Religious Implications of the Huari Offering Tradition." *Diálogo Andino* 4: 203–222. Arica, Chile.

———. 1987. "The Middle Horizon Ceramic Offerings from Conchopata." *Ñawpa Pacha* 22–23 (1984–1985): 49–90. Berkeley: Institute of Andean Studies.

———. 1992. "The Stone Ancestors: Idioms of Imperial Attire and Rank among Huari Figurines." *Latin American Antiquity* 3 (4): 341–364.

———. 1994. *Wari y Tiwanaku: entre el estilo y la imagen*. Lima: Pontificia Universidad Católica del Perú, Fondo Editorial.

———. 1999. "Deciphering Huari Temple Architecture and Ritual Activity from Iconography." Paper presented at the Sixty-fourth Annual Meeting of the Society for American Archaeology, Chicago, Ill.

Cordy-Collins, Alana. 1972. "The Tule Boat Theme in Moche Art: A Problem in Ancient Peruvian Iconography." Master's thesis, Department of Anthropology, University of California at Los Angeles, Los Angeles.

———. 1977. "Chavín Art: Its Shamanic/Hallucinogenic Origins." In *Pre-Columbian Art History: Selected Readings,* vol. 1, ed. Alana Cordy-Collins and Jean Stern, pp. 353–362. Palo Alto, Calif.: Peek Publications.

———. 1979a. "Cotton and the Staff God: Analysis of an Ancient Chavín Textile." In *The Junius B. Bird Pre-Columbian Textile Conference,* ed. Ann P. Rowe, Elizabeth P. Benson, and Anne-Louise Schaffer, pp. 51–60. Washington, D.C.: The Textile Museum and Dumbarton Oaks Research Library and Collection.

———. 1979b. "The Dual Divinity Concept in Chavín Art." *El Dorado* 3 (2): 1–31. University of Northern Colorado, Greeley.

———. 1980. "An Artistic Record of the Chavín Hallucinatory Experience." *Masterkey* 54 (3): 84–93.

———. 1982. "Psychoactive Painted Peruvian Plants: The Shamanism Textile." *Journal of Ethnobiology* 2 (2): 144–153.

———. 1983. *The Cerro Sechín Massacre: Did It Happen?* San Diego Museum of Man Ethnic Technology Notes No. 18. San Diego.

———. 1990. "Fonga Sigde, Shell Purveyors to the Chimú Kings." In *The Northern Dynasties: Kingship and Statecraft in Chimor,* ed. M. E. Moseley and A. Cordy-Collins, pp. 393–418. Washington, D.C.: Dumbarton Oaks Research Library and Collection.

———. 1992. "Archaism or Tradition?: The Decapitation Theme in Cupisnique and Moche Iconography." *Latin American Antiquity* 3 (3): 206–220.

———. 1993. "She's Got Lambayeque Eyes." Paper presented at the Institute for Andean Studies Annual Meeting, University of California, Berkeley.

———. 1994a. "An Examination of the Lambayeque Cultural Tradition from the Vantage of San José de Moro." Paper presented at the Society for American Archaeology Annual Meeting, Anaheim, Calif.

———. 1994b. "An Unshaggy Dog Story." *Natural History* 103 (2): 34–41.

———. 1996. "Lambayeque." In *Andean Art at Dumbarton Oaks,* vol. 1, ed. E. Boone, pp. 189–222. Washington, D.C.: Dumbarton Oaks Research Library and Collection.

———. 1997. "The Offering Room Group." In *The Pacatnamu Papers, Volume 2: The Moche Occupation,* ed. Christopher B. Donnan and Guillermo A. Cock, pp. 283–292. Los Angeles: Museum of Cultural History, University of California, Los Angeles.

———, and Rose A. Tyson. 1995. "An Early Moche Mortuary Temple at Dos Cabezas, Peru." Paper presented at the Latin American Symposium *Death, Burial, and the Afterlife,* San Diego Museum of Man.

Daggett, Richard. 1994. "The Paracas Mummy Bundles of the Great Necropolis of Wari Kayan: A History." *Andean Past* 4: 53–76. Cornell University Latin American Studies Program, Ithaca, New York.

Davidson, Judith R. 1980. "The Spondylus Shell in Chimú Iconography." Master's thesis, California State University, Northridge.

Delgado Sumar, Hugo. 1984. "Ideología Andina: El Pagapu en Ayacucho." Tesis para optar el Título de Antropólogo Social, Universidad Nacional de San Cristóbal de Huamanga, Ayacucho, Peru.

Demarest, Arthur A., and Geoffrey W. Conrad. 1992. *Ideology and Pre-Columbian Civilizations.* Santa Fe: School of American Research.

Dillehay, Tom D., ed. 1995. *Tombs for the Living: Andean Mortuary Practices.* Washington, D.C.: Dumbarton Oaks Research Library and Collection.

Dobkin del Rios, Marlene. 1980. "Plant Hallucinogens, Shamanism and Nazca Ceramics." *Journal of Ethnopharmacology* 2 (1980): 233–246.

Donnan, Christopher B. 1976. *Moche Art and Iconography.* Los Angeles: UCLA Latin American Center Publications.

———. 1978. *Moche Art of Peru: Pre-Columbian Symbolic Communication.* Los Angeles: Museum of Cultural History, University of California, Los Angeles.

———. 1986. "The Huaca 1 Complex." In *The Pacatnamu Papers,* vol. 1, ed. Christopher B. Donnan and Guillermo A. Cock, pp. 63–84. Los Angeles: Museum of Cultural History, University of California, Los Angeles.

———. 1988. "Unraveling the Mystery of the Warrior Priest." *National Geographic* 174 (4): 551–555.

———. 1990. "Masterworks Reveal a Pre-Inca World." *National Geographic* 177 (6): 17–33.

———. 1994. "Informe al Instituto Nacional de Cultura, La Libertad, de la Temporada 1994 en Dos Cabezas, Peru."

———. 1995. "Moche Funerary Practice." In *Tombs for the Living: Andean Mortuary Practices,* ed. Tom Dillehay, pp. 111–159. Washington, D.C.: Dumbarton Oaks Research Library and Collection.

———. 1997. "Deer Hunting and Combat: Parallel Activities in the Moche World." In *The Spirit of Ancient Peru: Treasures from the Museo Arqueológico Rafael Larco Herrera,* ed. K. Berrin, pp. 51–59. New York and San Francisco: Thames and Hudson and the Fine Arts Museums of San Francisco.

———, ed. 1985. *Early Ceremonial Architecture in the Andes.* Washington, D.C.: Dumbarton Oaks Research Library and Collection.

———, and Luis Jaime Castillo. 1992. "Discovery of a Moche Priestess." *Archaeology* 45 (6): 38–42.

———, ———. 1994. "Excavaciones de Tumbas de Sacerdocistas Moche en San José de Moro, Jequetepeque." In *Moche: Propuestas y Perspectivas,* ed. S. Uceda and E. Mujica, pp. 415–424. Trujillo, Peru: Universidad Nacional de La Libertad.

———, and Leonard Foote. 1978. "Appendix 2. Child and Llama Burials from Huanchaco." In *Ancient Burial Patterns of the Moche Valley, Peru,* ed. C. B. Donnan and C. Mackey, pp. 399–407. Austin: University of Texas Press.

———, and Donna McClelland. 1979. *The Burial Theme in Moche Iconography.* Studies in Pre-Columbian Art and Archaeology No. 20. Washington, D.C.: Dumbarton Oaks Research Library and Collection.

———, ———. 1999. *Moche Fineline Painting: Its Evolution and Its Artists.* Los Angeles: UCLA Fowler Museum of Cultural History.

Dover, Robert V. H., Katherine E. Seibold, and John R. McDowell, eds. 1992. *Andean Cosmologies through Time.* Bloomington and Indianapolis: Indiana University Press.

Dransart, Penny. 1995. *Elemental Meanings: Symbolic Expression in Inka Miniature Figurines.* University of London Institute of Latin American Studies Research Papers 40.

Duviols, Pierre. 1976. "La Capacocha." *Allpanchis: Revista del Instituto Pastoral Andino* 9: 11–57. Cusco.

———. 1986. *Cultura andina y represión: procesos y visitas de idolatrías, Cajatambo, siglo XVII.* Cusco, Peru: Centro de Estudios Rurales Andinos "Bartolomé de las Casas."

Dwyer, Edward, and Jane Powell Dwyer. 1975. "The Paracas Cemeteries: Mortuary Patterns in a Peruvian South Coastal Tradition." In *Death and the Afterlife in Pre-Columbian America,* ed. Elizabeth P. Benson, pp. 145–161. Washington, D.C.: Dumbarton Oaks Research Library and Collection.

Dwyer, Jane. 1971. "Chronology and Iconography of Late Paracas and Early Nasca Textile Designs." Ph.D. dissertation, Department of Anthropology, University of California, Berkeley.

———. 1979. "The Chronology and Iconography of Paracas-Style Textiles." In *The Junius B. Bird Pre-Columbian Textile Conference,* ed. A. P. Rowe, E. Benson, and A. Schaffer, pp. 105–128. Washington, D.C.: The Textile Museum and Dumbarton Oaks Research Library and Collection.

Eliade, Mircea. 1968. *Myths, Dreams and Mysteries: The Encounter between Contemporary Faiths and Archaic Reality.* London and Glasgow: Collins/The Fontana Library of Theology and Philosophy.

Faulkner, David K. 1986. "The Mass Burial: An Entomological Perspective." In *The Pacatnamu Papers,* vol. 1, ed. Christopher B. Donnan and Guillermo A. Cock, pp. 145–150. Los Angeles: Museum of Cultural History, University of California, Los Angeles.

Feldman, Robert Alan. 1980. "Aspero, Peru: Architecture, Subsistence Economy, and Other Artifacts of a Preceramic Maritime Chiefdom." Ph.D. dissertation, Department of Anthropology, Harvard University, Cambridge, Massachusetts.

———. 1985. "Preceramic Corporate Architecture: Evidence for the Development of Non-Egalitarian Social Systems in Peru." In *Early Ceremonial Architecture in the Andes,* ed. Christopher Donnan, pp. 71–92. Washington, D.C.: Dumbarton Oaks Research Library and Collection.

———. 1989. "A Speculative Hypothesis of Wari Southern Expansion." In *The Nature of Wari: A Reappraisal of the Middle Horizon Period in Peru,* ed. R. M. Czwarno, F. M. Meddens, and A. Morgan, pp. 72–97. B.A.R. International Series 525. Oxford.

Frame, Mary. 1989. *A Family Affair: Making Cloth in Taquile, Peru.* Museum Note 26. Vancouver, B.C.: U.B.C. Museum of Anthropology.

———. 1995. *Ancient Peruvian Mantles, 300 B.C.–A.D. 200.* New York: Metropolitan Museum of Art.

Franco, Régulo, César Gálvez, and Segundo Vásquez. 1994. "Arquitectura y Decoración Mochica en la Huaca Cao Viejo, Complejo el Brujo: Resultados Preliminares." In *Moche: Propuestos y Perspectivas: Actas del Primer Coloquio Sobre la Cultura Moche,* ed. Santiago Uceda and Elías Mujica, pp. 147–180. Trujillo, Peru: Universidad Nacional de La Libertad.

Frazer, James G. 1981 [1890]. *The Golden Bough: The Roots of Religion and Folklore.* New York: Avenel Books.

Gilfoy, Peggy S. 1983. *Fabrics in Celebration of the Collection.* Indianapolis: Indianapolis Museum of Art.

González Carré, Enrique, Enrique Bragayrac Dávila, Cirilo Vivanco Pomacanchari, Vera Tiesler Blos, and Máximo López Quispe. 1996. *El Templo Mayor de la Ciudad de Wari: Estudios arqueológicos en Vegachayoq Moqo-Ayacucho*. Ayacucho, Peru: Universidad Nacional de San Cristóbal de Huamanga.

Gose, Peter. 1986. "Sacrifice and the Commodity Form in the Andes." *Man* New Series 21/2: 296–310.

———. 1993. "Segmentary State Formation and the Ritual Control of Water under the Incas." *Comparative Studies in Society and History* 35 (3): 480–514. Cambridge.

———. 1994. *Deathly Waters and Hungry Mountains*. Toronto: University of Toronto Press.

Grant, Michael, and John Hazel. 1993. *Who's Who: Classical Mythology*. New York: Oxford University Press.

Guaman Poma de Ayala, Felipe. 1980 [1615]. *El primer nueva corónica y Buen gobierno,* 3 vols., ed. John V. Murra and Rolena Adorno. Mexico City: Siglo Vientiuno.

Harris, Olivia. 1982. "The Dead and the Devils among the Bolivian Laymi." In *Death and the Regeneration of Life,* ed. Maurice Bloch and Jonathan Parry, pp. 45–73. Cambridge: Cambridge University Press.

Hernández Príncipe, Rodrigo. 1923 [1621]. "Mitología andina." *Inca: Revista trimestral de estudios antropológicos* 1 (1): 25–68. Lima: Museo de Arqueología de la Universidad de San Marcos.

Heyerdahl, Thor, Daniel H. Sandweiss, and Alfredo Narváez. 1995. *Pyramids of Túcume*. New York: Thames and Hudson.

Hocart, A. M. 1970 [1936]. *Kings and Councilors*. Chicago: University of Chicago Press.

Hocquenghem, Anne Marie. 1978. "Les combats mochicas: Essai d'interprétation d'un material archéologique à l'aide de iconologie, de l'ethnohistoire et de l'ethnologie." *Baessler-Archiv* 26 (1): 127–157.

———. 1980. "Les offrandes d'enfants: Essai d'interprétation d'une scène de l'iconographie mochica." *Indiana* 6: 275–292.

———. 1987. *Iconografía Mochica*. Lima: Pontificia Universidad Católica del Perú.

Hosler, Dorothy, Heather Lechtman, and Olaf Holm. 1990. *Axe Monies and Their Relatives*. Studies in Pre-Columbian Art and Archaeology No. 30. Washington, D.C.: Dumbarton Oaks Research Library and Collection.

Iriarte, Francisco. 1967. "Projecto Huanchaco: Notas del campo." Ms. in Museo de Sitio, Chan Chan, Trujillo, Peru.

Isbell, Billie Jean. 1978. *To Defend Ourselves: Ecology and Ritual in an Andean Village*. Austin: University of Texas Press.

———. 1985. *To Defend Ourselves: Ecology and Ritual in an Andean Village,* 3d ed. Prospect Heights, Ill.: Waveland Press.

Isbell, William H. 1989. "Honcopampa: Was It a Huari Administrative Center?" In *The Nature of Wari: A Reappraisal of the Middle Horizon Period in Peru,* ed. R. M. Czwarno, F. M. Meddens, and A. Morgan, pp. 98–114. B.A.R. International Series 525. Oxford.

———. 1991a. "Huari Administration and the Orthogonal Cellular Architecture Horizon." In *Huari Administrative Structure: Prehistoric Monumental Architec-*

ture and State Government, ed. William H. Isbell and Gordon McEwan, pp. 293–315. Washington, D.C.: Dumbarton Oaks Research Library and Collection.

———. 1991b. "Honcopampa: Monumental Ruins in Peru's North Highlands." *Expedition* 33 (3): 27–36.

———. 1997. "Reconstructing Huari: A Cultural Chronology for the Capital City." In *Emergence and Change in Early Urban Societies,* ed. Linda Manzanilla, pp. 181–227. New York: Plenum Press.

———, Christine Brewster-Wray, and Lynda Spickard. 1991. "Architecture and Spatial Organization at Huari." In *Huari Administrative Structure: Prehistoric Monumental Architecture and State Government,* ed. William Isbell and Gordon McEwan, pp. 19–53. Washington, D.C.: Dumbarton Oaks Research Library and Collection.

———, and Anita Cook. 1987. "Ideological Origins of an Andean Conquest State." *Archaeology* 40 (4): 26–33.

———, ———. 1999. "Projecto Arqueológico Conchopata, 1999." Lima: Informe para el Instituto Nacional de Cultura del Perú.

———, and Gordon F. McEwan. 1991. "History of Huari Studies and an Introduction to Current Interpretations." In *Huari Administrative Structure: Prehistoric Monumental Architecture and State Government,* ed. William H. Isbell and Gordon McEwan, pp. 1–17. Washington, D.C.: Dumbarton Oaks Research Library and Collection.

Johnson, David. 1997. "The Relationship between the Lines of Nasca and Water Resources." Paper presented at the Sixteenth Annual Meeting of the Northeast Conference on Andean Archaeology and Ethnohistory, University of Maine, Orono.

Kauffmann Doig, Federico. 1966. *Mochica, Nasca y Recuay en la arqueología peruana.* Lima: Universidad Nacional Mayor de San Marcos.

Kolata, Alan L. 1993. *The Tiwanaku: Portrait of an Andean Civilization.* Cambridge, Mass., and Oxford, UK: Blackwell.

———. 1996. *Valley of the Spirits: A Journey into the Lost Realm of the Aymara.* New York: John Wiley & Sons.

Kosok, Paul. 1965. *Life, Land and Water in Ancient Peru.* Brooklyn, N.Y.: Long Island University Press.

Kroeber, Alfred L. 1930. *Archaeological Explorations in Peru. Part II. The Northern Coast.* Field Museum of Natural History, Anthropology, Memoirs 2 (2). Chicago.

———. 1956. "Toward Definition of the Nazca Style." *University of California Publications in American Archaeology and Ethnology* 43 (4): 327–432. Berkeley.

Kubler, George. 1948. "Towards Absolute Time: Guano Archaeology." In *A Reappraisal of Peruvian Archaeology,* assembled by Wendell C. Bennett. *Memoirs of the Society for American Archaeology* no. 4: 29–50. Menasha, Wisc.: Society for American Archaeology and the Institute of Andean Research.

Kutscher, Gerdt. 1983. *Nordperuanische Gefässmalereien des Moche-Stils.* Munich: Verlag C. H. Beck.

Lapiner, Alan. 1976. *Pre-Columbian Art of South America.* New York: Harry N. Abrams.

Larco Hoyle, Rafael. 1966. *Peru. Archaeologia Mundi.* London: Frederick Muller.

Lastres, Juan B. 1951. *Historia de la Medicina Peruana, Volumen I: La Medicina Incaica.* Lima: Universidad Nacional Mayor de San Marcos, Imprenta Santa Maria.

Lathrap, Donald W. 1973. "Gifts of the Cayman: Some Thoughts on the Subsistence Basis of Chavín." In *Variation in Anthropology: Essays in Honor of John C. McGregor,* ed. D. W. Lathrap and J. Douglas, pp. 91–105. Urbana: Illinois Archaeological Survey.

———. 1977. "Thoughts on the Subsistence Basis of Chavín." In *Pre-Columbian Art History: Selected Readings,* vol. 1, ed. Alana Cordy-Collins and Jean Stern, pp. 333–351. Palo Alto, Calif.: Peek Publications.

Lavalle, José Antonio de, ed. 1986. *Culturas Precolombinas: Nazca.* Serie Arte y Tesoros del Perú. Lima: Banco de Crédito del Perú en la Cultura.

———, and Werner Lang, eds. 1977. *Arte Precolombino: Museo Nacional de Antropología y Arqueología, Lima, primera parte: Arte textil y adornos.* Lima: Banco de Crédito del Perú.

———, ———. 1983. *Culturas Precolombinas: Paracas.* Colección arte y tesoros del Perú. Lima: Banco de Crédito del Perú.

Lavallée, Danielle. 1970. *Les représentationes animales dans la céramique Mochica.* Université de Paris, Mémoires de l'Institut d'Ethnologie, IV. Paris.

Lothrop, Samuel K., and Joy Mahler. 1957. "Late Nazca Burials in Chaviña, Peru." *Papers of the Peabody Museum of Archaeology and Ethnology* 50 (2): 3–61. Cambridge, Mass.

Lumbreras, Luis G. 1974. *Las Fundaciones de Huamanga: Hacia una prehistoria de Ayacucho.* Lima: Nueva Educación.

———. 1981. "The Stratigraphy of the Open Sites." In *Prehistory of the Ayacucho Basin, Peru. Volume II: Excavations and Chronology,* ed. Richard S. MacNeish, pp. 167–198. Ann Arbor: University of Michigan Press.

———. 1989. *Chavín de Huántar en el Nacimiento de la Civilización Andina.* Lima: Instituto Andino de Estudios Arqueológicos.

———, Elías Mujica, and R. Vera. 1982. "Cerro Baúl: Un enclave Wari en territorio Tiahuanaco." *Gaceta Arqueológica Andina* 1 (2): 4–5.

Lyon, Patricia. 1979. "Female Supernaturals in Ancient Peru." *Ñawpa Pacha* 16 (1978): 95–140. Berkeley: Institute of Andean Studies.

McClelland, Donna. 1990. "A Maritime Passage from Moche to Chimú." In *The Northern Dynasties: Kingship and Statecraft in Chimor,* ed. M. E. Moseley and A. Cordy-Collins, pp. 75–106. Washington, D.C.: Dumbarton Oaks Research Library and Collection.

McEwan, Colin, and María Isabel Silva I. 1989. "Que fueron a hacer los incas en la costa central del Ecuador?" In *Relaciones interculturales en el área ecuatorial del Pacífico durante la época precolombina,* ed. J. F. Bouchard and M. Guinea, pp. 163–185. Proceedings of the 46 Congreso Internacional de Americanistas/ International Congress of Americanists, Amsterdam, Netherlands, 1988. B.A.R. International Series 503. Oxford.

McEwan, Gordon F. 1987. *The Middle Horizon in the Valley of Cuzco, Peru: The Impact of the Wari Occupation of Pikillacta in the Lucre Basin.* B.A.R. International Series 372. Oxford: British Archaeological Reports.

————. 1998. "The Function of Niched Halls in Wari Architecture." *American Antiquity* 9 (1): 68–86.

Machaca Calle, Gudelia. 1983. "Secuencia cultural y nuevas evidencias de formación urbana en Ñawinpukio." Trabajo de investigación para optar el titulo de Licenciada en Arqueología, Universidad de San Cristóbal de Huamanga, Ayacucho, Peru.

Marcos, Jorge, and Presley Norton. 1981. "Interpretación sobre Arqueología de la Isla de La Plata." *Miscelánea Antropológica Ecuatoriana: Boletín de los Museos del Banco Central del Ecuador* 1: 136–154.

Menzel, Dorothy. 1964. "Style and Time in the Middle Horizon." *Ñawpa Pacha* 2: 1–105. Berkeley: Institute of Andean Studies.

————. 1968. "New Data on the Huari Empire in Middle Horizon Epoch 2A." *Ñawpa Pacha* 6: 47–114. Berkeley: Institute of Andean Studies.

————. 1976. *Pottery Style and Society in Ancient Peru.* Berkeley: University of California Press.

Millones, Luis, and Yoshio Onuki, eds. 1993. *El Mundo Ceremonial Andino.* Senri Ethnological Studies No. 37. Osaka, Japan: National Ethnographic Museum.

Molina, Cristóbal de. 1959 [1575?]. *Ritos y Fábulas de los Incas.* Buenos Aires: Editorial Futuro.

Montell, Gösta. 1929. *Dress and Ornaments in Ancient Peru: Archaeological and Historical Studies.* Gothenburg, Sweden: Elanders Boktryckeri Aktiebolag.

Montoya, María. 1997. "Excavaciones en la Plaza 3B." In *Investigaciones en la Huaca de la Luna 1995,* ed. Santiago Uceda, Elías Mujica, and Ricardo Morales, pp. 61–66. Trujillo, Peru: Universidad Nacional de la Libertad.

Moore, Gerry. 1996. *Architecture and Power in the Andes: The Archaeology of Public Buildings.* Cambridge: Cambridge University Press.

Morote Best, Efraín. 1952. "El Degollador (Nakaq)." *Tradición: Revista Peruana de Cultura* 11 (4): 67–91. Cuzco.

Moseley, Michael E. 1985. "The Exploration and Explanation of Early Monumental Architecture in the Andes." In *Early Monumental Architecture in the Andes,* ed. Christopher B. Donnan, pp. 29–58. Washington, D.C.: Dumbarton Oaks Research Library and Collection.

————. 1992. *The Incas and Their Ancestors: The Archaeology of Peru.* New York and London: Thames and Hudson.

————, and Alana Cordy-Collins, eds. 1990. *The Northern Dynasties: Kingship and Statecraft in Chimor.* Washington, D.C.: Dumbarton Oaks Research Library and Collection.

————, Robert Feldman, Paul Goldstein, and Luis Watanabe. 1991. "Colonies and Conquest: Tiahuanaco and Huari in Moquegua." In *Huari Administrative Structure: Prehistoric Monumental Architecture and State Government,* ed. William Isbell and Gordon McEwan, pp. 121–140. Washington, D.C.: Dumbarton Oaks Research Library and Collection.

Mostny, Grete, ed. 1957. "La Momia del Cerro el Plomo." *Boletín del Museo Nacional de Historia Natural* 27 (1): 1–120.

Murra, John V. 1962. "Cloth and Its Functions in the Inka State." *American Anthropologist* 64 (4): 710–728.

————. 1982. "El Tráfico de Mullu en la costa del Pacífico." In *Primer Simposio de Correlaciones Antropológicas Andino-Mesoamericano,* ed. J. G. Marcos and P. Norton, pp. 263–273. Guayaquil, Ecuador: Escuela Superior Politécnica del Litoral.

Museums of the Andes. 1981. New York and Tokyo: Newsweek and Kodanska.

Neira Avendaño, Máximo, and Vera Penteado Coelho. 1972–1973. "Enterramientos de Cabezas de la Cultura Nasca." *Revista do Museu Paulista,* Nova Série 20: 109–142. São Paulo.

Netherly, Patricia Joan. 1977. "Local Level Lords on the North Coast of Peru." Doctoral dissertation, Cornell University, Ithaca, New York.

Newman, Margaret. 1996. "Immunological Analysis of Organic Residue from a Wooden Mace from Huaca de la Luna, Peru." Unpublished report in the possession of Steve Bourget.

Ochatoma Paravicino, José. 1989. *Aqo Wayqo: poblado rural de la época wari.* Lima: CONCYTEC.

———. 1999. "Recientes Descubrimientos en el Sitio Huari de Conchopata, Ayacucho." Paper presented at the Sixty-fourth Annual Meeting of the Society for American Archaeology, Chicago, Ill. Published by the Facultad de Ciencias Sociales, Universidad San Cristóbal de Huamanga, Peru.

———, and Martha Cabrera Romero. 1998. "Recientes Descubrimientos en el sitio Huari de Conchopata-Ayacucho." Paper presented at the Sixty-fourth Annual Meeting of the Society for American Archaeology, Chicago, Ill.

O'Neale, Lila M. 1935. "Pequeñas prendas ceremoniales de Paracas." *Revista del Museo Nacional* 4 (2): 245–266. Lima.

Onuki, Yoshio. 1993. "Las Actividades Ceremoniales Tempranas en la Cuenca del Alto Huallaga y Algunos Problemas Generales." In *El Mundo Ceremonial Andino,* ed. L. Millones and Y. Onuki, pp. 69–96. Senri Ethnological Studies No. 37. Osaka, Japan: National Ethnographic Museum.

Paul, Anne. 1979. *Paracas Textiles: Selected from the Museum's Collections.* Etnologiska Studier 34. Göteborg, Sweden: Göteborgs Etnografiska Museum.

———. 1982. "The Chronological Relationship of the Linear, Block Color, and Broad Line Styles of Paracas Embroidered Images." In *Pre-Columbian Art History: Selected Readings,* ed. A. Cordy-Collins, pp. 255–277. Palo Alto, Calif.: Peek Publications.

———. 1990. *Paracas Ritual Attire: Symbols of Authority in Ancient Peru.* Norman: University of Oklahoma Press.

———. 1991a. "Paracas: An Ancient Cultural Tradition on the South Coast of Peru." In *Paracas Art and Architecture: Object and Context in South Coastal Peru,* ed. Anne Paul, pp. 1–34. Iowa City: University of Iowa Press.

———. 1991b. "Paracas Necropolis Bundle 89: A Description and Discussion of Its Contents." In *Paracas Art and Architecture: Object and Context in South Coastal Peru,* ed. Anne Paul, pp. 172–221. Iowa City: University of Iowa Press.

———, and Solveig Turpin. 1986. "The Ecstatic Shaman Theme of Paracas Textiles." *Archaeology* 39 (5): 20–27.

Paulsen, Alison C. 1974. "The Thorny Oyster and the Voice of God: Spondylus and Strombus in Andean Prehistory." *American Antiquity* 29 (4): 597–607.

———. 1983. "Huaca del Loro Revisited: The Nasca-Huarpa Connection." In *Investigations of the Andean Past: Papers from the First Annual Northeast Conference on Andean Archaeology and Ethnohistory,* ed. Daniel H. Sandweiss, pp. 98–121. Ithaca, N.Y.: Cornell University Press.

Pérez Calderón, Ismael, and José Ochatoma Paravicino. 1999. "Viviendas, talleres y hornos de producción alfarera Huari en Conchopata." *Conchopata: Revista de Arqueología,* No. 1. Ayacucho, Peru: Universidad Nacional de San Cristóbal de Huamanga, Facultad de Ciencias Sociales Oficina de Investigación.

Peru durch die Jahrtausende: Kunst und Kultur im Lande der Inka. 1984. Exhibition catalogue, Villa Hügel, Essen. Recklinghausen, Germany: Verlag Aurel Bongers.

Peters, Ann H. 1991. "Ecology and Society in Embroidered Images from the Paracas Necropolis." In *Paracas Art and Architecture: Object and Context in South Coastal Peru,* ed. Anne Paul, pp. 240–314. Iowa City: University of Iowa Press.

Pezzia, Alejandro. 1969. *Guía del mapa arqueológico pictográfico del Departamento de Ica.* Lima: Editorial Italperú.

Pijoan, Carmen María, and Josefina Mansilla Lory. 1990. "Prácticas rituales en el Norte de Mesoamérica: Evidencias en Electra, Villa de Reyes, San Luis Potosí." *Arqueología* 4: 87–96. Mexico City: Instituto Nacional de Antropología e Historia.

Pijoan, Carmen María, Josefina Mansilla, and Alejandro Pastrana. 1995. "Un caso de desmembramiento. Tlatelolco, D.F." In *Estudios de antropología biológica,* vol. 5, ed. Rosa María Ramos Rodríguez and Sergio López Alonso, pp. 81–90. México: Universidad Nacional Autónoma de México.

Porter, Nancy. 1991. "Prisoners and Captives in Peru: Ritual Sacrifice?" Paper presented at the Thirty-first Annual Meeting of the Institute of Andean Studies, Berkeley, Calif.

Pozorski, Thomas, and Shelia Pozorski. 1993. "Early Complex Society and Ceremonialism on the Peruvian North Coast." In *El Mundo Ceremonial Andino,* ed. L. Millones and Y. Onuki, pp. 45–68. Senri Ethnological Studies No. 37. Osaka, Japan: National Ethnographic Museum.

Pozzi-Escot, Denise. 1991. "Conchopata: 'A Community of Potters.'" In *Huari Administrative Structure: Prehistoric Monumental Architecture and State Government,* ed. William H. Isbell and Gordon McEwan, pp. 81–92. Washington, D.C.: Dumbarton Oaks Research Library and Collection.

Proulx, Donald A. 1968. *Local Differences and Time Differences in Nasca Pottery.* University of California Publications in Anthropology, vol. 5. Berkeley: University of California Press.

———. 1971. "Headhunting in Ancient Peru." *Archaeology* 24 (l): 16–21.

———. 1983. "The Nasca Style." In *Art of the Andes: Pre-Columbian Sculptured and Painted Ceramics from the Arthur M. Sackler Collections,* ed. Lois Katz, pp. 87–106. Washington, D.C.: Arthur M. Sackler Foundation and AMS Foundation for the Arts, Sciences and Humanities.

———. 1989. "Nasca Trophy Heads: Victims of Warfare or Ritual Sacrifice?" In *Cultures in Conflict: Current Archaeological Perspectives,* ed. Diana C. Tkaczuk and Brian C. Vivian, pp. 73–85. Proceedings of the Twentieth Annual Chacmool Conference, University of Calgary. Calgary, Alberta: Archaeological Association of the University of Calgary.

———. 1996. "Nasca." In *Andean Art at Dumbarton Oaks,* vol. 1, ed. E. Boone, pp. 107–122. Washington, D.C.: Dumbarton Oaks Research Library and Collection.

Purin, Sergio, ed. 1990. *Inca—Perú: 3000 ans d'histoire*. Brussels: Musées Royaux d'Art et d'Histoire.

Quilter, Jeffrey. 1989. *Life and Death at Paloma: Society and Mortuary Practices in a Preceramic Peruvian Village*. Iowa City: University of Iowa Press.

———. 1997. "The Narrative Approach to Moche Iconography." *Latin American Antiquity* 8 (2): 113-133.

Ravines, Rogger. 1977. "Excavaciones en Ayapata, Huancavelica, Perú." *Ñawpa Pacha* 15: 19-45. Berkeley: Institute of Andean Studies.

Rea, Amadeo M. 1986. "Black Vultures and Human Victims: Archaeological Evidence from Pacatnamu." In *The Pacatnamu Papers*, vol. 1, ed. Christopher B. Donnan and Guillermo A. Cock, pp. 139-144. Los Angeles: Museum of Cultural History, University of California, Los Angeles.

Reiche, Maria. 1968. *Mystery on the Desert*. Stuttgart: Heinrich Fink GmbH.

———. 1974. *Peruvian Ground Drawings/Peruanische Erdzeichen*. Munich: Kunstraum München E.V.

Reichel-Dolmatoff, Gerardo. 1974. "Funeral Customs and Religious Symbolism among the Kogi." In *Native South Americans*, ed. P. J. Lyon, pp. 289-301. Boston: Little, Brown and Co.

———. 1978. "The Loom of Life: A Kogi Principle of Integration." *Journal of Latin American Lore* 4 (1): 5-27.

Reinhard, Johan. 1992. "Sacred Peaks of the Andes." *National Geographic* 181 (3): 84-111.

———. 1996. "Peru's Ice Maidens: Unwrapping the Secrets." *National Geographic* 189 (6): 62-81.

———. 1997. "Sharp Eyes of Science Probe the Mummies of Peru." *National Geographic* 191 (1): 36-43.

Riddell, Francis, and A. Belin. 1987. "Informe del Proyecto de Rescate Arqueológico INC-CIPS en el Sitio de Tambo Viejo (PV74-1) Valle de Acarí, Departamento de Arequipa." Report to the Instituto Nacional de Cultura, Lima.

Roark, Richard. 1965. "From Monumental to Proliferous in Nasca Pottery." *Ñawpa Pacha* 3: 1-92. Berkeley: Institute of Andean Studies.

Rostworowski de Diez Canseco, María. 1975. "Pescadores, artesanos, y mercaderes costeños en el Perú prehispánico." *Revista del Museo Nacional* 41: 311-339. Lima.

———. 1996. *Estructuras andinas del poder*, 4th ed. Lima: Instituto de Estudios Peruanos.

———. 1997. "The Coastal Islands of Peru: Myths and Natural Resources." In *The Spirit of Ancient Peru: Treasures from the Museo Arqueológico Rafael Larco Herrera*, ed. K. Berrin, pp. 33-39. New York and San Francisco: Thames and Hudson and the Fine Arts Museums of San Francisco.

Rowe, John Howland. 1946. "Inca Culture at the Time of the Spanish Conquest." In *Handbook of South American Indians*, vol. 2, ed. Julian H. Steward, pp. 183-330. Smithsonian Institution, Bureau of American Ethnology, Bulletin 143. Washington, D.C.: Smithsonian Institution.

———. 1948. "The Kingdom of Chimor." *Acta Americana* 6 (1-2): 26-59. Mexico City.

———. 1995. "Behavior and Belief in Ancient Peruvian Mortuary Practice." In

Tombs for the Living: Andean Mortuary Practices, ed. Tom D. Dillehay, pp. 27–41. Washington, D.C.: Dumbarton Oaks Research Library and Collection.

———. 1996. "Inca." In *Andean Art at Dumbarton Oaks*, vol. 1, ed. E. Boone, pp. 301–320. Washington, D.C.: Dumbarton Oaks Research Library and Collection.

Rydén, Stig. 1930. "Une tête trophée de Nasca." *Journal de la Société de Américanistes* 22 (2): 265–271. Paris.

Salazar-Burger, Lucy, and Richard L. Burger. 1982. "La Araña en la Iconografía del Horizonte Temprano en la Costa Norte del Perú." *Beiträge zur Allgemeinen und Vergleichenden Archäologie* 4: 213–253.

Salomon, Frank. 1987. "Ancestor Cults and Resistance to the State in Arequipa, ca. 1748–1754." In *Resistance, Rebellion and Consciousness in the Andean Peasant World, 18th to 20th Centuries*, ed. Steve J. Stern, pp. 148–165. Madison: University of Wisconsin Press.

———. 1995. " 'The Beautiful Grandparents': Andean Ancestor Shrines and Mortuary Ritual as Seen through Colonial Records." In *Tombs for the Living: Andean Mortuary Practices*, ed. Tom Dillehay, pp. 315–353. Washington, D.C.: Dumbarton Oaks Research Library and Collection.

———, trans. and ed., and George L. Urioste, trans. 1991. *The Huarochirí Manuscript: A Testament of Ancient and Colonial Andean Religion*. Austin: University of Texas Press.

Samaniego, Lorenzo, Enrique Vergara, and Henning Bischof. 1985. "New Evidence on Cerro Sechín, Casma Valley, Peru." In *Early Ceremonial Architecture in the Andes*, ed. Christopher Donnan, pp. 165–190. Washington, D.C.: Dumbarton Oaks Research Library and Collection.

Sawyer, Alan R. 1961. "Paracas and Nazca Iconography." In *Essays in Pre-Columbian Art and Archaeology*, ed. S. K. Lothrop, pp. 269–298. Cambridge, Mass.: Harvard University Press.

———. 1962. "A Group of Early Nazca Sculptures in the Whyte Collection." *Archaeology* 15 (3): 152–159.

———. 1966. *Ancient Peruvian Ceramics: The Nathan Cummings Collection*. New York: Metropolitan Museum of Art.

———. 1968. *Mastercraftsmen of Ancient Peru*. New York: Solomon R. Guggenheim Foundation.

Schobinger, Juan. 1991. "Sacrifices of the High Andes." *Natural History* 100 (4): 63–69.

Schreiber, Katharina. 1987. "On Revisiting Huaca del Loro: A Cautionary Note." *Andean Past* 2: 69–79.

———, and Josué Lancho Rojas. 1995. "The Puquios of Nasca." *Latin American Antiquity* 6 (3): 229–254.

Schweigger, Erwin. 1947. *El litoral peruano*. Lima: Compañía Administradora del Guano.

Seler, Eduard. 1915. "Archäologische Reise in Süd- und Mittelamaerika, 1910–1911." *Gesammelte Abhandlungen zur Amerikanischen Sprach- und Altertumskunde* 5: 115–151. Berlin: Verlag Behrend.

———. 1923. "Die buntbemalten Gefässe von Nasca im südlichen Perú und die Hauptelemente ihrer Verzierung." *Gesammelte Abhandlungen zur Amerikanischen Sprach- und Altertumskunde* 4: 171–338. Berlin: Verlag Behrend.

Sharon, Douglas. 1972. "The San Pedro Cactus in Peruvian Folk Healing." In *Flesh of the Gods: The Ritual Use of Hallucinogens,* ed. Peter T. Furst, pp. 114–135. New York: Praeger.

Sherbondy, Jeannette E. 1992. "Water Ideology in Inca Ethnogenesis." In *Andean Cosmologies through Time,* ed. R. Dover, K. Seibold, and J. McDowell, pp. 46–66. Bloomington and Indianapolis: Indiana University Press.

Shimada, Izumi, and Jo Ann Griffin. 1994. "Precious Metal Objects of the Middle Sicán." *Scientific American* 270 (4): 82–89.

Silverblatt, Irene. 1987. *Moon, Sun, and Witches.* Princeton, N.J.: Princeton University Press.

Silverman, Helaine. 1990. "Beyond the Pampa: The Geoglyphs in the Valleys of Nasca." *National Geographic Research* 6 (4): 435–456.

———. 1991. "The Paracas Problem: Archaeological Perspectives." In *Paracas Art and Architecture: Object and Context in South Coastal Peru,* ed. Anne Paul, pp. 349–415. Iowa City: University of Iowa Press.

———. 1993. *Cahuachi in the Ancient Nasca World.* Iowa City: University of Iowa Press.

Sotheby's. 1981. "Fine Pre-Columbian Art, May 9, 1981" [auction catalogue]. New York: Sotheby Parke Bernet.

Stone-Miller, Rebecca. 1992. *To Weave for the Sun: Andean Textiles in the Museum of Fine Arts, Boston.* Boston: Museum of Fine Arts.

Strong, William Duncan, and Clifford Evans, Jr. 1952. *Cultural Stratigraphy in the Virú Valley, Northern Peru.* Columbia Studies in Archaeology and Ethnology, vol. 4. New York.

Taylor, Dicey. 1992. "Painted Ladies: Costumes for Women on Tepeu Ceramics." In *The Maya Vase Book,* vol. 3, ed. Justin Kerr, pp. 513–525. New York: Kerr Associates.

Tello, Julio C. 1918. *El uso de las cabezas humanas artificialmente momificadas y su representación en el antiguo arte peruano.* Lima: Casa Editora de Ernesto R. Villaran.

———. 1929. *Antiguo Perú: Primera época.* Lima: Comisión Organizadora del Segundo Congreso Sudamericano de Turismo.

———. 1959. *Paracas: Primera parte.* Publicación del Proyecto 8b del Programa 1941-42 de the Institute of Andean Research de Nueva York. Lima: Empresa Gráfica T. Scheuch S.A.

———, and Toribio Mejía Xesspe. 1979. *Paracas, Segunda parte: Cavernas y Necrópolis.* Publicación Antropológica del Archivo "Julio C. Tello." Lima: Universidad Nacional Mayor de San Marcos, and New York: Institute of Andean Research.

Tello, Ricardo. 1997. "Excavaciones en la unidad 12 de la Plataforma I." In *Investigaciones en la Huaca de la Luna 1995,* ed. S. Uceda, E. Mujica, and R. Morales, pp. 29–37. Trujillo, Peru: Facultad de Ciencias Sociales, Universidad de la Libertad.

Thompson, J. Eric S. 1970. *Maya History and Religion.* Norman: University of Oklahoma Press.

Tierney, Patrick. 1989. *The Highest Altar: The Story of Human Sacrifice.* New York: Viking.

Tomoeda, Hiroyasu. 1982. "Folklore Andino y Mitología Amazónica: Las Plantas

Cultivadas y la Muerte en el Pensamiento Andino." In *El Hombre y su Ambiente en los Andes Centrales,* ed. Luis Millones and Hiroyasu Tomoeda, pp. 275–306. Senri Ethnological Series 10. Osaka, Japan: National Ethnographic Museum.

Topic, John R., and Theresa Lange Topic. 1997. "Hacia una comprensión conceptual de la guerra andina." In *Arqueología, antropología e historia en los Andes: Homenaje a María Rostworowski,* ed. Rafael Varón Gabai and Javier Flores Espinoza, pp. 567–590. Lima: Instituto de Estudios Peruanos and Banco Central de Reserva del Perú.

Towle, Margaret. 1952. "Plant Remains from a Peruvian Mummy Bundle." *Botanical Museum Leaflets* 15 (9): 223–246. Harvard University, Cambridge, Massachusetts.

Townsend, Richard F. 1985. "Deciphering the Nazca World: Ceramic Images from Ancient Peru." *Art Institute of Chicago Museum Studies* 2 (2): 116–139.

Tuya, Angel de. 1949. "Las cabezas-trofeos de la ceramica Nasca." *Estudios de historia primitiva de América.* Madrid: Publicaciones del Seminario de Historia Primitiva del Hombre.

Tyson, Rose A. 1995. "Cuarto de los Cráneos." Notes on file, Anthropology Department, University of San Diego.

Ubbelohde-Doering, Heinrich. 1931. "Altperuanische Gefässmalereien, II Teil." *Marburger Jahrbuch für Kunstwissenschaft* 6: 1–63.

Ubelaker, Douglas H. 1992. "Hyoid Fracture and Strangulation." *Journal of Forensic Sciences* 37 (5): 1216–1222.

Uceda, Santiago, and José Canziani. 1993. "Evidencias de grandes precipitaciones en diversas etapas constructivas de la Huaca de la Luna, Costa Norte del Perú." *Bulletin de l'Institut Français d'Études Andines* 22 (1): 313–343.

Uceda, Santiago, and Elías Mujica. 1997. "Investigaciones en la Huaca de la Luna: A manera de introducción." In *Investigaciones en la Huaca de la Luna 1995,* ed. S. Uceda, E. Mujica, and R. Morales, pp. 9–15. Trujillo, Peru: Facultad de Ciencias Sociales, Universidad de la Libertad.

Uceda, Santiago, Elías Mujica, and Ricardo Morales, eds. 1997. *Investigaciones en la Huaca de la Luna 1995.* Trujillo, Peru: Facultad de Ciencias Sociales, Universidad de la Libertad.

Uhle, Max. 1901. "Die deformierten Köpfe von peruanischen Mumien und die Uta-Krankheit." *Verhandlungen der Berliner Gesellschaft für Anthropologie, Ethnologie und Urgeschichte,* vol. 33, pp. 404–408. Berlin.

———. 1903. *Pachacamac: Report of the William Pepper, M.D., LL.D., Peruvian Expedition of 1896.* Philadelphia: University of Pennsylvania.

———. 1908. "La esfera de influencia del país de los Incas." In *Trabajos de la II Sección Ciencias Naturales Antropólogicas y Ethnolológicas,* vol. 2, p. 269. Santiago de Chile: Impr. "Barcelona."

———. 1959. *Wesen und Ordnung der altperuanischen Kulturen.* Bibliotheca Ibero-Americana. Berlin: Colloquium Verlag.

———. 1991 [1903]. *Pachacamac: A Reprint of the 1903 Edition,* published with Izumi Shimada, *Pachacamac Archaeology: Retrospect and Prospect.* University Museum Monograph 62. Philadelphia: University Museum, University of Pennsylvania.

Urton, Gary. 1981. *At the Crossroads of the Earth and of the Sky: An Andean Cosmology.* Austin: University of Texas Press.

———. 1990. "Andean Social Organization and the Maintenance of the Nazca Lines." In *The Lines of Nazca,* ed. Anthony F. Aveni, pp. 173–206. Philadelphia: American Philosophical Society.

———. 1993. "Moieties and Ceremonialism in the Andes: The Ritual Battles of the Carnival Season in Southern Peru." In *El Mundo Ceremonial Andino,* ed. L. Millones and Y. Onuki, pp. 117–142. Senri Ethnological Studies No. 37. Osaka, Japan: National Ethnographic Museum.

Valcárcel, Luis E. 1932. "El gato de agua." *Revista del Museo Nacional* 1 (2): 3–27. Lima.

———. 1959. "Símbolos Mágicos-Religiosos en la Cultura Andina." *Revista del Museo Nacional* 28: 3–18.

———. 1964. *Historia del Perú Antiguo.* Lima: Juan Mejía Baca.

Vargas Llosa, Mario. 1993. *Death in the Andes.* New York: Penguin Books.

Verano, John W. 1986. "A Mass Burial of Mutilated Individuals at Pacatnamu." In *The Pacatnamu Papers,* vol. 1, ed. Christopher B. Donnan and Guillermo A. Cock, pp. 117–138. Los Angeles: Museum of Cultural History, University of California, Los Angeles.

———. 1992. "Prehistoric Disease and Demography in the Andes." In *Disease and Demography in the Americas,* ed. J. Verano and D. Ubelaker, pp. 15–24. Washington, D.C., and London: Smithsonian Institution Press.

———. 1994. "Características físicas y biología osteológica de los Moche." In *Moche: Propuestas y Perspectivas,* ed. Santiago Uceda and Elías Mujica, pp. 307–326. Travaux de l'Institut Français d'Études Andines 79 (7–8).

———. 1995. "Where Do They Rest? The Treatment of Human Offerings and Trophies in Ancient Peru." In *Tombs for the Living: Andean Mortuary Practices,* ed. Tom D. Dillehay, pp. 189–227. Washington, D.C.: Dumbarton Oaks Research Library and Collection.

———. 1997. "Physical Characteristics and Skeletal Biology of the Moche Population at Pacatnamu." In *The Pacatnamu Papers, Vol. 2: The Moche Occupation,* ed. Christopher B. Donnan and Guillermo A. Cock, pp. 189–214. Los Angeles: UCLA, Fowler Museum of Cultural History.

———. 1998. "Sacrificios humanos, desmembramientos y modificaciones culturales en restos osteológicos: Evidencias de las temporadas de investigación 1995–96 en la Huaca de la Luna." In *Investigaciones en la Huaca de la Luna 1996,* ed. S. Uceda, E. Mujica, and R. Morales, pp. 159–171. Trujillo, Peru: Universidad Nacional de La Libertad—Trujillo.

———, and Michael J. DeNiro. 1993. "Locals or Foreigners? Morphological, Biometric, and Isotopic Approaches to the Question of Group Affinity in Human Skeletal Remains Recovered from Unusual Archaeological Contexts." In *Investigations of Ancient Human Tissue: Chemical Analysis in Anthropology,* ed. Mary K. Sandford, pp. 361–386. New York: Gordon and Breach.

Vergara Figueroa, Abilio, and Freddy Ferrúa Carrasco. 1989. "Ayacucho: De nuevo los Degolladores." In *Pishtacos de verdugos a sacaojos,* ed. Juan Ansión, pp. 123–134. Lima: Tarea Associación de Publicaciones Educativas.

Wallace, Anthony F. C. 1966. *Religion: An Anthropological View.* New York: Random House.

Weiss, Eugenio. 1958. *Osteología cultural, prácticas cefálicas, cabezas trofeo trepanaciones, cauterizaciones,* vol. 2. Lima: Universidad Nacional Mayor de San Marcos.

Williams, Patrick Ryan. 1997. "Burning Down the House: Differential Patterns of Construction and Abandonment on Cerro Baúl." Paper presented at the Sixteenth Annual Northeast Conference on Andean Archaeology and Ethnohistory, Orono, Maine, October 1997.

———. 1998. "The 1997 Cerro Baúl Excavation Project." Report to the G. A. Bruno Foundation.

Wolfe, Elizabeth F. 1981. "The Spotted Cat and the Horrible Bird: Stylistic Change in Nasca 1–5 Ceramic Decoration." *Ñawpa Pacha* 19: 1–62. Berkeley: Institute of Andean Studies.

Yacovleff, Eugenio. 1931. "El vencejo (Cypselus) en el arte decorativo de Nasca." *Wira Kocha* 1 (1): 25–35. Lima.

———. 1932a. "Las falcónidas en el arte y en las creencias de los antiguos peruanos." *Revista del Museo Nacional* 1 (1): 35–111. Lima.

———. 1932b. "La deidad primitiva de los Nasca." *Revista del Museo Nacional* 1 (2): 103–161. Lima.

———. 1933a. "La jíquima, raíz comestible extinguida en el Perú." *Revista del Museo Nacional* 2 (1): 51–66. Lima.

———. 1933b. "Arte plumaria entre los antiguos peruanos." *Revista del Museo Nacional* 2 (2): 137–158. Lima.

———, and F. L. Herrera. 1934. "El mundo vegetal de los antiguos peruanos." *Revista del Museo Nacional* 3 (3): 241–322. Lima.

———, and Jorge C. Muelle. 1934. "Un fardo funerario de Paracas." *Revista del Museo Nacional* 3 (1–2): 63–153. Lima.

Young-Sanchez, Margaret. 1993. "The Shaman Theme in Paracas Art: Two Examples from the Collection of the Cleveland Museum of Art." Paper presented at the Twelfth Annual Northeast Conference on Andean Archaeology and Ethnohistory, Carnegie Museum of Natural History, Pittsburgh.

Zapata Rodríguez, Julinho. 1997. "Arquitectura y contextos Funerarios Wari en Batan Urqu, Cusco." In *La Muerte en el Antiguo Peru,* ed. Peter Kaulicke, pp. 165–206. Boletín de Arqueología PUCP, vol. 1. Lima: Pontificia Universidad Católica del Perú.

Zighelboim, Ari. 1995. "Mountain Scenes of Human Sacrifice in Moche Ceramic Iconography." In *Current Research in Andean Antiquity,* ed. Ari Zighelboim and Carol Barnes. *Journal of the Steward Anthropological Society* 23 (1 and 2): 153–188. Urbana: University of Illinois.

Zuidema, R. Tom. 1964. *The Ceque System of Cuzco: The Social Organization of the Capital of the Inca.* Leiden: E. J. Brill.

———. 1992. "Inca Cosmos in Andean Context." In *Andean Cosmologies through Time,* ed. R. Dover, K. Seibold, and J. McDowell, pp. 17–45. Bloomington and Indianapolis: Indiana University Press.

Index

Acarí, *xiii*, 125, 129, 130
Afterlife, belief in, 18, 38
Agriculture, 11, 12, 13, 23, 71–72, 119, 134, 147, 149
Allen, Catherine, 13
Alto Huallaga, 2, 5
Amat, Hernán, 150
Amazon, 12
Ancestors, 1, 11, 13, 71, 114, 135–136; animals as first, 72–73; communication with, 113–114, 161; cults, 117, 155, 161–162; effigy of, 59, 62, 86; garments for, 58–59; and mountains, 13, 161; offerings to (feeding, propitiation), 82–85, 88, 93, 97, 115, 117, 144, 161; recent dead, 59, 66, 76, 82, 85, 86, 87, 88; transition to, 66, 76; unity with, 18, 19, 100. *See also* Transformation
Ancón, *xiii*, 2
Animal sacrifice, ix, x, 1, 2, 10–11, 17, 147, 159; camelids (llamas), 10, 147, 167, 171; fetuses, 2; guinea pigs, 11; modern practices, 10. *See also* Hunting, ritual
Animals, mammals, x, 22, 56, 57, 59, 66–72, 77–89, 100, 120, 121, 122, 127, 134–135, 159; bats, 103, 105, 110, 114; camelids (llamas), 2, 10, 146, 147, 151, 154, 167; deer, 107, 112; dogs, 10; felines, 7, 70, 79, 81–83, 87, 132, 134, 151; foxes, 59, 105, 117; killer whales, 77, 79, 87, 122, 134; monkeys, 70, 71; sea lions, 10, 11, 13, 105, 108, 110, 112, 115, 117. *See also* Hunting, ritual
Animation: and blood nourishment, ix;

objects on Moche ceramics, 43; on Paracas textiles, 57, 63, 64, 87–88. *See also* Moche; Ritual, Animated Objects Ceremony
Animism, 1, 11, 62, 134. *See also* Fans
Ansión, Juan, 160
Apu. See Deities, supernaturals, and mythic beings: mountain
Apurímac, *xiii*, 149, 159
Aqo Wayqo, *xiii*, 147, 149
Architecture, ceremonial, 2, 7, 10, 15, 17, 21, 28, 29–30, 31, 45, 93–97, 102, 114, 115, 137–162, 166, 171, 173
Argentina, 15
Art and iconography, 39, 183; color symbolism in, 10, 36, 39, 129, 141–142, 144, 152, 155; Chimú, 176; Cupisnique, 21–22, 27; Huari, 137, 138, 139, 140, 141, 147, 154–156, 158, 161; Inca, 15; Lambayeque, 7, 40; Moche, 7, 14, 22, 25–28, 30, 36, 39–41, 42, 43, 46, 47, 48–52, 102–104, 105–109, 110, 112, 113–114, 115, 117, 173, 176, 181; Nasca, 6, 119, 120, 121–123, 125, 127–129, 130, 131, 132, 133, 134, 135, 172; Paracas, 56–57, 59–89, 172; Tiahuanaco, 7. *See also* Sacrifice, Andean: art and iconography
Arthropods: crab, 22, 108; scorpion, 22, 23; spider, 21, 22, 23, 25, 26–27
Aspero, *xiii*, 2
Astronomy/astrology, 13; Milky Way, 157; moon and lunar phases, 13, 23, 35 (*see also* Deities, supernaturals, and mythic beings: lunar); sun, 3, 5, 13, 14, 17, 18, 118n4 (*see also* Deities,

supernaturals, and mythic beings: sun). *See also* Calendar, ritual
Ayacucho, *xiii*, 7, 139, 140, 142, 146, 147, 149, 154, 156, 157, 158, 159, 161, 163, 168; valley, 137, 139, 149, 150, 155
Ayapata, *xiii*, 139

Batan Urqo, 153–154
Benavides, Mario, 142–143, 152
Benson, Elizabeth, 110, 112
Birds, 13, 21, 22, 59, 72–76, 79, 83, 109, 113, 121, 122, 127, 134; condor, 72, 74, 79, 87, 122, 134; falcon, 72–75, 87, 122, 134; feathers, 1, 50, 62, 120, 125; parrot, 127; vulture, 8, 82, 176, 181
Blood, ix, 3, 14, 35, 38, 56, 57, 63–66, 69, 71, 72, 82, 83–85, 86, 89, 103, 128, 110, 158, 161, 172, 181
Bourget, Steve, 2, 13, 176, 177, 181
Browne, David, 130, 133
Burial. *See* Mortuary practices
Burger, Richard, 77, 89

Caballo Muerto, *xiii*, 21
Cabrera Romero, Martha, 147
Cache, x–xi, 10, 23, 130, 132–133, 135, 139, 140, 147, 155, 168, 172
Cahuachi, *xiii*, 63, 120, 126, 127, 129, 130
Cajamarca, 5
Calendar, ritual, 10, 13–14, 23, 110. *See also* Astronomy/astrology
Callejón de Huaylas, *xiii*, 10
Cañete, *xiii*, 55, 89
Capac hucha (Capacocha). See Sacrifice, forms of
Captives and prisoners, 3, 7, 35, 40, 93, 100, 102, 104, 107, 109, 110, 112, 117, 125, 127, 128, 162, 171, 172–176, 178, 181, 182, 183
Carmichael, Patrick, 135
Casma Valley, *xiii*, 3, 24, 49, 169
Ceramics: Chimú, 9; Huari, 137, 138, 139, 145, 146, 147, 150–151, 155, 161, 162; jars, 30–31, 40, 41, 42, 43, 50, 85, 108–109, 110, 113, 115, 116, 130–

132, 137, 140–141, 147, 155; Moche, 30, 39, 42, 100, 101, 104, 107, 109, 110, 115, 174; Nasca, 55, 79, 119, 125, 127, 130, 131, 132; Paracas, 55; Topará, 88
Cerro Baúl, *xiii*, 149, 150, 151, 152, 154; 1997 Cerro Baúl Excavation Project, 152
Cerro Blanco, 94, 97
Cerro Carapo, *xiii*, 126, 130, 133
Cerro Colorado, *xiii*, 55
Cerro El Plomo, 16, 166
Cerro Sechín, site, *xiii*, 3, 4, 21
Chancay, *xiv*
Chan Chan, xi, *xiii*, 9, 10; Laberinto, 9, 10; Las Avispas, 9
Chavín, x, *xiv*, 5, 38, 39, 46, 89, 121, 167; de Huántar, *xiii*, 167; at Kotosh, 2. *See also* Cupisnique
Chaviña, 125, 130
Chicama Valley, *xiii*, 23, 24, 25, 94, 95, 170
Chicha/Soras Valley, 149
Child Sacrifice, 2–3, 7, 9, 19, 93, 98–100, 102, 103, 104–106, 112, 113–114, 115, 129, 147, 157, 177; in Genesis, 19; in Greek mythology, 18–19; in western Asia, New South Wales, and Africa, 19. *See also* Sacrifice, forms of: *Capac hucha*
Chile, 15, 16, 119, 156, 166
Chillón, *xiii*
Chimú, ix, xi, *xiv*, 7–9, 10, 35, 121, 169, 176
Chira, 24
Chroniclers, ix, 1, 2, 10, 17–18, 165; Betanzos, Juan de, 17; Cieza de León, Pedro, 10; Cobo, Bernabé, 2, 5, 10, 13, 18, 38, 75, 165, 171; Garcilasco de la Vega, Inca, 165–166; Guaman Poma de Ayala, Felipe, 160, 166; Hernández Príncipe, Rodrigo, 18; Molina, Cristóbal de, 15, 18
Cinnabar, 144
Cleveland Museum of Art, 63
Conchopata, *xiii*, 139–142, 146–147, 148, 149, 154, 155, 156, 158

Contisuyo Program, 150
Cook, Anita, xi
Cordy-Collins, Alana, 3, 107, 168, 172
Cosmology and worldview, Andean,
    ix, 1, 11, 13-14, 18, 19-20, 134, 136,
    156-158
Cupisnique, ix, x, xi, *xiii, xiv,* 5, 6,
    21-33, 38, 39, 47, 121, 158
Cups and goblets, 10, 39-40, 45, 47,
    50, 52, 110, 130-132
Cuzco (Cusco), *xiii,* 5, 13, 15, 17, 18,
    74, 152, 153, 154, 157, 166

Decapitation, x, 3, 4, 5-9, 21-33, 59,
    65, 100, 101, 103, 115, 121-125, 128,
    130, 155, 156, 159, 161, 168, 171-
    172, 174, 181, 183. *See also* Human
    remains: skulls and trophy heads;
    Sacrificers
Decapitator. *See* Sacrificers
Deities, supernaturals, and mythic
    beings, 3, 4, 5, 6, 11-14, 15, 18, 21,
    56, 57, 59, 71, 72, 83, 114, 136, 160;
    Bird Priest, 38; cosmic deity, 11;
    feline, 7; the Horrible Bird, 122,
    134; lightning, 15-16; lunar (moon
    goddess), 35, 45-46, 47; mountain,
    13-14, 137, 156, 157, 160, 161 (*see
    also* Sacred landscape); mythological
    beings, 56; Mythical Killer Whale,
    122, 134; Mythical Spotted Cat, 134;
    Old Lord, 38; sun, 13, 14, 15, 17, 18,
    45; thunder, 13, 16; Trophy Head
    Taster, 122, 134. *See also* Sacrificers
Donnan, Christopher, 107, 109
Dos Cabezas, *xiii,* 23, 24, 26, 28-33,
    38, 42, 93, 168; Dos Cabezas Project,
    23
Duality, 114-115
Duviols, Pierre, 17
Dwyer, Jane, 88

Early Horizon, *xiv,* 5, 88, 91n2, 167
Early Intermediate Period, *xiv,* 5, 7, 88,
    91n2
Ecosystem and environment, Andean,
    12-14, 137, 157. *See also* El Niño

Ecuador, 15, 35, 40, 43, 45
El Brujo, *xiii,* 23, 24, 25, 170, 171, 183;
    El Brujo Archaeological Project, 23,
    170
Eliade, Mircea, 14
El Niño, 12-13, 104, 115-117

Fans, 59, 60-63, 64, 65, 66, 67, 69,
    80, 81, 88
Farabee, William, 127
Feathers. *See* Birds: feathers
Feldman, Robert, 2
Fertility, vegetation, and regeneration:
    sacrifice and, 10, 14, 18, 56-57, 69-
    72, 85, 87-89, 117, 135-136, 158, 161,
    172
Figurines/statuettes, 15, 16, 100, 101,
    107, 109, 110, 144, 147, 153-155. *See
    also* Textiles and cloth: miniatures
Fish and fishing, 21, 22, 23, 25, 70, 75,
    79, 108, 115, 117; Master of Fishes,
    79-80; sharks, 77-79, 134
Frame, Mary, x
Frazer, James, 19, 138

Gallinazo, 22
Garagay, 21
García, Rubén, 130, 133
Geoglyphs, 121
Gods. *See* Deities, supernaturals, and
    mythic beings
Gose, Peter, 160
Guayaquil, Gulf of, 35

Hallucinogens, 130-131, 139
Hocart, A. M., 138-139
Honcopampa, *xiii,* 150-152, 154, 163
Huaca, 2, 19, 134
Huaca de la Cruz, 110, 112
Huaca de la Luna, *xiii,* 93-117, 173,
    176-183; Huaca de la Luna Ar-
    chaeological Project, 94
Huaca del Loro, *xiii,* 149
Huaca de los Reyes. *See* Caballo
    Muerto
Huancaco, 94, 95
Huancavelica, 139

Huanchaco, *xiii,* 23, 24, 93; Huanchaco Project, 23
Huari (Wari), ix, x, xi, 7, 121, 137–162; Cheqo Wasi sector, 142, 144, 145, 147, 149, 152, 154, 155, 162; Huari Urban Prehistory Project, 145
Huaricoto, *xiii,* 10
Huarmey, *xiii,* 24
Huaro Valley, 153, 154
Huarpa, 147
Human remains, 146, 149, 161, 171; appendages, 3, 6–7, 113, 144, 145, 171, 176, 177, 179, 182; defleshing, 60, 65, 181, 182; disarticulated or partial, 3, 98, 101, 102, 104, 162, 167, 174–175, 177, 181; secondary, 167–168; skulls and trophy heads, 5, 7, 28–29, 67, 119–136, 144, 145, 147, 155, 156, 158, 161, 167, 168, 171–176, 180, 181; treatment of bodies, 1, 168, 171, 172
Human sacrifice, ix, 1, 5–6, 8, 9, 15, 18, 19, 66, 138, 139–140, 147, 156, 157, 158, 160–162; mass sacrifice, 96, 100, 173–176, 181; retainers, 7, 169. *See also* Child sacrifice; Warfare, ritual
Hunting, ritual, 93, 112; Moche deer hunt, 10, 105, 109, 110, 113, 115, 117, 133; Moche fox hunt, 105, 117; Moche sea-lion hunt, 10, 105, 108, 110, 112, 115, 117

Ica, *xiv, xiii,* 89, 119, 156
Inca, *xiv,* ix–xi, 1, 3, 5, 10, 11, 13–14, 15–19, 38–39, 45, 75, 119, 121, 134, 142, 156–160, 165–167, 171–172, 175. *See also* Calendar, ritual; *Capac hucha;* Warfare, ritual
Ingenio River, *xiii,* 125, 129, 133
Initial Period, *xiv,* 36, 172
Insects, 41, 50, 51, 52, 86, 87, 102, 173
Isbell, William, 145, 149

Jauja, 159
Jequetepeque, *xiii,* 23, 24, 25, 26, 28, 30, 32, 38, 45, 173
Jumana, 130

Kogi, 38, 39, 46
Kolata, Alan, 10
Kotosh, *xiii,* 2
Kroeber, Alfred, 130
Kubler, George, 77
Kuntur Wasi, *xiii,* 5

Lake Titicaca, *xiii,* 13, 15, 89
Lambayeque, *xiii, xiv,* 7, 9, 23, 24, 38, 40, 46, 47, 117, 170
La Mina, *xiii,* 38, 42
La Paloma, *xiii,* 2
La Plata Island, 40
Las Avispas. *See* Chan Chan
Las Salinas, 124
Late Horizon, *xiv,* 36, 172
Late Intermediate Period, *xiv,* 7
Lightning. *See* Deities, supernaturals, and mythic beings
Loma Negra, *xiii,* 23, 24
Lumbreras, Luis, 168
Lurín, *xiii,* 15

McEwan, Gordon, 153
Manchan, *xiii,* 169
Maya, 38, 39, 45, 46, 47
Maymi, 139
Mesoamerica and Mexico, 38, 42, 45, 46, 47, 165, 182–183
Metal, 1, 15, 16, 137, 147; copper, 7, 30–31, 32, 33, 47, 120; gold, 5, 7, 8, 9, 15, 21, 30, 31, 45–46, 47, 63–64, 120, 151, 154, 171; silver, 7, 9, 15, 16, 31, 45–46, 47, 171; *tupu,* 147
Middle Horizon, *xiv,* 7, 15, 137–162
Minerals, 88, 120, 137; chrysocolla, 145, 147; mica, 2; obsidian, 6, 10, 124, 127, 128, 151; quartz (rock crystal), 2, 10; turquoise, 8, 9, 139, 147, 153, 154
Moche, *xiii, xiv,* ix, x, xi, 2, 7, 10, 14, 22, 23, 24, 25–33, 35–52, 93–117, 120, 121, 128–129, 137, 141, 156, 158, 168–183. *See also* Calendar, ritual; Hunting, ritual; Ritual, Animated Objects Ceremony; Ritual, Burial Ceremony; Ritual, Sacri-

fice Ceremony; Ritual, Tule Boat Ceremony

Mocollope, *xiii*, 94, 95

Mollusks: shell, 38, 43, 64, 98, 120, 137, 154; conch, 38, 52; snail, 117; Spondylus (thorny oyster), 10–11, 15, 35–52, 63, 132, 135, 145, 147, 154

Moquegua, *xiii*, 149, 150

Mortuary practices, 5, 10, 45, 71, 93, 108, 113, 114, 120, 130, 132, 135, 142, 146, 161–162, 167; burials, 2, 7, 9, 168, 171; cemeteries, 15, 55–56, 97, 124, 130, 154, 162, 165, 168; Chimú burials, 7–9, 169; Huari burials, 138, 147–148, 152, 154, 155, 156, 161; Lambayeque burials, 47; Moche burials, 30–33, 38, 96, 97, 98–100, 110, 114–115, 170–171, 183; Nasca burials, 120; Paracas burials, 55–57. *See also* Human remains; Human sacrifice

Mountains, 11, 14, 94, 117, 137, 156, 166, 168; as sources of water, 13, 157. *See also* Deities, supernaturals, and mythic beings

Moxeke, 21

Mummy bundles, 55–89, 130; as oracles, 1–2

Music, 130–131, 134

Muyu Orco, 149

Nakaq (Nacac). *See* Sacrificers

Nasca, x, *xiii*, xiv, 6, 55, 57, 79, 83, 85, 86, 88, 89, 119–136, 141, 149, 156, 158, 161, 171–172; River valley, 130. *See also* Geoglyphs

Nasca Lines. *See* Geoglyphs

Ñawinpukio, *xiii*, 147, 149, 154

Nepeña Valley, *xiii*, 24, 96

Nevada Ampato, *xiii*, 15, 167

Newman, Margaret, 110

Ochatoma, José, 147

Offerings, ritual, x, 1, 10–11, 15–18, 115, 136, 138, 139–142, 144–147, 149, 153, 154, 156, 157, 158, 161, 166, 167, 168; burned, 10, 17; coca, 1, 167; dedicatory, 13, 17–18, 30; food, 71,

85; maize and *chicha*, 17, 71, 167; *pagapu*, 156, 161; textiles, 1, 167. *See also* Animal sacrifice; Cache; Child sacrifice

Oracles: Delphic, 18; Pachacamac, 15

Pacatnamú, *xiii*, 173–176, 177

Pachacamac, *xiii*, 14, 15, 89, 165, 166, 168, 169

Pacheco, *xiii*, 139

Pagapu. *See* Offerings, ritual

Palpa, *xiii*, 129, 130

Pañamarca, *xiii*, 49, 96

Paracas, x, *xiii*, xiv, 6, 55–89, 119, 121, 122, 141, 156, 171, 172

Pérez, Ismael, 146

Peters, Ann, 79, 83–84, 86

Pijoan, Carmen, 182

Pikillacta, *xiii*, 139, 152, 153

Pisco, *xiii*, 55, 129, 156

Piura, *xiii*, 23, 24

Pozorski, Thomas, 9

Pozzi-Escot, Denise, 147

Pre-Ceramic Period, 121

Predators and predation, 77–86

Priest and priestess 38, 39–52, 59, 110, 130, 132, 134, 135, 136

Proulx, Donald, x, 6, 171

Pucará, x, *xiii*, 5, 141, 156

Punkurí, 22

Quilter, Jeffrey, 2

Reinhard, Johan, 15

Río Grande de Nasca, *xiii*, 120, 124, 125, 126, 129, 130, 133

Ritual, 12, 38, 96, 98–102, 109, 113, 115, 121, 130, 137, 139, 153, 156, 157, 165; Animated Objects Ceremony, Moche, 39, 41, 48, 52; Burial Ceremony, Moche, 39–40; Sacrifice Ceremony, Moche, 39, 40; straight-line processions, 17; Tule Boat Ceremony, Moche, 39–43, 46. *See also* Mortuary practices

Ritual space, 93, 98, 120, 135. *See also* Architecture: ceremonial

Ropes, 7, 8, 100, 102, 107, 109, 114,
124, 126, 130, 168–171, 173, 175
Rostworowski, Maria, 1, 11
Rulership, 138–139, 154, 157, 158, 160–
162

Sacred landscape, 121; caves, 13; lakes,
15; mountains, 13, 15, 134–135, 157,
160; places of origin (*pacarinas*), 13,
149, 157; rocks/hills, 95–96, 102,
114, 157. *See also* Ritual space
Sacrifice
Andean 1–20, 93; and ancestors, 93;
art and iconography, ix, x, 1, 3, 5,
7, 10, 14, 22, 23, 25–28, 29, 30, 31,
36, 39, 40, 48–50, 63, 64, 65, 66,
93, 102–104, 109, 113–114, 115, 117,
121–122, 125, 128–129, 133, 134, 135,
138, 139, 140–142, 147, 154–156, 158,
161–162, 172, 173, 176, 181, 183; as
nourishment, ix, 11, 14, 17, 83–84,
156; as political and social aspects,
10, 17–18; as reciprocity payment,
5, 10, 11, 13, 14, 15, 19–20, 22, 85,
100, 119, 135, 156, 161 (*see also* Animal sacrifice; Calendar, ritual; Child
sacrifice; Cosmology; Decapitation;
Fertility, vegetation, and regeneration; Human remains; Human
sacrifice; Offerings, ritual: dedicatory; Transformation; Warfare,
ritual)
forms of: auto-sacrifice, 5–6, 56, 61–
62, 66, 75, 88; *Capac hucha (Capacocha)*, xi, 15–19, 156–157, 166–168,
171, 172; heart sacrifice, 5, 62; stran-
gulation/garroting, 15, 18, 165–166,
168–171; throat slashing, 174, 178,
181 (*see also* Decapitation)
worldwide: ix, 1, 3, 13; in Greek mythology, 18–19; Khonds of India,
14
Sacrifice Ceremony, Moche. *See* Ritual:
Sacrifice Ceremony, Moche
Sacrificers, 3, 4, 14, 21, 22, 30, 31, 32,
47, 56, 137, 139, 140–141, 158, 161,
172; anthropomorphic bat, Moche,

14, 103, 104, 114; Anthropomorphic
Mythical Being, 122, 123, 134, 136;
anthropomorphic owl, Moche, 14;
of Dos Cabezas, 29–33; Front View
Sacrificer, 140, 141, 154, 155, 156,
158 (*see also* Staffs and staff-bearing
figures: Front Face Staff Figure); of
Huada de la Luna, 110–112; *Nakaq,
hacendados,* and *pistacu,* 159–160,
163n3; Profile Staff Sacrificer, 156
(*see also* Staffs and staff-bearing
figures: Profile Staff Figure); the Sacrificer, 158, 161, 162; Supernatural
Fish Decapitator, 22, 23, 25, 26, 33;
Supernatural Human Decapitator,
22, 28, 29; Supernatural Scorpion
Decapitator, 22, 23; Supernatu-
ral Spider Decapitator, 22, 23, 25,
26, 27; in transforming figures in
Paracas textiles, 80, 83–86. *See also*
Deities, supernaturals, and mythic
beings
Salinar, 22
Salomon, Frank, 91nn9,16, 92n22, 160
Sandoval, Abelardo, 146
San José de Moro, *xiii,* 38, 39, 45, 47,
52, 53n9, 183
Shell. *See* Mollusks
Sicán. *See* Lambayeque
Sifuentes, Eudosio, 160
Silverman, Helaine, 129, 130, 133
Sipán, *xiii,* 7, 23, 24, 31, 38, 42, 47,
114, 168, 169, 183; Sipán Project, 23
Skeletal remains. *See* Human remains
Spondylus (thorny oyster). *See* Mol-
lusks
Staffs and staff-bearing figures: Cerro
Sechín, 3, 4; Front View Staff Figure,
137, 140, 141, 155, 158 (*see also* Sacri-
ficers: Front View Sacrificer); Huari,
137, 140, 156, 158, 161; Nasca, 125;
Paracas, 59, 69; Profile Staff Figure,
137, 140, 141 (*see also* Sacrificers:
Profile Staff Sacrificer); Tiahuanaco,
140, 155, 158
Supernaturals. *See* Deities, supernaturals, and mythic beings

Tambo Viejo, *xiii,* 130
Tello, Julio C., 55, 90n4, 91n15, 124, 142, 146, 158
Textiles and cloth, 1, 7, 36; Aspero, 2; Chimú, 8, 169; garments, 58–59, 127; Huari, 137, 140, 154; Inca, 15, 16, 167; miniatures, 15–17, 58; Moche, 47, 98, 103, 109; Nasca, 119, 120, 121, 141, 158; Pachacamac, 168; Paracas, 6, 55–89; tools, 147. *See also* Offerings, ritual
Tiahuanaco (Tiwanaku), *xiv, xiii,* 7, 10, 140, 141, 155, 156, 158, 162
Tierney, Patrick, 3
Tiqnay, *xiii,* 149
Topará, 55, 88
Townsend, Richard, 134
Transformation, x, 18, 55–89, 85, 86, 110, 136, 161
Trepanation, 121, 127, 129
Tribute, 139, 156, 158, 161
Trophy heads. *See* Human remains: skulls and trophy heads
Tuberculosis, 11
Túcume, *xiii,* 10, 15
Tule boats, 39–45, 46, 48–51, 107. *See also* Ritual: Tule Boat Ceremony, Moche
Tumi. See Weapons

Uceda, Satiago, 94
Uhle, Max, 15, 103, 165–166, 168, 169
Uma. See Deities, supernaturals, and mythic beings: mountain
Underworld, 149
Urton, Gary, 14

Valcárcel, Luis, 155
Vargas Llosa, Mario, 137

Verano, John, 1, 19, 102, 129, 136
Vescelius, Gary, 150
Vicús, 22
Virú, *xiii,* 22, 24, 94, 96, 110

Wallace, Anthony, 22
Warfare: ritual, x, 3–5, 13–14, 93, 104, 107, 110–112, 117, 121, 125–129, 171; secular, 125, 127–129
Wari. *See* Huari
Wari Kayan, 55, 90n4
Warriors, 56, 65, 102, 110, 111, 125; Sipán's Warrior Priest, 31, 38, 45
Weapons, 65, 66, 72, 80, 81, 83, 88, 107, 120, 125, 127, 129; darts, 64–65; knives, x, 5–7, 10, 14, 19, 29, 31–32, 56, 62–65, 88, 102, 124, 127–128, 158; lances, 102; maces, 47, 49, 51, 102, 103, 104–105, 107, 108, 110, 111, 112, 122, 123, 124, 125, 127, 128, 181; rocks, 102; slings, 125, 127; spear throwers, 63, 105, 125, 127; *tumi,* 29, 31, 32
Whistling, 98, 102–104, 106, 107, 112, 113–114, 118n3
Williams, Patrick, 150
Women, 9, 15, 35–52, 103–104, 108–109, 113–114, 115, 165, 168–171. *See also* Deities, supernaturals, and mythic beings: lunar
Wounds, 27, 56, 59–66, 69–72, 84, 87–88, 121, 127, 128–129, 174, 176

Yako, *xiii,* 14

Zaña Valley, *xiii,* 5–6, 24
Zapata, Julinho, 153–154
Zuidema, R. Tom, 13, 20